J. M. Robertson

Essays in History and Politics

J. M. Robertson

Essays in History and Politics

ISBN/EAN: 9783337072841

Printed in Europe, USA, Canada, Australia, Japan

Cover: Foto ©Suzi / pixelio.de

More available books at **www.hansebooks.com**

ESSAYS

IN

HISTORY AND POLITICS.

BY

JOHN M. ROBERTSON.

PRICE ONE SHILLING AND SIXPENCE.

LONDON:
SOLD BY R. FORDER, 28 STONECUTTER ST., E.C.

1891.

LONDON:
PRINTED BY A. BONNER,
34 BOUVERIE STREET, FLEET STREET, E.C.

CONTENTS.

The Perversion of Scotland.

Royalism.

Thomas Paine. An Investigation.

Toryism and Barbarism.

Socialism and Malthusianism.

Overpopulation.

ERRATA.

Page 150, *note*.   *For* Tyler *read* Tytler.

,,   156, lines 19-20. *For* the passage "judged it prudent . . . . as regent" *read* "seems to have confided considerably in a leading clergyman, and in the ministers generally".

,,   162, line 15. *For* "no witch-burning" *read* "no systematic witch-burning".

IX.

THE PERVERSION OF SCOTLAND.
By JOHN ROBERTSON.

In the history of Scotland since the Reformation the term "the Church" has a more various significance than belongs to it in the records of any other modern State. Even in the Dark Ages, so-called, the early fraternity of the Culdees, by their independence of Roman control, gave a tinge of ecclesiastical diversity to Scotland's experience; and when once the Papal authority in matters spiritual and temporal was repudiated by the Scottish Parliament in 1560, the people entered on a period of religious vicissitude in which for a century and a half no single church polity prevailed for more than a generation, Presbyterianism and Episcopalianism alternating in varying strength as the various political forces fluctuated. Such a species of confusion, however, creates no difficulty for the onlooker who sees ecclesiastical history from the standpoint of religious neutrality. The general principle on which the State Establishment of religion is condemned, is, I take it, that any and every sect so established is certain to abuse its power, and that its form of government, while it may affect the nature and extent of the abuse, has little or nothing to do with the temper and attitude of the privileged body towards liberty and enlightenment. The mode varies, the spirit is the same.

In Scotland, as in England, it has been the custom to plead the cause of the Establishment as that of an institution beneficently bound up with the country's history, the molestation of which would be an outrage on the very spirit of national continuity. In Scotland even more than in England has the process of the Reformation been magnified and fabulised; the result there being the growth of an essentially mythological notion of the Reformation period and of the men who figured in it. To this day there circulate among the devout poor in Scotland narratives in which Reformation heroes are represented as either working miracles or having miracles worked in their behalf. The later editions of the "Scots Worthies" probably contain few of the old stories of supernatural interposition for the succor of the elect and the destruction of the wicked; but on such fables the ecclesiasticism of modern Scotland was to a large extent nourished; and the survival of the tradition has still some share in the temper of the resistance to the withdrawal of State recognition from the Church, though, as it happens, the tradition is not peculiar to the privileged sect. To show what the Reformation actually was and did, the manner of its occurrence, its effect on the political and social after-course of the people, and above all its influence on their intellectual development—to do this briefly is the purpose of the following pages.

It is by this time pretty well established that in Scotland as in England the immediately effective force in the Reformation was the temporal motive of a hankering after the Church's property among the powerful classes. In the north, no doubt, there was much more of a popular movement of hostility to the corrupt Romish Church than in the south: there always had been among the Scottish people a relatively closer participation in public affairs than can be traced in the early history of the commons of England, the difference arising in the main out of the constant turmoil in which Scottish life was so long kept by the two forces of hostile outside pressure and civil strife. But while the Scottish commonalty mixed closely in the uprising of Protestantism, it is sufficiently clear that the determining power was the interested adoption of their cause by the nobles. So much is admitted by clerical partisans of the Reformation. "It is a great mistake," says the younger McCrie ("Sketches of Scottish Church History", 2nd ed., p. 48), "to suppose that the Scottish Reformation originated with the common people, or in the spirit of rebellion. It would be much nearer the truth to say, that Scotland was reformed by her noblemen and gentlemen." And the impartial student can see very well what such a writer would not see, that what the noblemen and gentlemen were mainly interested in was the plunder. For over a century the issue had been strenuously led up to by the policy of the throne, which, always weak in that land of feudal strifes and scanty civilisation, assiduously sought to strengthen itself by strengthening the Church. As early as the thirteenth century the sons of St. Margaret had richly endowed religion; and at the death of James V. in 1542 the policy of that and previous Stewart kings had made the Scottish hierarchy wealthier in proportion to the country's total wealth than that of perhaps any State in Christendom. Not less marked than James's favor to the Church had been his hostility to the nobles, and at his death the enmity between the two classes had reached the highest pitch. Other influences had been spreading "Reformation principles"; but the adoption of anti-Romish doctrines by the nobility in general was essentially a phase of the struggle for existence between two powerful orders. The lords, growing ever stronger during the regencies of Mary's minority, naturally joined in the spiritual attack on their temporal enemies as a matter of tactics, seeing in the ministrations of the Protestant preachers an extremely serviceable engine for the overturning of an institution that could not subsist in the entire absence of popular attachment. In this spirit they sent abroad for Knox in 1559 as for a useful instrument to prosecute the work they had already carried so far. A few devotees there were among them, no doubt, just as there remained a few Catholics; but, as Dr. Burton critically observes of one group of the Protestant nobles of that time ("History of Scotland," revised ed., vol. v., p. 217): "it would be difficult to find in the Christian world men with less religion or more ruffianism". Even Mr. McCrie could not deny that when once the ecclesiastical revolution was carried the nobility unblushingly appropriated by far the greater part of the old Church's property. Only by strenuous efforts did the new clergy get any of it at all. The best arrangement they could force on the for-once united nobility—all-powerful for the moment in the interval between the death of the Queen Regent and the arrival of the young Queen Mary—was that the Church revenues should be divided into three parts, of which one was to be shared between the Crown and the Protestant ministers, while the other two were understood to remain with the disestablished Catholic dignitaries during their lives. What really happened, of course, was that the latter were promptly fleeced by the baronage, being only too glad to compound with the masters of the situation on any terms;

while the ministers were left to scramble for their fraction of a third. (See Burton's History, iv., 37—41; Knox's "History of the Reformation", Laing's ed. of his works, ii., 542; Calderwood's "History of the Kirk", Wodrow Society's ed., ii., 172; and Spottiswoode's "History of the Church", ed. 1851, vol. ii., p. 64.) The nobles, regretfully observes Mr. McCrie, "showed a degree of avarice and rapacity hardly to be expected from persons who had taken such active part in reforming the Church". Knox's comment was more dramatic. "Weill", he reports himself to have said "on the stoolle of Edinburgh" ("History of the Reformation", Laing's edition of his works, vol. ii., p. 310)—"Weill, yf the end of this ordour, pretended to be tacken for sustentatioun of the Ministeris, be happy, my judgment failleth me; for I am assured that the Spreit of God is nott the auctor of it; for, first, I see Twa partis freely given to the Devill, and the Thrid maun be devided betwix God and the Devill". "Who wold have thought", he exclaims again, "that when Joseph reulled Egypt, that his brethren should have travailled for vitallis, and have returned with empty seckis unto their families?" And, again (p. 312): "O happy servandis of the Devill, and miserable servandis of Jesus Christ; yf that after this lyef thair war nott hell and heavin!" (see also pp. 128–9). The chagrined ministers loudly demanded that they should have the entire reversion of the endowment. They "seem to have made the mistake", as Dr. Burton judicially puts it (iv., 39), "of supposing that the active energy with which their lay brethren helped them to pull down Popery was actually the fruit of religious zeal; and to have expected that they took from the one Church merely to give to the other. The landholders, on their part, thought such an expectation so utterly preposterous that they did not condescend to reason with it; but, without any hypocritical attempt to varnish their selfishness, called the expectations of the ministers 'a fond imagination'." And such it certainly proved to be. The condition of the new clergy for many a day was one of distinct hardship, their pittances being so irregularly paid that some fairly abandoned their calling (Spottiswoode, ii., 64).

It is only just, in this connexion, to acquit them in part of a charge often brought against them—that of bringing about the general destruction of the old religious edifices.

Certainly the clergy were zealous to annihilate all the artistic adjuncts, which for them were mere "idolatry"; and the rank and file were responsible for the destruction as well as the plunder of many monasteries, some of which were noble buildings. But, while there would have been some practical cogency in the view so often attributed to Knox, that "the best way to drive off the rooks is to pull down the nests", as a matter of fact Knox was for a different policy, though, as we shall see, the temper of demolition was not absent from the clerical body. There has been, on this subject, a seesaw of sweeping aspersion and equally sweeping vindication of the Reformers, in which the truth has been alternately made too white and too black. In the earlier part of this century, an influential antiquarian movement fostered the view among Episcopalians and unbelievers that the Reformers were a mere set of frenzied fanatics who sought to destroy every scrap of architecture associated with Papistry. Cooler research noted that the great monasteries in the southern counties had been burned in the English invasion under Hertford, during Mary's infancy, in 1545—the second under that leader; and the more liberal Presbyterians eagerly proclaimed that no guilt of that kind lay with their forefathers. But to speak so is to ignore some of the plainest facts of the Reformation. The invading English general did indeed display his zeal in the service of his master and the cause of Protestantism by burning, in addition to 243 villages and 192 separate structures, the Abbeys of Kelso, Melrose, Dryburgh, Roxburgh, and Coldingham (Burton, iii., 247-8); as he had burned Holyrood Abbey and Palace, with the town of Edinburgh, in 1544 (Laing's Knox, ii., 121, *note*); but there is not the least reason to assume that the southern edifices, if not so destroyed, would have escaped the Reformation mobs any more than did the monasteries of the north. The Protestants had already destroyed the monasteries at Dundee and sacked the Abbey of Lindores in their first outbreak in 1543 (Burton, iii., 250), two years before Hertford's second invasion; they had at the same period attacked the church of Arbroath and the Blackfriars Monastery at Edinburgh; and in 1559 they wrecked monasteries all over the country. But it is important to notice on this head that the main devastation of the latter year was not only not wrought at the behest of the clerical and aristocratic leaders, but was done in spite of their resistance. The failure of Dr. McCrie to vindicate Knox in this regard is a curious illustration of the helplessness of a partisan in his own walk when he has to hold the scales between sections of his party. Knox's History shows in the clearest way that the leading Reformer opposed the wrecking of the fabrics even of the monasteries. Describing the opening outbreak at Perth, involving the ruin of the Greyfriars', Blackfriars', and Charterhouse monasteries—the third "a buylding of a wonderouse coast and greatness"—he writes that the riot was begun against the exhortations of the preacher present and of the magistrates, by a multitude, "not of the gentlemen, neyther of thame that war earnest professouris, but of the raschall multitude" (i., 322); and in this he is followed by Calderwood (History of the Kirk, i., 441). Again, dealing with the burning of the Abbey and Palace of Scone (pp. 360–2), he tells how Murray and Argyle on the first day saved the buildings, and how it was only on the breaking out of a fresh riot on the second day, over the stabbing of a Dundee plunderer by the bishop's son, that "the multitude, easelie inflambed, gave the alarme", and a fresh mob from Perth set Abbey and Palace on fire. "Wharat", says Knox, "no small nomber of us war offended, that patientlie we could nocht speak till any that war of Dundie or Sanct Johnestoun" [*i.e.*, Perth]. His superstition, indeed, makes him incline to suspect that there must have been a divine dispensation in the matter; just as he seems fain to make out, in his own despite, that the mischief-makers at Perth had after all been disinterested religionists,[1] anxious "onlie to abolish idolatrie, tho places and monumentis thereof"; but of the Scone business he expressly says in his conclusion (p. 362) "assuredlie, yf the labouris or travell of any man culd have saved that place, it had nocht bein at that tyme destroyed; for men of greattest estimatioun lawboured with all diligence for the savetie of it". On the same page, his common-sense again coming uppermost, he tells that the utter destruction

---

[1] The inconsistencies of Knox's text on this head are so marked as almost to suggest some tampering with the original MS. before its publication; but revisals in different moods would probably suffice to lead into self-contradiction a man naturally clear-headed, but always incitable to vaticination by his theistic fervor.

of the friaries at Stirling was accomplished by the "rascheall multitude" before the arrival of the occupying force under Murray and Argyle; and yet again (p. 363) he records that at Edinburgh " the poore" had "maid havock of all suche thingis as was movable", in the monasteries of the Black and Gray Friars, "befoir our cuming, and had left nothing bot bair wallis, yea, nocht sa muche as door or windok; wharthrow we war the less trubilled in putting ordour to suche places." It was thus the common people of the towns who, eager to fleece the monks whose gross venality and hypocrisy they knew so well, proceeded from plunder to the savage destruction of the fine buildings for which they had no appreciation whatever; while men like Knox and Murray would gladly have preserved such edifices. The Churchmen had left themselves no friends. As the writer of the "Diurnal of Remarkable Occurrents" says: "In all this tyme all kirkmennis goodis and geir wer spoulzeit and reft fra thame, in euerie place quhair the samyne culd be apprehendit; for euerie man for the maist pairt that culd get anything pertenyng to any kirkmen, thocht the same as wele won geir" (p. 269). The people were wreaking vengeance rather than assailing an alleged idolatry; they pulled down the houses for hatred of the dwellers. The destruction was general and deplorable, the already defaced and poverty-stricken country being thus deprived by its own children of a large part of what little show of material wealth it had left. Knox (ii., 167) tells how the Protestants of the West "burnt Paislay . . . . kest down Failfurd, Kilwynning, and a part of Crossragwell"; and from Balfour (Annals i., 316) and the English envoy Sadler (Burton, iii., 353, *note*) and other sources we know that similar destruction was wrought at Cambuskenneth, Linlithgow, Dunfermline, and St. Andrews; while the clergy themselves everywhere saw to the smashing of "images" and altars. Nay, the ministers did not entirely spare the churches as is claimed for them by Burton (p. 353). When the historian asserts that "the fabric of the churches did not excite their destructive indignation," he overlooks the record that in the very first General Assembly of the new Church, held in December 1560, it was resolved "that the kirk of Restalrig, as monument of Idolatry, be razed and utterly casten downe and destroyed"

("Booke of the Universall Kirk of Scotland," ed. 1839, p. 3). Further, though the admission is not decisive, it is to be noted that Dr. McCrie accepts for the Reformation the responsibility of the destruction of the Chapel of Loretto at Musselburgh ("Life of Knox", Crichton's ed., 1840, p. 151, *note*). The residual truth is that, setting aside the demolition of one or two churches, presumably of a highly ornamental type, and the utter annihilation of all ecclesiastical art work, the Protestant clergy are not chargeable with the ruin of the fabrics of the great cathedrals and churches. Apart from the declarations of Knox, they must have the credit, such as it is, of the preserved letter of instructions by Argyle, Murray, and Ruthven, in which the lairds of Arntilly and Kinvaid are directed to burn all the images, altars, and monuments of idolatry in the Cathedral of Dunkeld, with the proviso: "Faill not, bot ze tak guid heyd that neither the dasks, windocks, nor durris be ony ways hurt or broken, eyther glassin wark or iron wark". (McCrie's Life of Knox, Appendix, p. 372.) That McCrie should not have given any effect in his biography to Knox's repudiation of the pulling down of the monasteries must apparently be attributed to his unwillingness to put on record that the Reformation was in any sense a work of reckless mobs[1]—an unwillingness paralleled in his son's reluctance to admit that the Protestant aristocracy were mostly hungry land-grabbers. The facts, looked at fairly, are seen to relate naturally to the known principles of human nature. The natural instincts of the rude populace led to the wreckage of the monasteries: the clergy, fanatically eager to destroy the signs of "idolatry", might well seek to preserve the buildings; and nobles like Murray would readily help them. It was specially to the interest of the clergy to retain such buildings. There seems to be no good authority for Spottiswoode's story, made so familiar by Scott in "Rob Roy", that Glasgow Cathedral was only saved by the armed resistance of the city craftsmen to an attempt against it by the zealots (see Burton, vi., 222, *note*); and there is on the other hand documentary evidence that the clergy bitterly reproached the greedy landowners, who were the last and

---

[1] He seems, however, to have been unaware that the southern monasteries were destroyed by Hertford. See his second note on p. 151, and the text.

worst culprits, for the sordid apathy with which they let the preserved edifices, great and small, fall into utter ruin for sheer lack of ordinary repairs. The roofs of cathedrals were soon stripped of their lead for purposes of war, and the Protestant nobility, alike in their private and in their public capacities, refused to lift a finger for their maintenance. On them must fall the final reproach. Glasgow Cathedral, on the other hand, was preserved by municipal supervision; and "there is abundant testimony that the clergy of the Reformation did their best for the preservation and good order of the fabrics of the churches" (Burton, iv., 355); though their poverty disabled them for that particular form of self-aggrandisement. What the new Church did as such, when thus disappointed of the rewards for which its clergy had hoped, was to get hold of the popular mind with a thoroughness which would otherwise have been impossible, and, accordingly, to exert to the utmost its influence for the restriction and subjection of the people's intellectual and social life. Wealth and power have been natural objects of desire to every established Church, and if that of Scotland after the Reformation could not acquire the former it could still attain the latter.

Scarcely was the legislative process of the Reformation accomplished when the clerical passion for power began to manifest itself. The political change was effected by the Estates in August 1560, and in .1561, just before the arrival of Queen Mary from France, the secular-minded among the people of Edinburgh had a taste of the quality of the new institution. Under Romanism the people of Scotland, like those of other European countries, had regularly practised such ancient semi-pagan semi-Christian mummeries as the Bacchic feast of the Ass, and such customs naturally gave them a taste for pageants in general. Accordingly, in the summer of 1561 the Edinburgh tradesfolk proposed as of old to celebrate the pageant of Robin Hood. But the new clergy had set their faces against all such performances, and, armed with an Act of Parliament, the Lords of the Congregation, which at that time meant the clergy *plus* the countenance of the nobles, prohibited the undertaking. The craftsmen persisted; disturbance followed; and a "cordinar" or shoemaker, charged with both theft and rioting, was put in jail—in the old "Heart of Midlothian"—and sentenced to death.

To John Knox, as being the most influential public man at the moment, the friends of the condemned man applied for mercy; but the Reformer and the magistrates, in the words of the contemporary chronicler, would "dae nothing bot have him hangit". Only by a forcible riot and storming of the gaol was the representative of popular rights saved. (See Burton iv., 27; Knox's History, ii., 157-9; and the "Diurnal of Remarkable Occurrents", published by the Bannatyne Club, pp. 65-6.) The magistrates were terrorised, and the clergy had to be content with holding the "haill multitude excommunicat" till, so says Knox, they "maid humble sute unto the kirk". The preachers of course knew that they could only maintain their position by an absolute moral control over the mind of the populace. That they in the long run acquired, and there was virtually an end in Scotland of popular pageants, and of every form of dramatic, musical, and imitative art, for many generations.

The uppermost thought of the Protestant clergy, of course, was to complete the suppression of the old faith. The Act of 24th August, 1560, had provided that the administering, or being present at the administration, of the mass, should be punishable on a first offence by forfeiture of possessions and corporal punishment; on a second, by banishment; and on a third by death. (Scots Acts of Parliament, ed. 1814, vol. ii., p. 534.) This pointed, considering the spirit of the times, rather to a minimising of bloodshed than to an absolute desire to take the lives of Papists in any number; and in point of fact the history of the extirpation of the old faith in Scotland, so far as we have it, is a much less sanguinary record than the corresponding narrative for England. What happened in the first instance was a wholesale expulsion. (See Diurnal of Occurrents, p. 69.) But three points have to be kept in view: first, that Queen Mary came to her kingdom immediately after the ecclesiastical revolution, and that she always evaded the ratification of the Reformation Acts, which were so distasteful to her; second, that, apart from the Queen's unwillingness to let Catholics be persecuted, a large section of the nobility looked very coldly on the pretensions of the Presbyterian clergy to exercise civil power; and, third, that many of the criminal records of that period have been lost. (See Burton, v.,

10.) It will be found on examination, too, that only a few heretics had been put to death in Scotland by the Romish Church in the days of its power; and it may have been that the Protestant laity were unwilling to take more lives than the old church had done. But if, with Protestant partisans, we take the line of arguing that it was not for lack of will that the Romish priesthood had burnt so few Protestant emissaries, it will be impossible to reject a similar conclusion in regard to the Protestant policy after the overturn. Certainly nothing could be more fiercely intolerant than the declarations of the Reformers in regard to the doctrines they had overthrown. To them the mass was in dead earnest "idolatry", properly punishable with death. Knox insisted on this constantly; and there were few things which exasperated him more than the suggestion that there might be no harm in leaving the Papists alone. (See the "History of the Reformation", ii., 265-6.) The principle of toleration had in fact no more place in the Calvinistic system than in the Papal; and if it be granted that the Protestants knew the Queen and the Catholic party would be glad to put them down as they had put down Catholicism, it is none the less certain that their motive was not mere self-preservation, but just such an innate lust for the suppression of heresy as actuated Catholic persecutors in that age. And, motive apart, the forcible suppression of Catholic worship was completely and relentlessly accomplished. Knox at one point triumphantly writes that the "Papists war so confounded that none within the Realme durst more avow the hearing or saying of Messe, then the theavis of Lyddesdaill durst avow thair stowth [stealth=stealing] in presence of ane upryght judge" (History, ii., 265). How much bloodshed this really represented it is impossible now to say. That it meant countless acts of gross tyranny is perfectly clear from the many references to prosecutions, finings, and banishments. But it is impossible to believe that in such a community as the Scotland of that day no worse outrages than these were inflicted on a downtrodden and detested sect by their triumphant enemies. A passage or two from the old "Diurnal of Occurrents" gives us some idea of the temper of the time. Under the date April 11th, 1574 (pp. 340-1) the Diarist tells how one Robert Drummond committed suicide by stabbing himself at the cross when he was about to be burnt in the cheek for persisting in bigamy. He had first been made to do penance in the kirk; then, for continued contumacy, he had been banished; now, having returned and proved incorrigible, he was to be branded, when he suddenly took matters in his own hands and escaped his tormentors. And the Diarist incidentally explains how, after the second punishment, "the Magistratis, being movit with pittie, brocht him in the toun, becaus he had been ane lang servand, and *ane greit seikar and apprehendar of all preistis and papistis*". Of such unrecorded persecution there must have been an abundance; and another detail in the same record, overlooked or ignored by historians, points to an unascertainable, though doubtless small, number of random executions. In the same year is the entry (p. 341): "Wpoun the fourt day of Maij thair wes ane preist hangit in Glasgow, callit   , for saying of mes." The name is either awanting or illegible in the manuscript, it appears; and it is evident that the writer did not think the matter one of much consequence. Such an entry is a sufficient disproof of the allegation that no Papist suffered death for his religion in Scotland, and of the generally accepted statement of Calderwood ("History of the Kirk of Scotland", iii., 196) that Ogilvie the Jesuit, hanged at Glasgow in 1615, was the first priest put to death in Scotland after the execution of Hamilton, the Archbishop of St. Andrews, hanged on his capture in 1571 as a Queen's-man too dangerous to be allowed to live. There appears to be no truth in the story (found in Leslie's History and in Dempster's "Historia Ecclesiastica", and cited in Robert Chambers' "Domestic Annals") that a priest named Black was stoned to death by an Edinburgh mob in 1562; Black having really been mysteriously killed on the night of Darnley's murder in 1567 (see Laing's Knox, ii., appendix, 592—5); but such an outrage would have been possible enough, and would have given small concern to the Protestant ministers. What is certain is that from the fall of Mary down to the end of the seventeenth century the Romanists left in Scotland could not indulge in the ceremonies of their Church, even in semi-private fashion in rural districts, without risk of instant prosecution, and, that they ran the most serious dangers when they secretly harbored

Catholic priests. Even Mary was compelled to prosecute and imprison the members of her own faith, being, indeed, menaced from the first in her own practice of it. When, on the first Sunday after her arrival, she attended mass in her private chapel at Holyrood, an attack was made on the building by a Protestant mob, a priest was ill-treated, and the interior would certainly have been wrecked but for the interference of Mary's brother Lord James Murray, afterwards Regent. Even by such an act as this, Murray, Protestant as he was, incurred the resentment of Knox, who approved of and probably encouraged the riot. (See his History, ii., 271.) Shortly after, at a meeting of the "Congregation", the clergy voted unanimously against allowing the Queen to exercise her own worship in her own household, and only the lay votes carried a contrary resolution (Burton, iv., 34). It is not here argued that the Protestant clergy had no reason to fear a return of Catholic ascendancy: the point is that their spirit was precisely that of the Catholics. It may indeed be claimed for the early Protestants, by those who will, that whereas the Catholics practised oppression while in power and professed principles of tolerance when in the minority, the Protestants were as pronounced in their intolerance when weak as when strong. (*Ibid.*, 119.) From the first they defied the Court. In March, 1562, "Sir" James Arthur, a priest, was prosecuted for solemnising baptisms and marriages "in the old abominable Papist manner"; and if he escaped punishment it was only by the determined exercise of the queen's "mercy", on which he threw himself (p. 56). Mary, of course, was too consummate a tactician not to save her fellow Catholics in the long run, but in May 1563 she had to permit the indictment of forty-eight Papists, including the Archbishop of St. Andrews and other eminent ecclesiastics, for celebrating mass and endeavoring to restore Popery in Paisley and Ayrshire; and of the number several had to go through the form of imprisonment at the Queen's pleasure. (*Ibid.*, 63.) The manner of the offences charged had involved no attack on the Protestant authorities, but consisted simply of the more or less secret performance of Catholic worship, just as the Covenanters of a later generation performed theirs. In 1565, again, we find a priest, "Sir" John Carvet, seized for saying mass, and pilloried and pelted with eggs on two successive days; being apparently only saved from lynching at the hands of a riotous mob on the second day by the interference of the town guard. A royal letter, demanding the prosecution of the rioters, secured his release, but no such prosecution took place; and the bare idea of such a demand on the part of the Crown moved the clergy to wrathful activity. (Knox ii., 476; Burton, iv., 118.)

It cannot be too strongly insisted that the Protestant Church all along aimed at secular power. With the example of Geneva before their eyes, the Reformers held it their function to control the body politic and the body social alike; and only the self-interest of the aristocracy prevented their fully gaining their ends, just as it baulked them of the revenues of the fallen Church. The issue as to temporal power was effectively raised in 1561, over the attempt of the clergy to have their "Book of Discipline" made part of the law of the land. "The Protestant nobles and lairds", observes Burton (iv., 34), "were ready to accept all denunciations of Antichrist and Popish idolatry, nor did they hesitate at accepting the Calvinistic doctrines of the new faith just as Knox and his assistant ministers set them forth: they had, hence, at once adopted the Confession of Faith in Parliament. But the Book of Discipline affected practice as well as faith, and enforced certain stringent restraints to which it would have been inconvenient for some, who were the readiest to subscribe propositions of theological metaphysics, to submit." So that, though some approved, and even these under suspicion of hypocrisy, the lay notabilities resisted the clerical proposal; one telling Knox to "stand content—that Buke will nott be obteaned" (Burton, iv., 35; Hist. of Ref., ii., 297). For the time the preachers were left to impotent declamation; but in the summer of 1565, after the Carvet riot, they attempted more vigorous measures. Frustrations in other ways they had borne, but they would not endure that there should be any approach to toleration of Romish practices. Accordingly they resolved in General Assembly: "Imprimis, that the Papisticall and blasphemous masse, with all Papistrie and idolatrie of Paip's jurisdictione, be universallie suppressed and abolished throughout the haill realme, not only in the subjects, but in the Q. Majestie's awn persone, with punishment against all persones that shall be deprehended to transgresse and offend the same; and that the sincere word of God and His true religion, now presently receaved, might be established, approven, and ratified throughout the whole realme, as well in the Queen's Majestie's owne persone as in the subjects, without any impediment, and that the people be astricted to resort upon the Sunday at least to the prayers and preaching of God's word, like as they were astricted before to the idolatrous masse; and thir heads to be provided be act of Parliament, with consent of the Estates and ratification of the Queen's Majestie" ("Booke of the Universall Kirk", p. 28; compare Burton, iv., 48). At the same time, besides requiring that provision should be made for the ministers, they demanded, what they had ordained in 1560, that no one should be permitted to teach in schools, colleges, or universities, or even in private, save such as were authorised by the Church; further, that Parliament should make adequate provision for the punishment of crime, "witchcraft, sorcerie, and inchantment" being among the offences singled out for special mention. There could not be a more explicit attempt on the part of a purely ecclesiastical body to lay down and control the laws of the land; and it was only the extreme uncertainty of the political situation at the moment—just before Mary's marriage with Darnley—that prevented any effective action being taken when the Queen diplomatically evaded the Assembly's demands (Burton, pp. 119—21).

Nor was the Protestant spirit of intolerance strong merely against the Church of Rome. The hatred of the Presbyterians to all other sects was tolerably impartial. As Tytler observes ("History of Scotland," Nimmo's ed., iii., 130), "it was the opinion of many of the leaders of the Reformation . . . . in Scotland that the hierarchy of England, as established under Elizabeth, was nearly as corrupt as Rome itself". And when in 1562 steps were taken to arrange a meeting between Mary and Elizabeth, the Scottish clergy, Knox heading them, bitterly opposed the plan, preferring, says Tytler (p. 161), "that their queen should remain an obstinate Papist, rather than take refuge in a religion which had as little ground in the word of God". How this temper took effect when the opportunity arose we shall see later. In the meantime the Reformers had almost no species of Dissent to trouble them. Calderwood much later chronicles the arrival of a few Brownists (iv., pp. 1, 2) as an incident that came to practically nothing; and we may surmise that the English Anabaptists, from what they knew of Knox's sentiments in regard to them, would be very chary of seeking proselytes in the north. He thought some of their writings deserved punishment by death as blasphemous (Laing's Knox, v., 14); and his voluble treatise on Predestination, written by way of combatting their doctrines, stands in the front rank of the most rancorous controversy of the period. They shrank, poor men, from the theory that the Deity had foreordained the eternal perdition of the majority of his own creatures, and they sought to account for the moral confusion of the world, as more pretentious thinkers have done before and since, by the old suggestion of two supernatural principles: all which was as brimstone in the nostrils of a good Calvinist. But the creed of Geneva had not to contend with such aberrations of humane sentiment in Scotland. There the iron of inhuman dogma wholly entered the national soul, with what dark results of intellectual and social perversion it is now proposed to show.

Printed by ANNIE BESANT and CHARLES BRADLAUGH, 63, Fleet St., E.C.—1886.

X.

THE PERVERSION OF SCOTLAND.
By JOHN ROBERTSON.
(II.)

WE have seen how the class interest of the nobles had effected the main part of the Reformation, and how, their purpose served, they for the most part turned their backs on their preaching allies. The ultimate result of this course was the democratisation of the Kirk's polity, but the effect came about slowly. At the outset its members had no thought of abolishing the hierarchical system; and there can be little doubt that if the nobles had fairly shared their plunder with their auxiliaries Scotland would to-day have been as Episcopalian as England. The allowances originally proposed to be made to them varied from one hundred to three hundred merks a-year, a rate of income of which it was said that few Scotch lords had then as much in spare cash (Burton, iv., 41—2; Calderwood, ii., 172); and the clergy insisted that it was no more than they needed, arguing that, looking to the importance and dignity of a minister's services, provision ought to be made not only for his comfort but for the "education and up-setting [establishment] of his sons, and for his daughters being virtuously brought up and honestly doted",—that is, dowered (Burton, iv., p. 36). Such an arrangement would have made of the ministry a class with aristocratic habits and sympathies; among whom an order of bishops would be regarded as in every way desirable: as it was, the old hierarchical titles were not legally abolished in 1560; and the spirit of episcopacy was exemplified in the Kirk's institution of the new order of "superintendents" holding office during life, of whom Spottiswoode observes that "their power was episcopal; for they did elect and ordain ministers, they presided in synods, and directed all church censures, neither was any excommunication pronounced without their warrant" (ii., 167). It has been pretended that as these Superintendents were themselves chosen by the Church there was nothing episcopal in their functions, but the essential point is that, as Buckle decisively points out in his citations ("History of Civilisation", iii., 99), they exercised a special authority, which the Assembly upheld. It was required "that punyschment suld be appointed for suche as dissobeyid or contemned the Superintendentes in thair functioun", (Knox ii., 161) and in 1562 "it was ordeaned, that if ministers be disobedient to superintendents in aniething belonging to edificatioun, that they must be subject to correctioun". (Calderwood, ii., 184). In the "Book of Discipline", indeed, it is also provided that the Superintendent "must be subjected to the censur and correctioun of the Ministeris and Elderis . . . . of the hoill Province", (Knox ii., 20); but for obvious reasons that stipulation did not prevent the superintendent from being in actual fact a person in authority. Such an arrangement was the more natural because a considerable number of the new ministers had been inferior clergy in the old Church. (Burton, iv., 328). But as years passed and the ruling class made no better provision for the ministry, there naturally arose a temper more and more averse to a system which created within the church a small semi-aristocratic class. In 1567, after Mary's forced abdication and during her incarceration at Lochleven, matters seemed to come to a definite issue. The clergy invited to their Assembly, as lay coadjutors, the Protestant landholders in general, calling on them to co-operate in the task of securing to the Church its proper patrimony, and some eighty of the "most notorious impropriators of Church lands" actually attended and professed zeal in the cause ("Booke of the Universall Kirk," pp. 54–58; Burton, iv., 324); while the Parliament went so far as to draw up a statute ordaining that "the haill thriddis of the haill benefices of this Realme sall now instantlie, and in all tymes to cum, first be payit to the Ministeris of the Evangell of Jesus Christ and thair successouris." And even this purported to be but a temporary arrangement, holding good until "the Kirk come to the full possession of thair proper patrimonie, quhilk is the teindis" [tithes]; while an annotated draft suggests a restoration of the "hale patrimony", which would mean the temporalities of all kinds. (Burton, iv., 324–5; Acts of Parliament, iii., pp. 24 and 37.) The whole was a grim and impudent mockery on the part of the nobles. It "bore no fruit, if we may except the historical conclusion, that the statesmen of the day were anxious to secure the co-operation of the clergy" (Burton, p. 325).

Why they should have been so anxious it is needless to inquire minutely: the substantial fact is that if the ruling classes ever found the support of the clergy useful, the clerical influence none the less was impotent as against the aristocratic. In one direction only did it play freely and irresistibly, namely, in the coloring and moulding of the ignorant and plastic popular mind; though, of course, where the superstition of the nobles chimed with that of clergy and people, there was unity of fanatical action, just as there had been union when the nobles' personal interests coincided with the progress of the new doctrines. Scottish history will be misunderstood at several conjunctures if this factor of the interested action of the nobility is not kept clearly in view. Just as the throne, alike under James V., his widow, and his daughter, had the nobility against it because of its wish to aggrandise the Catholic Church, so did Murray prejudice his position as Regent the moment he gave his fellow nobles cause to suspect that he wished to help the Protestant clergy from the confiscated revenues (Burton, iv., 358). Buckle seems to me to make far too much of the political power of the clergy when he declares (iii., 113) that "it was they who taught their countrymen to scrutinise, with a fearless eye, the policy of their rulers"; and he lapses into sheer extravagance[1] when he further announces that "It was they who pointed the finger of scorn at kings and nobles, and laid bare the hollowness of their pretensions". The clergy never showed regal and aristocratic pretensions to be hollow in any sense save one which simply substituted their own pretensions for those they challenged; and in point of fact there was as much popular criticism of the rulers by the populace in the old times as in the new. How much the political action of the ministry was an affair of declamation may be

---

[1] Such a criticism should not be advanced by a student of Scotch history without a counterbalancing acknowledgment of the excellent service Buckle has done in bringing the main factors of that history into luminous relief and reducing the whole to rational bases, besides making an important research in quarters almost entirely ignored by specialist historians. My own debt to him is great.

seen from their powerlessness to protect even their own class against Regent Morton. That Protestant ruler, who, powerful and unscrupulous as he was, could not in the long run preserve himself against the ferocious intriguing of the nobles hostile to him, declared that there would never be peace in Scotland until some ministers were hanged; and he did torture and hang one in 1572 ("Diurnal," pp. 262, 293), without thereby securing special order, it must be said. The political lot of the clergy under the Protestant Regencies of James's minority is a mere record of impotent resentment of contemptuous oppression. In 1572 the Privy Council compelled them to accept a systematic establishment of the whole set of superior ecclesiastical offices under the old titles, it being provided that the names, titles, and dioceses of archbishops and bishops were to "stand and continue in time coming as they did before the reformation of religion", while the dignities of the abolished monastic system were also to be preserved by way of maintaining "the ecclesiastical Estate in Parliament" (Calderwood, iii., 173; Burton, v., 74—77). What Knox thought of this arrangement as such is not quite clear, but the truth seems to be that he was not anti-episcopalian at heart; and though he had a quarrel of some duration with Murray, he does not appear ever to have protested against Murray's retention of the Priorship of St. Andrews. In August of 1572 we find him subscribing "with my dead hand but glaid heart, praising God", the official ratification of a certain sermon preached before the regent; and this below the signature of "J. Sanct Androis"—a circumstance which Dr. McCrie does not mention in his account of the matter ("Life," p. 292. Compare Burton, v., 80). Nor did the populace show any presbyterian zeal against the arrangement; their comment taking the shape of one of those nicknames, their talent for which has been noted —and inherited—by Carlyle. The true purpose of the re-establishment of the hierarchy was to retain ecclesiastical funds in the hands of the landowners by a new device, the new bishops being simply the tools of the ruling nobles, and their function that of drawing revenues the greater part of which they surrendered to their patrons. On perceiving which, the popular mind classed them with the domestic invention of the "tulchan"—the stuffed figure of a calf which in the husbandry of those days it was customary to place beside a cow at milking time to induce her to give her milk freely. The "tulchan bishops" are perhaps the most happily nicknamed body in history, and the popular feeling against them apparently went little further than the nickname.

If the Kirk could be defrauded thus under the Regencies of Lennox and Mar, while the sorely tried country was being convulsed by fresh invasions and a miserable civil war, it was not likely to manage much better under the iron rule of the Earl of Morton when quiet had been restored. Morton "had the address to persuade the Presbyterian clergy that it would be the best thing for their interest to resign at once into his hands the thirds of the benefices which had been granted for their support. . . . Their collectors, he said, were often in arrear; but his object would be to make the stipend local, and payable in each parish where they served. . . . The moment Morton became possessed of the thirds, his scheme of spoliation was unmasked. The course he followed was to appoint two, three, or even or four churches to one minister, who was bound to preach in them by turns; and at the same time he placed in every parish a reader whose duty was to officiate in the minister's absence, and to whom a miserable pittance of twenty or forty pounds Scots was assigned. Having thus allotted to the Church the smallest possible sum, he seized the overplus for himself; and when the clergy . . . . petitioned to be reinstated in their property . . . . they were at first met with many delays, and at last peremptorily told that the appointment of the stipends ought properly to belong to the regent and council" (Tytler, iv., 2; see also Spottiswoode, iii., 195-6). Instead of the people being now more democratically impatient of tyranny than in the past, they were positively oppressed by Morton in a way they never had been under their kings. He exacted fines in all directions from those who had been on the other side in the civil war, and the circuit courts, under his administration, "became little else than parts of a system of legal machinery invented to overawe and plunder all classes of the community. To supply them with victims he kept in pay a numerous body of informers, whose business it was to discover offences. . . . Ground was found for every species of prosecution; against merchants for transporting coin out of the realm, *against Protestants for transgressing the statute by eating flesh in Lent*, against the poorer artisans or laborers for the mere remaining in a town or city which was occupied by the queen's forces. As to those whose only offence was to be rich, their case was the worst of all; for to have a full purse, and 'thole' [undergo] a heavy fine to the regent, were become synonymous terms" (Tytler, iv., 3). Against this tyranny by a Protestant noble, one of the pillars of the Reformation, the clergy could not and did not help the people. Their comparatively efficient criticism of the ruling powers only began under the weak and ignoble rule of James VI., when the throne was in its old position of conflict with the baronage.

Such was the tenor of ecclesiastical history in Scotland from the Reformation till after the death of Knox; and for us who study the influence of the Kirk as a political and social institution the question arises, What had it done thus far for the nation? Did it improve men's morals or spread light and knowledge, or further justice, or increase liberty, or raise the people, or in any way specially promote civilisation? The answer of the impartial historian must be that it had done none of these things. Taking its rise in sectarian hatred, and finding its life in persecution, it could not vindicate justice, or consecrate liberty; and, making neither for freedom nor tolerance, it could not be said to advance morality. The one thing that can be claimed for it thus far is that its influence was directed against "immorality" in the clerical sense—that is, against unlegalised intercourse between the sexes. When a leading reformer was found to have broken his marriage vow his brethren promptly expelled him (Burton, iv., 90); but of any inculcation of a high general morality their teachings show no trace. It is the bare truth to say that in an age of lawlessness and crime they never protested against lawless violence save when it was used against themselves or their party. Men like Knox, not personally inclined to acts of outrage, availed themselves without scruple of the aid of the most depraved criminals.[1] The murderers of

---

[1] The suspected complicity of Wishart the martyr in the English plot to assassinate Beaton being still insufficiently proved, I offer no statement on the question here. The charge, however, must be kept in view. Compare Tyler, iii., 365 *et seq.*, and Burton, iii., 256-261. As the evidence stands, there is clear ground for suspicion against

Cardinal Beaton, with whom he threw in his lot in 1546, were admittedly a set of grossly licentious ruffians (Burton, iii., 263). Of one of them the clerical historian Robertson has declared that he was "the most corrupt man of his age", a description accepted by Burton, with the remark that it is "an expression condensing within it a terrible mass of criminality" (p. 268); while Knox himself (History, i., 23) afterwards spoke of others of the gang as having become "enemies of Christ Jesus and to all vertew" —which may mean either that after murdering Beaton they cooled in their zeal for Protestantism, or that their later lives were in keeping with that beginning. It proves Knox's entire failure to rise above the ethics of his time that he justified the acts of such men without hesitation when they happened to meet his own wishes. He was even more lawless than his lay contemporaries, not less so. When a layman like Lyndsay could say of the Beaton murder that

"Although the loon was weill away,
The deed was foully done,"

Knox had no regret or scruple whatever. The Rev. Dr. Crichton feels constrained to urge (McCrie's "Life", p. xxxv.) that "the arguments of Knox, drawn from heathen antiquity, to palliate the assassination of Cardinal Beatoun, the ill-timed merriment he displays in relating that foul deed, and the countenance which his comments on that act were calculated to give in a fierce age, to promote murder or unrestrained vengeance—deserved, upon the whole, a severer reprehension, a more decided condemnation than they have found in the pages of his biographer". And the Beaton business was not a solitary case. Knox was always ready to condone and extol a murder which removed an enemy of his cause. Much indignation has been expressed by Presbyterian partisans at a statement of Tytler's (iii., 216, and appendix) that Knox was privy to the murder of David Rizzio. The charge is in point of fact quite reasonably supported;[1] but

---

Wishart, and no satisfactory vindication. The argument relied on by the younger McCrie ("Sketches", p. 41, *note*) is childish.

[1] The case stands thus. The envoy Randolph wrote from Berwick to Elizabeth's minister Cecil in March, 1565-6, naming certain men, and alluding to others unnamed, as having been mixed up in the assassination; and to this letter, in the State Paper Office, was

if it were not, the outcry would still be ridiculous in the face of the unquestioned fact that Knox, in his history (i., 235), declares that "that pultron and vyle knave Davie *was justlie punished*", and complains that the titled assassins, Morton, Ruthven, and Lindsay, and the rest, "*for thare just act, and most worthy of all praise*, ar now unworthely left of thare brethren, and suffer the bitterness of banishement and exyle". Dr. McCrie ("Life," p. 253) concedes that "it is probable" Knox had "expressed his satisfaction" at the murder, but does not think fit to cite the above passage. One wants to know what great moral difference there is between pronouncing a given assassination, after the event, to have been a just act, worthy of all praise, and being privy to it beforehand? I am not making it an indictment against Knox that in an age of blood he gave his countenance to deeds of blood: I simply state the facts, and submit that he was doing nothing to purify his age.

It is claimed for the Reformers, with inveterate fatuity, that they introduced a higher moral tone when they denounced Mary for the killing of Darnley. There could be no more decisive test of the abject empiricism of the ethics of the eulogists and the eulogised. Here was the leading Reformer proclaiming the murder of Rizzio, guilty only of zeal for his mistress and his Church, to be a noble and laudable action, while the murder of the really vile Darnley, most scoundrelly of traitors and most filthy of adulterers, at the instance (real or presumed) of his outraged and nauseated wife, was execrated as the grossest of crimes. Morality becomes a farce in the face of such decisions. No rational reader of history will dispute for a moment that for such an act as the murder of her secretary any

---

found pinned a list of names, dated "Martii, 1565" [= 1566 by modern reckoning], in the hand of Cecil's clerk, with the endorsement, "Names of such as were consenting to the death of David". At the bottom of the list are the names of Knox and his colleague Craig, and there is subjoined a statement beginning: "All these were present at the death of Davy and privy thereunto". It is known that all those named were not present, and Tytler argues that the and = or, a perfectly probable construction. The ecclesiastics, with professional candor, found on the fact that Knox was *not* present, and declare that the construction *and = or* is monstrous. They ignore the fact that the literal construction would make Randolph a crazy gossip.

contemporary sovereign in Mary's place would have felt justified thrice over in beheading the assassins; and looking to the fact that Darnley was one of the framers of the plot, the execration of Mary resolves itself into saying that for a Queen to put her husband to death is the worst of crimes even when he has deserved death by her country's laws. The fact is that the current of popular feeling against Mary in Scotland was determined by the obvious folly of her course and not by its guilt. A mediæval populace never detested a guilty or perfidious sovereign who carried crime regally and remained master of the situation: witness the popular attitude towards Henry VIII. in England and towards his daughter Elizabeth. Mary Stewart, bringing to a desperately difficult situation one of the cleverest heads queen ever had, contrived to lose it more hopelessly than queen ever did; carrying her race's unwisdom in affection to the last stage of possibility. The crowd pardons everything in a ruler save weakness; though, as in Mary's case, it will readily fasten its outcry on a crime by way of justifying its wrath, once aroused. It has, of course, one moral code for kings and another for queens; but, even in that view, to pretend that the clamor raised in Scotland over the killing of Darnley meant pure moral horror at the taking of life—even at the taking of a husband's life—is to water history into a moral tale for the domestic hearth. In these matters the Protestant clergy were exactly on a par with their lay contemporaries alike in the barbarism of their ethics and their transparent personal bias; just as in the next reign they approved of the kidnapping of the King because the kidnappers were in the Protestant interest, while the king was supposed to lean to Catholicism. Their professed respect for law was even as that of the barons, an ingrained cant—for the sixteenth century had its cant like the nineteenth. And so far as Murray, the most reputable of the Protestant leaders, directed the administration of justice, there was even a retrogression from the standards of the time; the poor men concerned in the Darnley tragedy being zealously put to death, while their masters, notoriously the true criminals, went scot free.

In the matter of liberty there is really not the shadow of a case for the early Kirk. As we have seen, it had never entertained the principle of freedom, as such, for a moment. From the first it sought to keep social life under its thumb, taking up the threads where the Church of Rome had dropped them. As early as 1563 we find the ecclesiastical Superintendent of Fife delating four women for witchcraft, and the Assembly calling on the civil power to act, the new Church thus early rivalling the old in sanguinary superstition ("Acts and Proceedings of the General Assemblies," Bannatyne Club ed., Pt. 1, p. 44). Then in 1567 a baronet who harbors an excommunicated man is ordered by the Assembly to send him forth (*Ibid.*, p. 98). Two years later the new clerical power takes upon it to assert an absolute censorship of the press and to order that the Edinburgh printer of the day, Thomas Bassandine, " is not to print without license of the supreme magistrate, and revising of such things as pertain to religion by some of the Kirk appointed to that purpose" (*Ibid.*, p. 126); and in 1574 a Committee of Assembly is appointed "to oversee all manner of books or works that shall be proposed to be printed, and to give their judgment thereupon if the same be allowed and approved by the law of God or not". New Protestant was but old priest writ large, and when the Protestant became a full-fledged Presbyter the correspondence was still more emphatic. We have seen how, at his outset, he laid his hand on popular amusements; and we shall see later the full effect of his censorship of the press and his general intellectual influence. Meanwhile, simultaneously with the definite establishment of the censorship, the Assembly made elaborate arrangements for the extinction of the love of beauty in the popular mind, with what results innumerable later comments on the squalor and uncleanliness of the Scottish common people can testify.

The reverend brethren thus express themselves on the subject of dress: "We thinke all kynd of brodering vnseimlie; all vagaries of velvett on gownes, hoses, or coat; and all superfluous and vaine cutting out, steiking with silks; all kynd of costlie sewing on passments, or sumptuous or large stoiking with silks; all kynd of costly sewing or variant hews in sarks; all kynd of light and variant hewes in cloathing, as red, blew, yeallow, and sicklyke, *whilk declares the lightnes of the mynd*; all wearing of rings, bracelets, buttons of silver, gold, or other mettall; all kynd of superfluitie of cloath in makeing of hose; all vsing of plaids in the Kirk be Reidars or Ministers . . .; all kynd of gowning, coating or doubliting, or breiches of velvett, satine, taffettie, or sicklyke; all costly gilting of whingers and knyves, or sicklyke; all silk hatts, or hatts of divers and light collours. But that their haill habite be of grave collour, as black russet, sad grey, sad browne, or serges, wirsett chamlet, growgrame-lytes, wirsett, or sicklike" (*Ibid.*, p. 335). And a "daring obligation", as Dr. Burton terms it, was undertaken by the brethren for "their wives to be subject to the same ordour". The significance of such a piece of sumptuary legislation goes further than the unspeakable catalogue of haberdashery it presents, further than its mere direct prohibitions. Such a list of forbidden embellishments is the work of men who were capable of carrying priestly inquisition into the minutiæ of life as no clergy had ever done before, and who were determined to get hold alike of the bodies and the souls of the multitude around them, crushing all individual instinct within their rigid scheme and deadening all the hues of life to their own joyless monotone of asceticism.

This was in 1573, and after the final fall of Morton in 1581 the Church year by year gained in social and even in political influence, though its constitution had still vicissitudes before it. In 1580, before Morton's arrest, the Assembly is found deciding that "the office of ane bishop, as it is now used and commonly taken within this realm, has no sure warrant, authority or good ground out of the scripture of God, but is brought in by folly and corruption, to the great overthrow of the kirk of God". The office accordingly was abolished, and the existing bishops were called on to surrender their functions, under pain of excommunication (Burton v., 201—2). Next came the "Second Book of Discipline", in which the Kirk's Constitution is placed on a definitely Presbyterian basis, that polity being now strenuously urged by a new school of ecclesiastics, at the head of whom was Alexander Melville, lately returned from the continent, and bringing with him the latest developments of Protestant ecclesiasticism, as Knox and others had brought the creed of Geneva. The Parliament, as before, refused to give legal force to the Church's scheme of discipline (*Ibid.*, 204) but the clergy adhered to it for themselves; and in the beginning of 1581 they obtained the boy king's signature to a document wordily repudiating "all kinds of Papistry", variously known as the First Covenant, the Second Confession of Faith (the First being that of 1560), the King's Confession, and the Negative Confession. With the King on their side, the clergy forcibly imposed this Covenant on the nation, a royal mandate being obtained empowering them to compel the signatures of their parishioners and to proceed against Recusants according to civil and church law. (*Ibid.*, 208.) Presbyterianism now began to take hold of the popular mind (p.210). The boy king remained a childish monarch at maturity; and only his passion for absolutism—a revulsion from the democratic teachings of his tutor George Buchanan—prevented the clergy from fully attaining the political power it sought. The episode known as the Raid of Ruthven, the kidnapping of the young King in 1582, had their full approbation as being the work of Protestant lords; but though James had many skirmishes with the Kirk, he judged it prudent to leave an influential clergyman instead of a noble to act as regent during his matrimonial expedition to Denmark in 1589; and in 1592 episcopacy was formally abolished and Presbyterianism established by Act of Parliament; this step being followed up in 1593 by an Act "for punishment of the contemners of the decreets and judicatories of the Kirk" (Burton, iv., 277—80). Thus in the period from 1560 to 1592, Scotland saw established, first a Protestant system with something like virtual episcopacy, under which Catholic hierarchical titles were still recognised; then a regular and legalised Protestant episcopacy; and then a system of pure Presbyterianism.

And how did the national life develop all the while? Dr. Burton, dating the strictly Presbyterian movement from a "religious revival" about 1580, sums up the moral history of the previous twenty years in the sentence: "On the present occasion, speaking of the mere social and moral influences set at work, a stranger might welcome the advent of efforts which, whether spiritually orthodox or not, yet had something in them tending to check or modify the spirit of ferocity, rapacity, and sensuality that was spreading moral desolation over the land" (v., 201). His own account of the state of things thirty years later still, tells us how far such a hypothetical hope had been fulfilled. But first let us hear the old historian of the Kirk proclaiming at once the triumph of Presbyterian polity and the concurrent demoralisation, civil and religious, of the land: "The Kirk of Scotland was now come to her perfection, and the greatest puritie that ever she atteaned unto, both in doctrine and discipline, so that her beautie was admirable to forraine kirks. The assembleis of the sancts were never so glorious, nor profitable to everie one of the true members thereof, than in the beginning of this yeere" [1596] (Calderwood, v., 387). And in the Assembly of the spring of this very year, as reported by the same writer (p. 409), official complaint is made of "the commonn corruptions of all estats within this realme", as follows: "An universall coldnesse and decay of zeale in all estats, joyned with ignorance and contempt of the Word, ministrie, and sacraments; and where knowledge is, no sense or feeling. . . . Superstitioun and idolatrie is interteaned, which uttereth itself in keeping of festivall dayes, bone-fires, pilgrimages, singing of carrolls at Yuille. Great blasphemie of the holie name of God in all estats, with horrible banning and cursing in all their speeches. Profanation of the Sabboth, and speciallie in seed-tyme and harvest. . . . Little care, reverence, and obedience of inferiours to their superiours, as siclyke of superiours in discharging of their duteis to their inferiours. . . . A flood of bloodshed and deadlie feuds rising thereupon; an universall assisting of bloodsheds, for eluding of lawes. Adulteries, fornications, incests, unlawfull marriages, and divorcements . . . .; excessive drinking and waughting; gluttonie, which is no doubt the cause of the dearth and famine . . . .; Sacrilege in all estats, without anie conscience, growing continuallie more and more, to the utter undoing of the Kirk; . . . . cruel oppression of the poore tenents, whereby the whole commouns of the countrie are utterly wracked. . . . . A greate number of idle persons without lawfull calling, as pypers, fiddlers, songsters, sorners, plesents, strong beggars, living in harlotrie, and having their children unbaptized, without all kinde of repairing to the Word. . . . . Universall neglect of justice both in civil and criminal causes . . . .; no executioun of good lawes made against vices, or in favour of the kirk. In parliament sacrilegious persons, as abbots, pryours, dumbe bishops, voting in name of the kirk, contrare the laws of the countrie. . . . . The sessioun [*i.e.*, the law courts] is charged with buying of pleyes [pleas] delaying of justice, and briberie." It is further stated, on p. 416, that "the land is overflowed with Atheisme and all kinds of vice, there being above foure hundreth parish kirks destituted of the ministrie of the Word, by and attour [*i.e.*, over and above] the kirks of Argile and the Iles." And it is proposed, by way of reforming the pastorate, "That suche as are light and wantoun in behaviour . . . . in speeche, in using light and profane companie, unlawfull gaming, as dancing, cairding [*i.e.*, card-playing], dyeing [dicing] and suche like . . . . be sharpelie and gravelie reproved by the presbyterie. . . . . That ministers being found swearers . . . . profainers of the Sabboth, drunkards, fighters, guiltie of all these, or anie of them, to be deposed *simpliciter*. . . . . That ministers given to unlawfull and uncompetent trades and occupations for filthie gaine, as holding of ostlareis [hostelries], taiking of ocker [usury] beside [against] conscience and good lawes, and bearing worldlie offices in noble and gentlemen's houses, merchandice and such like, buying of victualls, and keeping to dearth . . . . be admonished . . . . and if they continue therein, to be deposed" (pp. 404-5). Such were the concomitants of purity and perfection in the assemblies of the saints: such the palmy days of primeval Presbyterianism. At the end of the report of this Assembly's proceedings (p. 420) Calderwood writes: "Heere end all the sincere Assembleis Generall of the Kirk of Scotland, injoying the libertie of the Gospell under the free government of Christ", the statement having reference to the fact that in 1597 the political see-saw again brought about an establishment of episcopacy by the Estates. On the whole it might be thought that the intermission of the "sincere Assemblies" was a good thing. On their own showing they had co-existed not only with general demoralisation but with the most scandalous backwardness in those very matters of religion which the clergy professed to have specially at heart. And the situation is not hard to understand. The moral and intellectual elevation of any people is a complex process, in which the pursuit of the liberal arts and of commerce is a most important element. In a nation accustomed to violence there is no other way of attaining peaceful civilisation. But instead of availing itself of these means of amelioration the Kirk was positively hostile to the first and cold towards the second. Its trusted spiritual weapons were those of fanatical exhortation, of monition, of ascetic denunciation: violence it opposed with violence, justifying its own deeds as wrought in the service of God, though accomplished with the weapons of carnal wickedness; and trampling the idea of religious tolerance under foot. Such a policy made men neither just nor humane, neither pure nor charitable; while all the special fruits of intense superstition were present in rank luxuriance. To that end the Kirk exercised a double influence, spreading fanaticism by direct methods on the one hand, and on the other crushing out all leanings towards intellectual light. A close study of Scottish history suggests that the nation's ecclesiastical experience has something to do with the growth of one species of intellectual capacity, but against this service, be it worth what it may, there is to be set a tremendous account of disservice to the nation's best interests. Before the Reformation Scotland had begun to build up a literature of poetry and drama; and the prosperity of Catholicism insured a certain effort towards art. True, the progress of the country under the Stewarts had been but slow. There are many reasons for accepting the conclusion of Dr. Burton (iii., 432, 438) that the country had been substantially richer before the War of Independence in the thirteenth century than it was in the middle of the sixteenth; the explanation being that the constant struggle with England on the one hand, and on the other the unending civil convulsions—arising out of the military power inevitably acquired by the nobles in a country constantly at war—were always draining the nation of material wealth; the poverty so induced making the nobles still more bent on plunder and ever more factious. In the strong though short reign of James the Fourth, however, the country had progressed remarkably alike in wealth and in culture; and it was in the troubled reign of his son, which began in a long minority, that the Reformation movement began. The question is, then, whether that movement, as taking shape in the Protestant Kirk, tended to the nation's intellectual progress, putting the matter of wealth aside; and when we find that it absolutely made an end for a whole age of literature proper and of every form of art, the question is pretty well answered in the negative.

Confining ourselves to the two reigns of the Fourth and Fifth Jameses, we have literature represented by the many-sided poet Dunbar and the satiric and dramatic poet Sir David Lyndsay, two names which will compare with any in English literature up to the same period, with the one exception of Chaucer. But Dunbar, if on the whole less important and permanent, is in his way not less unique and really not less powerful than Chaucer; so unique and so powerful that there is no Scottish lyric poet who can be named beside him down to the time of Burns; and on Lyndsay's chief dramatic work, the morality play of "The Thrie Estaitis", we have the verdict of Mr. Ward that in vigor and variety it "far exceeds any English effort of the same species", and is further "by far the most elaborate and powerful of all the mediæval Moralities" ("History of English Dramatic Literature", i., 70—71). Put beside these writers' works those of Bishop Gavin Douglas, the translator of the Æneid, and the poems attributed to James V., and it becomes clear that Scotland was at the beginning of the sixteenth century far on the way to the possession of a literature at once brilliant and popular—the surest manifestation of an upward tendency in civilisation. A people with such a literature promised to become enlightened, artistic, and free from superstition. What the rise of the Protestant Kirk made them was the direct antithesis of all these.

XI.

THE PERVERSION OF SCOTLAND.
By JOHN ROBERTSON.
(III.)

BLOODY civil strife is always injurious to culture; and in 1560 the impulse given by Dunbar, Douglas, and Lyndsay, was certainly not obviously bearing fruit. But it was the work of the Kirk that instead of a reaction towards culture the whole back-swing of the nation's mind was substantially towards an arid fanaticism. The inner spirit of the new movement was hostile to literature and art as such. I say this advisedly, with full recognition of all that can be said as to the learning of a few of the first Reformers, and of men like Andrew Melville in the generation immediately following. The essence of living literature, living thought, living science, and living art, is the free play of the mind in all these various directions, and to the Reformers the idea of giving free play to the mind in any direction whatever was rank profanity. Melville might indeed discuss the classics with a scholar's gusto, and, basing himself on the new scholastic infallibilism of the Bible, might boldly challenge in the schools the supremacy of Aristotle; but here even his intelligence set bounds to its critical action; and while he could not but have some personal influence for light, if not for sweetness, his power was fatally greater in the narrow sphere of doctrine than in the broad sphere of knowledge. At best, his culture had no help for the common people. The very praise given him for his services in furthering the classical movement in Scotland is decisive as to his worse than failure to promote the national literature. On the one hand an imitative, insincere, academic classicism; on the other a vulgarised Calvinism—such was the literary message of the Reformation for Scotland. The classicism never took hold of life at all; the Calvinism blighted life at every point of contact. A moral code arbitrarily deduced from the Bible was made to apply to every species of action whatever, with the result of finding evil in nearly everything men found pleasure in doing. Much has been said in praise of the scheme of the universities and schools projected by Knox and his colleagues (see Knox, ii., 213, *et seq.*), and it may freely be conceded that if the avarice and barbarism of the landowning class had allowed that scheme to be carried out, some beneficial spread of knowledge might have resulted. But such a result could only have accrued by indirect means, not at all by reason of the kind of policy the kirk would have pursued in education. The typical learned Presbyterian of the age was Andrew Melville, in whom the most copious scholarship bore little save the Dead Sea fruit of factitious polemics. Knox himself has left positively nothing of permanent human value save his vivid record of the movement in which he bore part. And when we set beside this negative indictment, this destitutution of healthful teaching, the positive performance of the Kirk in the way of sowing superstition and deepening mental darkness, it is hard to see what room there is left for crediting it with any service to national progress.

Presbyterian partisans, hard pressed to vindicate their ancestors on the subject of witch-burning, take the line of asserting that the witchcraft mania was an inheritance from Romanism. The ruse is puerile. The Reformers would have made short work of a colleague who refused to see that the exhortation to witch-killing and the authority for the belief in sorcery came from Holy Writ. What historically concerns us here to-day is that whereas in Catholic times there was no witch-burning in Scotland, the Protestant clergy were as zealous in that walk as they were in denouncing Popery and sexual license. The first legal enactment against witchcraft in Scottish history is the Act of the Protestant Parliament of 1563, in which the penalty of death is enacted "alsweill . . . aganis the usar, abusar, as the seikar of the response or consultatioun" (Acts, ii., 539); this being one of the few things in which the Estates conformed to the wishes of Knox (Burton, iv., 72). As we have seen (*ante*, p. 154), the clergy at once sought to give effect to the new statute. It is difficult, however, to trace their achievements closely. Pitcairn ("Criminal Trials in Scotland", I., part ii., p. 49) speaks of the case of Bessie Dunlop in 1576 as one of the earliest witchcraft trials of which detailed record remains; the only previous case in his compilation, I think (save one in which a woman was only banished), being that of Janet Boyman in 1572 (*Ibid.*, p. 38). I find in his collection accounts of fifty-seven prosecutions for witchcraft in all, the accused being burned in nineteen cases and beheaded in three. But he notes (iii., 597) that during the reign of James VI. "hundreds of helpless creatures were destroyed under form of law" on the charge of witchcraft; "for those who were tried before the High Court of Justiciary bore a very small proportion to the very great numbers who were tried and condemned by the Lords of Regalities, Baron Bailies, and by the Royal Commissioners. A very striking fact mentioned by Baron Hume in his valuable Commentaries [ref. to Hume on Punishment for Crimes, ii., 559] may be here briefly noted, that no fewer than *fourteen* Commissions for Trial of Witches were granted [*note :* by the Lords of Privy Council] for different quarters of the country, *in one sederunt*, of the 7th of November, 1661; which year seems to have been the most fertile period of this sort of accusation." That is to say, the mania reached its highest point in Scotland one hundred years after the Reformation, the superstition having steadily intensified from the time of Knox, down through the historic Covenanting period under Charles I., when the nation became most thoroughly Presbyterian and devout.

The influence of the clergy to this end, implied in the main facts, is made clear by the details collected by Pitcairn in regard to trials for witchcraft. "There was generally in all cases of this nature," he writes (I., Pt. ii., p. 49), "a previous Precognition [*i.e.*, examination] taken before the Privy Council, most frequently after repeated examinations before the Kirk Session or the Presbytery. . . . . Such inquisitions generally proceeded upon a Special Commission issued by the Privy Council; when the evidence of neighbors was taken down, whose lamentable ignorance and superstitious fears would magnify into Sorcery and Witchcraft the simplest actions of the life of the suspected Witch." It is unnecessary here to go into any description of the ghastly mediæval mania in question. The case of Bessie Dunlop is typical, it being perfectly evident from the records that that poor woman became insane after childbirth, and that her illusions were taken as a reason for burning her. Pitcairn's account of the manner of witch-worrying in Puritan Scotland, however, has present importance. "Solitary confinement," he goes on, "cold and famine, extreme thirst, the want of sleep, and the privation of all the comforts, even the commonest necessaries of life, the desertion of their affrighted relations and friends, added to the cruellest tortures, generally induced them at length, weary of life, to make their 'Confession' as it was called. One of the most powerful incentives to 'Confession' was systematically to deprive the suspected witch of the refreshment of her natural rest and sleep; and the cruellest means were often resorted to, to accomplish this heinous purpose. Even the indulgence of lying in a reclining posture on their handful of straw was frequently denied them. This engine of inhuman oppression was perhaps more effectual in extorting confessions than the actual application of the torture or *question* itself. Iron collars, or 'witches' bridles', are still preserved in various parts of Scotland which had formerly been used for such iniquitous purposes. These instruments were so constructed, that by means of a hoop which passed over the head, a piece of iron, having four points or prongs, was forcibly thrust into the mouth, two of these being directed to the tongue and palate, the others pointing outward to each cheek. This infernal machine was secured by a padlock. At the back of the collar was fixed a ring by which to attach the witch to a staple in the wall of her cell. Thus equipped, and night and day 'waked' and watched by some *skilful* person appointed by her inquisitors, the unhappy creature, after a few days of such discipline, maddened by the misery of her forlorn and helpless state, would be rendered fit for 'confessing' anything, in order to be rid of the dregs of her wretched life. At intervals, fresh examinations took place, and these were repeated from time to time, until her 'contumacy', as it was termed, was subdued. The Clergy and Kirk Sessions appear to have been the unwearied instruments of 'purging the land of witchcraft'; and to them, in the first instance, all such complaints and informations were made."

As regards the practice of judicial torture, it is clear that the clergy were assiduous in that insanest of all forms of cruelty the world has seen. Tytler notes (iv., 231) that when the Jesuit Morton was captured in 1595, "the ministers of the Kirk insisted that this unhappy person should be subject to the torture of the boots, as the only means of obtaining a full confession "; and we know from Pitcairn that the victims of the witch mania were tortured in the presence of ministers, who signed the reports. Some of the refinements of atrocity achieved in the pursuit will compare not ineffectively with the choicest exploits of the Holy Inquisition; witness the case of Alison Balfour, who was tortured in the "caschielawis" for forty-eight hours on end, during part of which time her aged husband, her eldest son, and her little daughter, aged seven, were all tortured before her, not as being themselves guilty, but simply in order to extort her confession. That being obtained, she was loosed, whereupon she at once revoked the statement wrung from her (Pitcairn, I., part ii., p. 375). Two ministers assisted at her execution. The superstition, of course, soon pervaded all classes, King James being one of the devoutest believers; and in time the magistrates became as zealous as the clergy in destroying the wretched women who came under the insensate suspicion of the populace. Here is one contemporary piece of narrative, a memorandum by Thomas, Earl of Haddington, in his Minutes of the Privy Council Proceedings, under date December 1st, 1608 (Haddington MSS. A. 4, 22, Advocates' Library, quoted by Pitcairn, iii., 597): "The Erle of Mar declairit to the Counsall that sum wemen were tane in Broichtoun" [before the Baron Baillie of the Regality of Broughton, near Edinburgh, Pitcairn explains] "as Witches; and being put to ane Assyse and convict, albeit thay perseverit constant in thair denyell to the end, yit thay wer burnit quick, efter sic ane crewell manner, that sum of thame deit in despair, renunceand and blaspheamand; and otheris, half brunt, brak out of the fire, and wes cast in quick in it agane, quhill thay wer brunt to the deid." Burning "quick" [*i.e.*, alive] was a late development, the witch having usually been "wirreit" or strangled before being burned in the early days. The people seem to have passed from cruelty to cruelty precisely as they became more and more fanatical, more and more devoted to their Church, till after many generations the slow spread of humane science began to counteract the ravages of superstition; the clergy, as we shall see, resisting reason and humanity to the last. This is the most salient feature in the mental life of the Scottish people for a century after the Reformation as contrasted with their life before it—this shifting of the balance of superstition from the mainly absurd accessories of Catholicism to the deadly belief in diabolic influences. Hallam has flatly declared ("Literature of Europe," part 1, c. iv., sec. 61) that the theology of Luther was no more acceptable to reason than the theology he assailed: he might similarly have said that in Scotland the Reformation, on the intellectual side, meant for the people the replacement of folly by frenzy, of delusion by mania, of twilight by darkness—a darkness which its few lights of scholarship only serve to make more visible in the retrospect. In the essential mattters of social brotherhood and beneficence I can detect no gain from the theological change in Scottish history. When in 1569 famine and pestilence visited the harassed land, the new cultus bore no fruit in pity or human kindness. "The public policy was directed rather to the preservation of the untainted than to the recovery of the sick. In other words, selfishness ruled the day. The inhumanity towards the humbler classes was dreadful. Well might *Maister Gilbert Skeyne, Doctor in Medicine*, remark in his little tract on the pest, now printed in Edinburgh: 'Every ane is become sae detestable to other (whilk is to be lamentit), and specially the puir in the sight of the rich, as gif they were not equal with them touching their creation, but rather without saul or spirit, as beests degenerate fra mankind!' This worthy mediciner tells us, indeed, that he was partly moved to publish his book by 'seeand the puir in Christ inlaik [perish] without assistance or support in body, all men detestand aspection, speech, or communication with them'" (Chambers' "Domestic Annals of Scotland", i., 52—53). Here the new religion failed, on test, to inspire brotherly compassion, about as utterly as any pagan creed ever did; and its doctrine of witchcraft wrought directly and enormously for the searing of humane feeling. "Towards those who came under the suspicion of diabolical dealing there was no pity left in the human heart. . . . . Where the suspicion alighted it carried belief with it, so as to render this chapter in the history of human wrongs perhaps the very darkest and saddest of them all" (Burton, vii., 115). Such is the feeling of the latest and most temperate historian of Scotland, contemplating the condition of his country as its religious "re-

formation" determined it for a hundred years.
those who represent the ecclesiastical change as a
amelioration of the national life, moral and 1
weigh against their theological gains the immortal ......,
of that awful murder roll.

The history of the Kirk after the Presbyterian climax of
1592 is to the full as chequered as that of the generation
before. So soon afterwards as 1597 the Estates at the
wish of the king passed an Act once more providing that
any pastors or ministers on whom the king should confer
the office and title of bishop or abbot, or any similar distinction, should sit and vote in Parliament freely as of old
(Acts, iv., 130; Burton, v., 314). This has been so often
represented as a tyrannous interference with the Kirk's
internal affairs that it may be well to state plainly how
matters really stood. The clergy were as far as could well
be conceived from desiring merely to be left alone in their
spiritual functions. The Second Book of Discipline (of
1581) had expressly stipulated that while the civil power
had no right to interfere in Church management, beyond
"commanding the spiritual to exercise and do their office
according to the Word of God", on the other hand "the
spiritual rulers should require the Christian magistrate to
minister justice and punish vice, and to maintain the liberty
and quietness of the Kirk within their bounds" (Burton,
v., 203). Thus, as Burton comments, "the State could
give no effective orders to the Church, but the Church
could order the State to give material effect to its rules and
punishments". The State did not grant the modest demand, but such was the clerical scheme. Again we find
Row ("History of the Kirk," Wodrow Society's ed., p.
184), representing the clergy in 1597 as perceiving that
"plotts were laid down for the alteration of religion or the
bringing in of *libertie of conscience at the least.*" When, on
the contrary, the Estates re-established episcopacy in 1597,
they did nothing to give the bishops any spiritual jurisdiction in the Church (Burton, p. 315). Some juggling took
place in the Assemblies, in which bribery seems to have
played a part, by way of getting the ministers to accept
the situation; and on this being partially secured in 1600,
two or three bishops were created (Calderwood, vi., 96;
Spottiswoode, iii., 82). A strong spirit of time-serving had
become conspicuous among the ignorant and ill-paid clergy;

the king's party in the 1598 Assembly being described by Calderwood, their spiritual brother, as "a sad, subservient rabble", led by a "drunken Orkney asse" (v., 695). Financial or fanatical self-interest was indeed the one political light the clergy possessed;[1] and accordingly when, in 1600, the crazy Gowrie Conspiracy to assassinate James made its futile sputter, the high Presbyterian section almost to a man championed the cause of the would-be assassins, unjustly enough, for the simple reason that the house of Gowrie was known to be strongly Presbyterian, while James was at least Episcopalian and his wife was Catholic.

About this time, however, the fortunes of the Puritan party began to sink very low. There is clear reason to conclude that it was only in contrast with the personal folly and weakness of James that they had been politically influential; and when in 1603 James acceded to the throne of England, and Scotch affairs were attended to for him by the Privy Council, consisting of nobles now no longer in conflict with the crown, the clergy, as of old, went quickly to the wall before the compact force of the aristocracy. All along, the northern districts, of which Aberdeen may be termed the capital, had been mainly royalist; standing for Catholicism in Mary's time and for Episcopalianism in James's; the power of the Melville party being chiefly confined to the south, the west, and Fifeshire. To the people of the northern districts the Puritan party were "the popes of Edinburgh" (Burton, v., 431). Accordingly when, in 1605, the aristocratic party gainsaid "the popes" on the question of the king's relation to the Church, there was a singular collapse on the clerical side. The battle, says Burton (v., 433), "was fought on the question whether General Assemblies belonged to the Crown, and were called and adjourned in the king's name, or were bodies acting in self-centred independence". "This question," he adds, "oddly enough, is not yet settled, and is evaded by a subterfuge so abundantly ridiculous as to be a standing butt for the jests of

---

[1] On this head I may cite the judgment of Mr. Robert Louis Stevenson in his essay on "Knox in his Relations to Women", reprinted in his "Familiar Studies of Men and Books". That admirable writer's standpoint is different from mine, but he is explicit as to the political benightedness of the Reformation clergy in Scotland, with the partial exception of Knox.

the profane "—the allusion being to the annual hocus-pocus between the Queen's Commissioner and the General Assembly. What happened was that the Melville party, more brave than prudent, called an Assembly at Aberdeen; which being forbidden by royal proclamation, there met only nine members, these of course being Melvillites. At a second "Assembly", also prohibited, they mustered nineteen; whereupon the Privy Council interfered, and imprisoned fourteen of them. In January, 1606, six of these, including John Welch, Knox's son-in-law, were brought to trial for treason and found guilty by a small majority of the jury; and in October, 1606, they were sentenced to banishment; while about the same time the unsubduable Melville, his nephew, and six others, were formally invited to the English Court to "treat" with his majesty. The end was that a Latin epigram of Melville's brought him into sharp collision with the king and council; he further assailing Episcopalianism in their presence with such audacity and vehemence that he was imprisoned in the Tower for four years, obtaining his liberty only on condition of leaving the country; while his companions were put under surveillance in different towns, English and Scotch. Melville, who was sixty-six years old at the time of his banishment, henceforward drops out of Scottish history, living mainly as a wandering scholar till his death at Sedan in 1622. "His death," remarks Dr. Burton (v., 439), "was almost unnoticed, and his fame faded away from all memories save those of the remnant of his own peculiar people. His name will not be found in the biographical dictionaries save in a few of recent times, for his fame in the present day is due to its resuscitation by a man who lived in the present generation" [*i.e.*, Dr. McCrie].

It thus appears that after a period of fanatical activity the Puritan movement positively subsided before the cold hostility of the Scots governing class, acting together with none of the vacillation and none of the childishness which characterised the personal policy of the king, though refusing to go as far as James required. Doubtless the flame of fanaticism had for the time gone far to exhaust itself. On the expulsion of Welch and his friends, the remnant of the Presbytery of Edinburgh professed to rejoice at the exhibition of his majesty's "just anger", declaring the offenders to be persons whom "the Kirk here has at last been forced to cut off and excommunicate from her society" (Burton v., 436). So far did the reaction go that in 1606 the Estates passed yet another Act for the establishment of Episcopacy, this time professing to give the bishops not only their honors and dignities but their ancient revenues as well (Burton, v., 441; Acts iv., 281; Calderwood, vi., 496); and James, now thoroughly attached to the English system, set about getting the consent of the clergy to the installation of the bishops and archbishops as "constant moderators", or supervisors, of Presbyteries, Synods, and Assemblies. There was some fight left in the high Presbyterians; and a story is told of a conflict, involving a personal scuffle and some profanity, between the King's emissary Lord Scoon and the Synod of Perth in 1607—(see McCrie's "Sketches", p. 151, and references there). But James was able to obtain in 1610 the positive acceptance of the Act of 1606 by a General Assembly, "by dint of bribery and intimidation" as is explained by the true-blue Presbyterians of modern times. It does not appear to be realised by these loyal partisans that the very occurrence of such wholesale bribery as they allege is the most damning impeachment of the Kirk of their devotion. On their own showing, it was then two-thirds corrupt. The evidence is decisive. Sir James Balfour, the annalist (ii., 18) states that in 1606 the Earl of Dunbar, James's Commissioner and Scottish Lord Treasurer was notoriously understood to have "distributed amongst the most neiddey and clamorous of the ministrey to obtain ther voyces and suffrages, (or ells moue them to be neutralls) forty thousand merkes of money to facilitate the bussines intendit, and cause matters goe the smouthlier one;" the fact being made certain by the later discovery of Dunbar's accounts. And the clerical historian Row—who, says the younger McCrie, "may have somewhat exaggerated the sum"—states ("History of the Kirk", p. 289) that in buying the benefices of the bishops "out of the hands of the noblemen that had them, in buying votes at Assemblies, in defraying of all their other charges", the King "did employ (by the confession of such as were best acquainted with, and were actors in these businesses) above the summe of three hundreth thowsand pounds sterlin money—that is, sixe and thirtie hundreth thowsand pounds, or fiftie-four hundreth thowsand merks Scots money". There can be no manner of doubt that Mr. Row exaggerated extensively, but the fact of the bribing remains; and there is no evidence of any special "intimidation" in the business. Money sufficed to procure a majority for episcopacy in the Glasgow Assembly of 1610; the distribution of golden angels being such as to secure the addition of "the angelical Assembly" to the list of Scotch historic nicknames. By this arrangement the Kirk positively agreed to have its annual Assembly regarded as called and constituted by the Crown; and to place its provincial synods under the permanent supervision of the bishops, who were further to have jurisdiction in matters formerly in the hands of presbyteries. The clergy indeed proposed that the bishops should be subject to the censure of the General Assembly, but when the Estates finally ratified the new arrangement in 1612 they simply ignored the stipulation. Here again the aristocratic party nominally arranged the Kirk's constitution to their own taste; but here again their invincible greed eventually brought about the frustration of their own scheme. The landowners were willing and even eager to retain episcopacy, enacting it again and again as we have seen; but nothing could induce them to provide properly for the class they wanted to establish. The new bishops in their degree had to endure precisely the same sort of financial hardships as the general clergy underwent formerly (see Burton, v., 444–461); and this circumstance, as we shall find, at length indirectly brought about a new and intenser development of Presbyterianism, a deeper and more enduring popular fanaticism.

All this while there was the reverse of a falling-off in the denunciation of Popery and the burning of witches; venal and fanatical ministers being alike "sound" and zealous on these heads. After the Gunpowder Plot, James's Protestantism was pretty well above suspicion, and that and other Romish scares gave the Scotch clergy abundant pretext for the inculcation of their first principle—the damnableness of Papistry. In 1600 the clergy called upon the king to prevent the French ambassador from having mass in his own house (Calderwood, vi., 27); an insanity which the British Solomon declined to commit. In 1615 came the execution of the Jesuit Ogilvie, already mentioned; an event in regard to which the pious Calderwood, with characteristic Christian charity, notes (vii., 196) that "some interpreted this execution to have proceedit rather of a care to blesse the king's governement than of anie sincere hatred to the Popish religion. Some deemed that it was done to be a terrour to the sincerer sort of the ministrie not to decline the king's authoritie in anie caus whatsoever." Similarly the reverend historian, telling how three citizens of Edinburgh, who had been sentenced to death for entertaining priests, were reprieved at the scaffold, states (vii., 202) that "the people thought this forme of dealing rather mockerie than punishment". It is plain from whom "the people" would get the hint. The clergy were positively disgusted that a priest's execution should not be indisputably on the sole ground of his religion; and angry when the civil power had the clemency to spare at the last moment three doomed citizens whose sole crime was the harboring of the priests of their faith. It is worth noting on the other hand, by way of offset to official Catholic misdeeds, that when in 1599 the king was sued by the Rev. Robert Bruce for withheld stipend, and the king in person tried to browbeat the Court of Session to decide in his own favor, the president, Sir Alexander Seton, who was a Catholic, and as such denied the right to the practice of his worship by Bruce's sect, firmly resisted the royal interference, and joined in a judgment against the king (Tytler, iv., 270).

Expressly trained in religious hate, steeped in the darkest superstition, and withheld from all art and culture by the precept and example of a clergy who were confessedly coarse and ignorant where not intensely fanatical—held aside thus from civilisation on all hands, the Scottish people of all classes still naturally made slow progress in the matter of social order. The Earl of Haddington, whom we have seen exposing the cruelties of the witch mania, is found in 1617 declaring ("State Papers . . . . of Thomas, Earl of Melrose", published by Abbotsford Club, 1837, i., 273) that whereas his contemporaries could remember a time when disorder was universal, they had now arrived, under the glorious rule of James, at a condition of prosperity and good government unequalled anywhere; and he gives a frightful catalogue of notorious oppression, bloodshed, and crime, to bear out the first part of the statement. This Dr. Burton accepts (vi., 16) as a substantially accurate description of the condition of Scotland at the union of the Crowns. The picture would probably hold more precisely true of an earlier part of James's reign, some improvement having taken place before 1603; but on the other hand the Earl's account of matters in 1617, drawn up as it is in a letter from him to the king, is certainly untrustworthy in its courtly optimism. Progress was no doubt made after James's departure, under the rule of a vigorous executive, and of such statesmen as Binning himself; but lawlessness was still rife. Apart from the virtual barbarism of the Highlands and the Isles, we find it incidentally noticed by Calderwood (vii., 201) that highway robbery was practised round about Edinburgh in 1615 by "certaine bair and idle gentlemen" whom the common people called "Whilliwhaes"; and the fact is significant of the condition of the country in general. The same writer briefly tells (vii., 118) how in 1610 a batch of thirty-six pirates was brought to Edinburgh, and twenty-seven hanged *en masse* at Leith. It was with such recent memories, with such deeds going on around them, with such practice to show for their theological system, that the clergy and their more devout adherents waxed hysterical over the attempts of James, on his Scottish visit in 1617 and later, to impose on the Kirk the methods of worship in vogue in England. Rapine and murder, perennial violence and rank vice, might elicit their lamentations, but what touched them to the quick was the suggestion that certain ceremonies should be performed kneeling which had been usually performed sitting or standing; that Christmas should be kept as a holiday; and that baptism or communion might be gone through in private. James nevertheless contrived to get a majority in the Perth Assembly of 1618 for five such revolutionary changes; and though the minority predicted the most awful consequences, it does not appear that during the twenty years which elapsed before another Assembly was held there was any special alteration in the social life of the country, save in that progressive perversion of the national mind which made trivial formalities and empty shibboleths more and more the main subjects of intellectual exercise.

When James's fussy meddling with church ceremonies is dignified, as it is by Buckle (iii., 113), with the title of an attempt to "subvert the liberties of Scotland"—as if the serious liberties of the people had ever yet been gained at all—it is natural that the further and more blundering interferences of his son Charles should be regarded as a still more desperate stretch of tyranny. But these popular notions, hastily adopted as they have been by men of high ability, are seen in the light of later research to be mostly empirical, and to be founded chiefly on clerical prejudice and rhetoric. Even the resistance to the ritualistic innovations of James had behind it the ever-vigorous force of the pecuniary interest of the baronage and landowners. An Act of 1617 (Acts, iv., 529) provided for the recovery of the minor temporalities formerly attaching to deaneries, canonries, and prebendaries; and this measure no doubt was felt by the nobles, as Dr. Burton suggests, to be a means towards the feathering of their own nests; but in the circumstances they could not well refuse the further Act (*Ibid.*, p. 531) appointing a Parliamentary commission to effect the better remuneration of ministers. This had practical results. "The minimum allowance [fixed by the commission] was equivalent to 500 merks, a sum estimated at £27 15s. 6d. sterling; the maximum reached 800 merks, estimated at £44 9s. sterling. As ecclesiastical lawyers and antiquaries find that the complaints of the Churchmen about their incomes were much modified after this commission began its work, there is the inference that it gave them some satisfaction. We may further infer, that to the extent to which the clergy were pleased and satisfied, the several greedy unscrupulous classes of men who had got possession of the tithes became discontented and hostile" (Burton vi., 45). How much force there is in this inference we shall better estimate when we have looked behind the preposterous assumption generally made by Scotchmen, fanatical and latitudinarian alike, that the *quasi*-religious rising in the reign of Charles I. was set in motion by the inspired rowdyism of a mythical apple-woman.

The popular notion of the rise of the Covenant movement is that when in 1637 Charles and Laud sent down to Scotland a liturgy offensive to the Presbyterianism of the country, an Edinburgh woman of the name of Jenny Geddes, who sold greengroceries, flung a stool at the head of a dean who read the new service, whereupon the whole country incontinently plunged into insurrection. The historical facts, as now ascertained, are rather more complex; and the Jenny Geddes element is found to be apocryphal.

One of the first public acts of Charles I., after his accession in 1625, was the marrying of a Catholic princess; and his next act of importance, from the point of view of the Scotch, was a proclamation at the cross of Edinburgh, in the winter of the same year, to the effect that the new king formally revoked all grants by the Crown, and all appropriations to the Crown's prejudice, whether before or after his father's Act of Annexation—made on James's attaining majority in 1587. These Acts of Revocation by father and son were in similar terms, but there was the substantial difference that that of Charles included the tithes appropriated by the landowners, whereas James left the tithes alone (Burton, v., 270). This proclamation of Charles, says Burton (vi., 75), "professed to sweep into the royal treasury the whole of the vast ecclesiastical estates which had passed into the hands of the territorial potentates from the Reformation downwards. . . . He held that what the Crown had given the Crown could revoke. . . . This revocation swept up not only the grants made by the Crown, but the transactions, made in a countless variety of shapes, by which those in possession of Church revenues at the general breaking up, connived at their conversion into permanent estates to themselves or to relations, or to strangers who rendered something in return. . . . It was maintained, on the king's part, that the receivers of these revenues, which had belonged in permanence not to the men who drew them, but to the ecclesiastical offices to which they were attached, were illegal; and had this view been taken at the beginning, instead of standing over for upwards of sixty years, we, looking back upon it from the doctrines of the present day, must have pronounced it to be a correct view." This, as Sir James Balfour held in that generation ("Annals," ii., 128), was the real origin of the later Scottish insurrection, and consequently of the civil war; and Balfour effectively indicates the tone of the propertied classes when he declares that "whoeuer wer the contriuers of it deserue, they and all ther posterity, to be reputted by thir three kingdomes infamous and accursed for euer".

It was, of course, one thing to proclaim a revocation,

and another thing to carry it out. Charles, according to Bishop Burnet ("History of My Own Time", Book I., ed. 1838, p. 11), tried deep diplomacy, only to overreach himself. In order "that the two great families of Hamilton and Lennox might be good examples to the rest of the nation, he by a secret purchase, and with English money, bought the abbey of Aberbroth of the former, and the lordship of Glasgow of the latter, and gave these to the two archbishoprics. These lords made a show of zeal after a good bargain, and surrendered them to the king. He also purchased several estates of less value to the several sees; and all men who pretended to favor at court offered their church lands to sale at a low rate." This, however, was not sufficient, and ere long[1] Charles sent down the Earl of Nithsdale, a noble of Papist leanings, to attempt to bring the tithe-holders to submission; but the effort was fruitless, Nithsdale finding the service "desperate", and being, according to one story (see Burnet, as cited), in actual danger of his life. It is needless here to discuss the legality of the king's action or the nature of his motives. There was probably truth in his statement (Burton, vi., 79) that the teinds were rapaciously and brutally enforced by the lay impropriators, and had become "the cause of bloody oppressions, enmities, and of forced dependencies". But the certain and important matter is that, while an arrangement was ultimately made for the commutation of the tithes, the propertied classes cherished a grudge against the king for his interference, and a constant suspicion of further attempts (*Ibid.*, pp. 84, 225); and that, the purpose of the king and Laud having notoriously been to enrich the bishops and promote episcopacy, "the aristocracy and the more plebeian party in the Church were arrayed against the crown and the prelates" (p. 78).

---

[1] Burton (vi., 77) says, in 1628; but Mr. Gardiner ("History of England", vii., 278) holds that it cannot have been so late, and writes 1626. The latter date is that given by Laing ("History of Scotland", 2nd ed., iii., 91). But Burnet's narrative (as cited above) would give 1627.

XII.

THE PERVERSION OF SCOTLAND.
By JOHN ROBERTSON.
(IV.)

NEXT came the permanent establishment of an impost in the nature of an income-tax (p. 85); and, the king persisting in enforcing the policy of Laud, there arose a general fear of a reversion to Romanism, complicated and intensified by the crowning consideration that all these acts of Charles were virtually attempts to subject the polity of Scotland to that of England. "The history of Scotland", as Burton observes (vi., 132), "will not be truly understood by anyone who fails to see that to force any English institution upon the people would be accepted as a gross national insult. This stage of political infatuation had been reached by the Book of Canons, of which Clarendon said: 'It was thought no other than a subjection to England, by receiving laws from thence, of which they were most jealous, and most passionately abhorred.'" Here then were at work the three forces of the interested enmity of the landowners to the church policy of Charles and Laud, which always menaced their revenues; the panic-fear that Laud was re-introducing Romanism; and the potent spirit of nationalism, fiercely jealous of the influence of the "auld enemy", England. Added to all this there was the impulsive force of the agitation against Charles's absolutism in England— a kind of influence which had before operated powerfully at the Reformation, when the natural hunger of the Scottish nobles for the Church's wealth was whetted and stimulated by the spectacle of the doings of Henry VIII. As for the offending liturgy in particular, its purport will be found carefully set forth in Burton's History; but it must be left to the zealots of ceremonial to explain how a tumult over such a matter can be held by rational people to be a serious vindication of "religious liberty". Nothing could be more ridiculously unworthy of a great cause than the indecent scuffle usually pointed to as the historic origin of the rebellion. Shrewish clamor and stool-throwing by a number of ignorant and disorderly women of all classes is the precious fountain-head of the "religious liberty" of the Covenant, as clerical historians see the matter; and the canonised figure of the fabulous Jenny Geddes[1] fitly poses as the genius of the scene. Whether or not there was any truth in the contemporary theories that the riot had been pre-arranged and that some of the rioters were men in women's clothes; or whether the clergy were the instigators of "the she-zealots" in Edinburgh and elsewhere —for the "devouter sex", as a contemporary called them, showed fight in several places (Burton, pp. 153-4 and 204)—in any case the subsequent movement was a vastly more complex affair than the protest against a liturgy. That weak and blind obstinacy on one hand, and more or less foolish popular excitement on the other, should

---

[1] The Jenny Geddes story is a demonstrated myth; and, apart from that, the exhibition of the historic stool in Edinburgh is a sufficiently impudent absurdity. There is no contemporary trace whatever of any Jenny Geddes in the riot; and the story of her address to the Dean is obviously trumped up out of two narratives in which a "good Christian woman" or "she-zealot" is represented as having slapped in the face, either with her hand or her Bible, a gentleman who said "Amen" to the Dean's reading of the service, charging the offender with saying Mass at her ear. Compare the contemporary account printed in the Bannatyne Club's edition of Rothes' "Relation", p. 199, and the narrative of Gordon of Rothiemay ("History of Scots Affairs," Spalding Club, ed. I., 7). Kirkton, born about 1620, expressly says it was "ane unknown, obscure woman who first threw a stool" ("Secret and True History of the Church of Scotland", Sharpe's ed., p. 31). Wodrow, writing in 1705 ("Analecta", Maitland Club ed., i., 64) notes a "constant believed tradition" that the thrower of the "first stool" was a Mrs. Mean. The first historic trace of any Jenny Geddes is in 1660, when an Edinburgh greengrocer of that name uproariously burnt her trade-gear publicly in honor of the restoration of Charles II. (See Burton, vi., 151, *note*). If that personage is the heroine of the Covenant, the fact should be kept properly in view. And if tradition is to be founded on, we should not lose sight of the other tradition that on the Sunday before the historic riot Jenny Geddes had done public penance in the Kirk for fornication. (See Kirkpatrick Sharpe's note on Kirkton, pp. 31-2.)

Another constantly retailed figment is the story of John Knox's daughter having told King James that she would rather "kep" her husband's head in her apron than persuade him to accept the bishops. This fable, as always told by clerical writers, represents Knox's daughter as saying that her father had no sons. Yet these writers cannot have been unaware that Knox had two sons, one of whom became an English vicar (Dr. McCrie's "Life", p. 416).

thus turn the course of a nation's history, is an impressive enough reflection; but our business here is to trace in particular the effect of the Covenant movement on Scottish life, leaving the other historical issues alone.

First, then, the "Covenant" was a piece of policy in which, as regards its inception, religion had about as much share as in any other stroke of state at the time. It "took" brilliantly; but it was diplomacy that led fanaticism, not piety that ruled diplomacy. "The strength of the opposition," writes Burton of the situation late in 1637 (p. 160), "was still in its political element," though "common cause was made between the politicians and the clergy; and there was always enough about the grievances of the consciences of the serious to secure their co-operation" —this though many of the nobility were known profligates. For the rest, the Covenant was considerably more offensive than defensive, being in the main simply the old repudiation and execration of Popery prepared by the Protestants of the first generation. And, warlike action once begun, there was at least no more thought of allowing liberty of conscience to others than had been shown on the side of the King. Under the powerful organisation of the executive body known as "The Tables", "the parochial Committee saw that each adult member of the parish signed, or otherwise gave his adhesion to the Covenant. . . . . Over the districts where the organisation had the mastery, no one worth claiming as a partisan was permitted to evade the pledge. Those who would not yield had to seek refuge in the districts where the Cavaliers prevailed." "In Inverness the town's drummer or crier proclaimed the obligation of signing the Covenant, with the alternative of heavy penalties against all who were obstinate or slothful" (*Ib.*, p. 205; compare pp. 279–80, 287, and 355). So Burnet: "They forced all people to sign the Covenant" ("Own Times" Book I., p. 21). And the important Assembly of 1638 was packed in the anti-royalist interest:—"The Tables undertook the working of the elections so as to produce a thoroughly Covenanting Assembly" (Burton, vi., 225). There, however, as at the Reformation, the aristocratic interest was plenipotent; the lay leaders of the movement adroitly reviving an old Act of Assembly which provided that each presbytery should elect one lay member of Assembly as well as two clergymen, and that the royal burghs should send lay commissioners in addition. The clergy vainly protested (pp. 225, 229). They "could not but see that this nominally rigid adherence to their standards was transferring them into the hands of new masters. They could not be blind to the reason why the office destined for men of a religious turn and serious walk in life was wanted for a haughty powerful nobility, many of them profligate livers. Among them, indeed, were men fighting their own personal battle for the preservation of the old ecclesiastical estates, which they believed to be in danger—all had a personal dislike of the bishops, as assuming a superiority over them. But it was in such men that the strength of the Assembly as a hostile declaration against the Court lay, and they prevailed in the elections" (pp. 225-6). And thus yet once again was Episcopacy abolished in Scotland, and a pure Presbyterianism set up.

For the war itself, the general fortune of that was indisputably the outcome, not at all of religious enthusiasm, but of the important fact that the peace of Westphalia had thrown idle a large number of trained Scots soldiers, and among others an extremely able general, David Leslie. It was the winding up of the Thirty Years' War that "threw loose the materials that were to revive into the civil wars of Britain" (Burton, p. 217). And the covenanting leaders —among whom, at first, was Montrose, it should be remembered—conducted their business much as did the other European campaigners of the period; offering to pay the powerful Marquis of Huntly's debts for him if he would join them (p. 216); and not even scrupling to seek aid from the Papist king of France (p. 288)—a proceeding perhaps about as easy to reconcile with patriotism as with religious sincerity. Again, when the "Covenanting" army under General Monro occupied Aberdeen in 1640, their conduct was tolerably like that of other European forces— the delating of sixty-five unwed mothers before the Covenanting church courts being one of the symptoms (p. 322). As for the dealings of the Covenanting nobility with those of their feudal enemies who were now at their mercy, these were precisely like the old civil wars, full of "limitless plunder, destruction, and bloodshed" (p. 323).

It was not for nothing, however, that such a movement, however fundamentally political and bound up with class interests, was associated with the profession of a religious covenant and the cause of the popular church. Through all the cool generalship, the unscrupulous diplomacy, the military rapine and debauchery, the seed of fanaticism was being sown and ripened; growing up, indeed, in the breasts of reprobates and ruffians, as freely as in the merely ignorant and credulous populace. Dr. Burton, I think, goes too far when he says (p. 354) that "some thirty years before, the Scots were a people somewhat indifferent about religious matters"; but it is clear that from the time of the Covenant they became much more generally fanatical than ever before.

During the war the clergy were naturally at the highest pitch of fanatical excitement. The "Large Declaration" drawn up for Charles by Walter Balcanquall tells how the Covenanters for a time did homage at Edinburgh to a Mrs. Margaret Nicholson, who had raving fits which were regarded as inspired trances. "The multitude was made believe her words proceeded not from herself, but from God. Thence was that incredible concourse of all sorts of people—noblemen, gentlemen, ministers, women of all ranks and qualities—who watched or stayed by her day and night during the time of her pretended fits, and did admire her raptures and inspirations as coming from heaven. . . . So soon as she was ready to begin, the news of it was blown all the town over, and the house so thronged that thousands at every time could find no access. . . . Rolloc, her special favorite, . . . being desired sometimes by the spectators to pray with her, and speak to her, answered that he durst not do it, as being no good manners in him to speak while his Master was speaking in her" (Burton, vi., 277-8). Religious excitement of a more normal species was naturally abundant. It is extremely difficult to trace closely the interplay of the various influences through the Covenanting movement, but while we have seen that in its origin it was mainly political, it is clear that the clerical element was that which most tended to aggrandise itself. Once Charles was repelled, it was no part of the interest of the aristocracy to go further. Some king they must have: They ultimately realised, indeed, that, whether or not they had made a blunder in beginning, the game had gone out of their hands; and we must largely attribute to this the fact that on Charles' execution the Scottish nation decided for his son. Not that the clergy were any more Republican or Cromwellian than the nobles: on the contrary, it seems certain that they remained as devoted to the abstract principle or sentiment of kingship as the nation had always done through its many rebellions and revolutions. The prominent minister, Robert Baillie, who had been a sufficiently zealous Covenanter, is found execrating the regicide. Mere clerical sympathy with the decapitated king's son, however, would never have floated the rising in his favor if the powerful classes had not been at least willing to see it take place. Of course the blind impulse of national sentiment again came into play; and a Covenanting army, of a curiously mixed quality, mustered for Charles II. against Cromwell, with the most disastrous results. Leslie was no longer the best general in Britain; and his clerical allies contrived that he should lead against the Ironsides not even the cream of his old troops. It is beyond doubt that, whether or not the preachers forced him to precipitate the battle of Dunbar, they had fatally weakened his army by expelling all the troops who did not satisfy clerical requirements in the matter of piety. Naturally, the men who had been trained in the Thirty Years' War in many cases fell below the standard. "Thus they drove away, as an astonished onlooker [Sir Edward Walker] tells us, four thousand men, and these, as old experienced soldiers, the best in their army" (Burton, vii., 15). The same onlooker describes them as "placing for the most part in command ministers' sons, clerks, and such other sanctified creatures, who hardly ever saw or heard of any sword but that of the Spirit" (p. 21)—which strictly agrees with Leslie's own account of his defeat (p. 26). If it were true that it was religion that made the movement against Charles I.; it was certainly religion that lost Dunbar and Worcester.

As the civil war went on, the fanatics became if possible still more fanatical. The pretence of safeguarding their own liberties with which they had started was now played out; but they were as zealous in positive as in negative intolerance. Before the battle of Dunbar the prince was made to declare: "He doth now detest and abhor all Popery, superstition, and idolatry, together with Prelacy, *and all errors, heresy, schism, and profaneness; and resolves not to tolerate, much less allow of these in any part of his majesty's dominions,* but to oppose himself thereto and endeavour the extirpation thereof to the utmost of his power" (*Ib.*, p. 19; compare p. 67). That is the essential note of the Covenant. The main reason why the Scotch clergy and Cromwell never made friends was simply his "damnable doctrine of toleration" (p. 31). To the devout Row ("Contin. of Blair's Autobiography, p. 335; cited by Buckle, iii., 195) he is "that old fox" even when death has struck him down; so little of brotherhood, not to speak of chivalry, was there in the Puritan sectarianism of the time. But nothing is more curious in the history of Scotland—or of England, for that matter—than the fashion in which the strong man, hedged by no regal divinity, but using the great engine of his own welding, his army, set his foot on all the forces with which the weak king could only meddle to his own undoing. A study of Cromwell's dealings with the Covenanters makes short work of the notion that the policy of Charles I. was an intolerable despotism. The things which the king tried in vain to do were trifles beside those which the Protector carried through with iron determination and utter completeness. The Estates of the Realm, that grim and turbulent senate, the ancient defier of kings and oligarchies, he absolutely extinguished. But "one important thing had yet to be done. The theologians who had kept Scotland in uproar for so many years had to be silenced as well as the politicians. The two opposing parties—the Resolutioners and the Remonstrants [*i.e.*, the royalists and their critics]—were girding their loins for a war of extermination. After a long contest, with much surrounding disturbance, the end would be that the majority would drive forth the minority. In July 1653 the General Assembly met in Edinburgh, each side charged with material for hot debate" (Burton, vii., 49). Whereupon, as Baillie narrates, a body of Cromwellian musketeers and troopers beset the church, and the reverend brethren were with all possible simplicity marched through the streets, escorted one mile beyond the town, and instructed that henceforth they "should not dare to meet any more above three in number." And they did not dare. The end of the movement of the Covenant was that Scotland was deprived of its Parliament, and the Kirk of its very right of assembly. In view of which consummation it becomes desirable that the hues of the customary rhetoric against the ecclesiastical and other tyranny of Charles should be somehow harmonised with the colours of the adjoining picture. The prevailing anomaly is a trifle absurd, if we are to proceed on any more plausible principle than this, that the unpardonable sin on the part of a tyrant is failure.

But it was not to idleness that Cromwell relegated the clergy when he suppressed their Assembly. What they could do to thwart progress by methods of State they had pretty well done. In Episcopalian Aberdeen, before the Covenanting outbreak, there was "a society more learned and accomplished than Scotland had hitherto known" (Cosmo Innes's preface to *Fasti Aberdonenses*, published by Spalding Club, p. xli.); and its university, made famous in Europe by the learning of the "Aberdeen doctors", was quite the most important centre of light in the country. "One cannot," says Robert Chambers, "reflect without a pang on the wreck it was destined to sustain under the rude shocks imparted by a religious enthusiasm which regarded nothing but its own dogmas, and for these sacrificed everything. The university sustained a visitation from the Presbyterian Assembly of 1640, and was thenceforth much changed. 'The Assembly's errand', says Gordon of Rothiemay, 'was thoroughly done; these eminent divines of Aberdeen either dead, deposed, or banished; in whom fell more learning than was left in all Scotland beside at that time. Nor has that city, nor any city in Scotland, ever since seen so many learned divines and scholars at one time together as were immediately before this in Aberdeen. From that time forwards, learning began to be discountenanced. .... Learning was nicknamed human learning, and some ministers so far cried it down in their pulpits, as they were heard to say: *Down doctrine, and up Christ*'" ("Domestic Annals", ii., 121). Their most decisive work, however, was probably that done in ordinary course by the ordinary ecclesiastical machinery; the account of which by Buckle is well known to the general reader. Never was an inquisition more comprehensive, a tyranny more minute. A few pages of any of the old presbytery records will give a sufficiently clear idea of how the clergy occupied themselves throughout the country. Here are a few illustrations from the "Selections from the Registers of the Presbytery of Lanark", published by the Abbotsford Club:

1627. February. "Ordaines Wm. Weir, pyper, for playing

at Yuile at the gysing [masking] in Douglas, to be summoned with a lybellit summonds" (p. 5).

1633, September 5. "Mr. Thomas Ballentyne [a minister] censured for travailling and goeing abroad upone the *Saturdayes*, and is exhorted to mend that fault" (p. 9).

1646. September 3rd. "The qlk day compeires the Lady Glespen, and confessing shee said, if Montrose and his people were present, she would not be worse vsed than be our awine [by our own], is ordained to confesse her fault privatelie before the sessione—" (p. 53).

From the early pages of the "Extracts from the Presbytery Book of Strathbogie", published by the Spalding Club, I cull the following:

1636. July. "It is ordained that stockes shall be made for the punishment of stubborne and unruly delinquents" (p. 7).

September. "Margaret Fraser suspect of witchcraft, and having broken waird in Aberdene, is ordained to bring ane testimoniall of her bygone conversation, or otherwyse the receipters [receivers or entertainers] of the said Margaret to be punished" (26).

September. "Barbara Lowrie compeared also in sackcloth and confessed her adulterye with John Stewart. She was ordained to stand in the jogges and brankes [iron collar, etc.] till the congregation be satisfied, becaus she had no gear" [*i.e.* no money to pay a fine]. Stewart, who is also accused of an attempt at rape, is merely "ordained to sit in sackcloth till the people be satisfied, and to pay twenty markes penaltye" (p. 8).

In the same month it is reported that one George Gordoune had been cited before the session at Rynie for "prophaneing the Sabboth, by gathering grosers [gooseberries] in time of sermon" (p. 9).

September 29. "It is ordained that drinkers in tyme of divyne service shall be punished as fornicatours" (p. 10).

1637. March. "It was ordained that every brother should make intimation out of his pulpit, that none of their parishioners receipt Margaret Charles, who was lately parted with chylde in the parish of Dumbennand" (p. 14).

This sort of prying oppression was going on wholesale all over the country at the very time the attempt of Charles to impose a liturgy was being shrieked over as an act of tyranny. These—in addition to the constant prosecutions of witches—were but a few of the normal forms of ecclesiastical interference with liberty. The mere staying away from Church, not to speak of holding intercourse with papists, was an offence constantly being proceeded against and often punished by the penalty of excommunication, which, where effectual, involved something like entire social ostracism. (Compare Strathbogie Extracts, pp. 15 and 42; "The Church and Churchyard of Ordiquhill", by Wm. Cramond, Banff, 1886, pp. 44, 47, 49, 50; and Extracts from Aberdeen Presbytery Records, Spalding Club, pp. 97, 102-3, 109, 139, 143.) In Aberdeen, in 1607, occasional residents abstaining from church attendance were sought to be expelled from the city (Presbytery Records, cited by Buckle, iii., 222). But there was nothing that the Presbyteries did not interfere with. They ordered heads of households to keep rods for the chastisement of children or servants using improper language (see extract in Buckle's notes, iii., 208); they censured boys and servants for Sabbath-breaking (*ib.*); they searched private houses during sermon time, besides scouring the streets, to find absentees (p. 209); they paid spies and secretly terrorised servants to give testimony against their masters (*ib.*); they passed censure for omission to salute a minister (p. 210); they imposed penalties for the employment of pipers at weddings (p. 258); they imprisoned wandering singers and forbade others to give them meat or drink (p. 259); they prohibited poor people from giving their children more than two or four godfathers and godmothers (p. 260); they caused women to be whipped (p. 262); they ordered merchants not to travel to Papist countries (p. 264); they caused it to be directed in all the Edinburgh pulpits that no women should be employed as waiters in taverns (*ib.*); they insisted that widows should either re-marry or go into service, and not live alone (*ib.*); they compelled families to break up (*ib.*); they rebuked those who travelled, or paid visits, or strolled in the fields or streets, or slept in the open air, on Sunday (pp. 265—6); they tried to prevent boys from swimming on any day (*ib.*); they compelled mothers to refuse shelter to their own sons when excommunicated (p. 278). During the wars, too, they carried to the most extraordinary lengths their aggressions against members of the aristocracy suspected of papistical or cavalier leanings. Of one case the Editor of the Lanark Records writes:—"The treatment of the Marquess and Marchioness of Douglas by the Presbytery of Lanark exhibits a system of ecclesiastical oppression almost without parallel. They were compelled to profess their belief in the doctrines of a church of which they had never been members,—to join in its ordinances under pain of excommunication (then drawing with it the most serious civil consequences) and of being denounced to the ruling powers as malignants and enemies of their country. They were deprived of all control over the education of their children, —latterly even of their society ....; and they were forced to receive into their family a nominee of the Presbytery; ostensibly as a chaplain, but truly as a spy on their proceedings. They were under the necessity of dismissing their confidential servants at the bidding of the Presbytery; and for a series of years were fain to cultivate its forbearance by the most abject and humiliating submissions." And "at the time when the Presbytery was most rigorous in its measures against the Marquess to compel his family's adherence to the Church, it was making repeated complaints against his interference with the consciences of his tenantry" (Preface, p. x.). In view of such proceedings, it is the less surprising that when the tables were turned at the Restoration, and Episcopacy was set up in a more complete form than ever before, the royalists trampled on the Presbyterians.

Scottish ecclesiastical history is popularly told so as to bring into high relief the persecutions under Charles II. and James II., leaving the immediately preceding period in the vague as one of general religious well-being. Certainly the Episcopalian persecution was infinitely the bloodier of the two. Apart from the perpetual torturing and burning of suspected witches, the Presbyterian zealots cannot be accused of carrying their tyranny, odious as it was, to the point of savage cruelty. Such a diabolical act as the drowning of eleven gipsy women in the Nor' Loch of Edinburgh in 1624 is doubtless to be set down in the dreary catalogue of the crimes of racial animosity. At all events, it was left to the Episcopal *régime* to carry sectarian hatred to the point of shooting, sabring, hanging, and drowning, men and women who persisted in following their own form of worship. From the point of view of the non-sectarian student, of course, the fact only constitutes one more historical proof that the establishment of any form of religion means oppression, to the extent of the power of the established sect to oppress. It will be well, however, to keep in view the circumstances which determined the specially sanguinary character of the Episcopal persecutions. First let it be remembered that the Protestant laws had from the first prescribed the death penalty against all persistent Papists, and that this was only evaded by the wholesale flight of the more devoted Catholics and the practice of more or less complete dissimulation by the others. What was done to the extreme Presbyterians between 1660 and 1688 was strictly what they had always said *ought* to be done to Papists. At the Restoration a number are found, as before Dunbar, calling on Charles II. to employ his power "in the reformation of religion in the kingdoms of England and Ireland in doctrine, worship, discipline, and government"—that is, in subverting English religious liberty by enforcing Presbyterianism—" and to the extirpation of Popery, Prelacy, superstition, heresy, schism, profaneness, and whatsoever shall be found contrary to sound doctrine and the power of godliness; and that all places of power and trust under your majesty may be filled with such as have taken the Covenant" (Burton, vii., 124). The fanatics who made this demand were now in a minority. "There can be no greater mistake than to suppose, as some people have from what afterwards befell, that these men represented the prevailing feeling of the Scots at the juncture of the Restoration. Whatever remnant of the old frenzy remained with these zealots of the west, the country at large, Presbyterian and Episcopalian, had little sympathy with it." "With the zealous Covenanters the landowners had now no common cause. A quarter of a century had passed since the climax of their terror, that the Church property gathered by them during the previous seventy-five years would be torn from them. A new generation now held these lands" (p. 126). Under a restored episcopacy, therefore, there was no choice for the zealots between surrender and suffering. But they were made of sterner stuff than the Papists had been; and, besides, had no such opening of escape to friends on the Continent as the Papists had at the Reformation, supposing they had possessed means enough to travel. Last, but not least, it has to be remembered that the new king had at command the military material worked up by the civil war and placed at his disposal by Monk; and that a military persecution was now possible such as would have been practically out of the question in Scotland in the previous reigns.

Apart from the direct cruelty and iniquity of the persecution under Episcopalian auspices, it of course had the usual indirect effect of promoting the other form of bigotry against which it was directed; Episcopalianism having thus its ample share in that "perversion of Scotland" to barren fanaticism which we have been tracing. The Abjuration Act of the "drunken Parliament" [really a meeting of Privy Council] of 1662, by which three hundred and fifty clergymen were driven from their benefices, was a blunder even from the Episcopalian point of view (Burton, vii., 160, 178); and though a number of the expelled were led back by the Act of Indulgence of 1669, sufficient harm had been done to considerably strengthen the ranks and the prestige of the minority, to say nothing of the misery and bloodshed between.

Between the old forces of spontaneous or instilled zealotry and the ferocious persecutions carried on under Charles II. and James II., the unhappy bias of the country towards fanaticism was developed to an extent now difficult to realise. In England, with the computed issue of 30,000 pamphlets on mere Church questions between 1640 and 1660, there was a sufficiently lamentable waste of energy in polemics; but in Scotland there seems to have been no other intellectual life whatever. Divisions within divisions reduced all public or social action to a dreary delirium of words, in which the light of political as of every other sort of reason would seem to have gone out. A brief sketch of the disintegration of the Covenant movement will show as well as a lengthy dissertation the value of an impulse of fanaticism as a means to the attainment of good government:

"The original quarrel was between Covenanters and Episcopalians—called otherwise Cavaliers, and, after the manner of the the primitive Christians in naming their persecutors, Malignants.

"The 'Engagement' of 1647, to assist the king and march into England, told off the Engagers, leaving the Nonengagers, otherwise called Abhorrers.

"The 'Act of Classes', under Argyle's Government in 1650, secluded from power all the Engagers, with some other persons, all being divided into classes according to the extent of their iniquities. The parties among the Covenanters were now Argyleites and Classites.

"The 'Resolution' to acknowledge Charles II. made Resolutioners, and Remonstrants or Protesters. In the earlier part of Charles II.'s reign the Presbyterians were divided into the Indulged and the Covenanters of the original Covenant, who were again subdivided into Resolutioners and Protesters.

"By the 'Sanquhar Declaration'" a party of the Protesters withdrew under a new Covenant, and were called Sanquharians, Cameronians, Society men, Hill men, Mountain men, and Wild Westland Whigs" (Burton, vii., 248-9).

And the effect of it all was that the liberties of Scotland were still more utterly submerged than those of England. Where Cromwell had been tyrannous only in form[1], dealing with institutions, Charles II. was able to and did oppress in the most grinding fashion; and the extortions and atrocities of his military administrators failed to provoke anything like an effectual rising. Now that the propertied classes had no object in exploiting fanaticism, it was helpless against the military power of the Crown; and in the absence of any appeal to national sentiment those who did attempt insurrection were contemned by their compatriots. In connexion with the rising in 1666 of west country Covenanters, which ended in the battle of Pentland, "we hear of more sufferings to the remnant of their army from the peasantry around the place of their defeat, than from the victorious enemy, cruel as their general was reputed to be." (*Ib.*, p. 172). The abject democratic collapse of 1660—intelligible enough as the result of the enfeebling paternal autocracy of Cromwell—was at least as complete in Scotland as in England. Lauderdale and Rothes, who had been leading Covenanters of the profligate aristocratic type, became consummate instruments of monarchism; and the Estates, now a mere gathering of royalist gentry, voted away funds and liberties alike with an infinite complacency. Licence flourished more freely than ever did bigotry, and it seemed as if any spontaneous democratic life, fanatical or otherwise, was at an end for ever. That this was not so was clearly not the outcome of the old ecclesiastical influences.

---

[1] With a few exceptions. There is a doubtful story of his sentencing one minister to six months' imprisonment for saying, in the discussion which he held with the clergy in Edinburgh, that he had perverted Scripture. (See Wodrow's Analecta, Maitland Club, ii., 283-4). It is certain that Scotland enjoyed considerable prosperity under his despotism.

It would indeed be unwarrantable to say that such persecutions as those of Charles and James would never have provoked an effectual rebellion. It appears that after the failure of 1666, and still more during the reign of James, increasing sympathy had begun to be felt for the sufferers; and we can gather that the dangers of conventicle worship were gradually exercising an extending fascination. We have, for instance, an account of an open-air service at which 3,200 persons took the communion (McCrie's "Sketches", p. 466). But it is plain that the prospects of the conventicling party were still very black towards the end of James's reign; and here again, as in the previous crises of 1560 and 1637, the all-important element of pecuniary interest is found to be the decisive factor in precipitating change—so far, at least, as the affairs of Scotland separately are concerned. "Looking through the mismanagements of the period for the causes of the coming Revolution", writes Burton of the situation about the time of James's accession, "less will be found in these cruel inflictions on the western zealots, than in a project for extracting money from certain men of substance[1] throughout the country. They were called 'fugitives', as being persons who were liable to punishment under some one or other of the multitudinous penal laws then at work. They were a selected body of about two thousand. The position in which each was put was, that if he would frankly confess his offence and pay a stipulated fine, he would thenceforth be as exempt from all prosecution for the offence he had compounded for, as if he had received a remission under the great seal" (vii., 255-6; ref. to Wodrow, iv., 13). Add to this not only the deeply-rooted prejudice against the toleration of Papists, but the well-grounded conviction that James wished to restore Catholicism, a step which would soon involve an opening up of the old question of the appropriated Church lands and revenues, and we have the determining forces of the Revolution of 1688, from the Scottish standpoint.

Looking to the miseries endured by the conventiclers in the "Killing Time", it may seem invidious to lay stress on the intellectual disservice done by the sufferers to the

---

[1] They seem to have largely consisted of well-to-do people of the middle and artisan class. See Wodrow's list.

interests of the nation; but this is an element we cannot ignore. Suffering as they did from bigotry, bigotry was the inspiration of their own cause. The minister James Guthrie, hanged in 1661, had denounced toleration as a sin only a few months before his execution (Burton, vii., 155); and similarly James Renwick, the last of the "martyrs", on the scaffold in 1688 lifted up his "testimony against Popery, Prelacy, Erastianism; against all profanity and everything contrary to sound doctrine"; against the king's claim to absolute power; "and against this toleration flowing from this absolute power" (*Ib.*, p. 279; citing Wodrow, iv., 454). These men and their followers had no notion of the gospel of human brotherhood bound up in later struggles for liberty. When, under William IV., the Cameronian regiment, formed to resist the royalist movement of Viscount Dundee, was employed on the Continent, the protesting Cameronians at home were horrified, not at any practical acts of their former brethren, but at their fighting under the same banner with "Papists, Lutherans, Erastians, Cocceians, Bourignians" (Burton, vii., 325). They had neither political nor ethical principles to guide them. One of their worst grievances against James II. was that he proposed to include them under the same toleration with Papists (p. 270); and Wodrow, the zealous historian of their sufferings, is found lamenting that the Quakers had been allowed to spread so terribly, the "good Act" of 1663, which had proposed to drive them out of Edinburgh, having been allowed to lie comparatively idle (*Ibid.*, p. 271; "History of the Sufferings", ed. 1829, i., 377). He could bring no tolerable argument against the Episcopalian persecution. "That the Restoration Government had taken a lesson from the Covenanters was so obvious that Wodrow had in some measure to admit it, along with a palliation not likely to pass current with all men, in saying: 'It is not my province now to compare the matter of the one with the other here. The difference there is prodigiously great, there being evidently in the Covenants nothing but what was agreeable to the moral law, and what people were really bound to, whether they had sworn them or not'" (Burton, vii., 192; Wodrow, ii., 390).

XIII.

THE PERVERSION OF SCOTLAND.
By JOHN ROBERTSON.
(V.)

FINALLY, the body of later Covenanting zealots included many men of a lawless type, such as the fanatical ruffians who murdered Archbishop Sharp; and it is noted that the Cameronian regiment, "ere it gradually lapsed into the uniform modified licentiousness of other military bodies, exhibited a mixture of fanaticism and profligacy which deeply perplexed its hapless chaplain Shields" (Burton, vii., 326, and ref.). What may truly be said of them all is that they were brave men; indeed they brought their worst hardships upon themselves by the wild audacity with which they declared war on Charles II., (by the "Sanquhar Declaration") as a tyrant and usurper, and excommunicated (by the "Torwood Excommunication") the king, his brother, and the leading men in the government of Scotland. As to the "rabbling" of the west-country Episcopalian curates at the Revolution, Macaulay's account may be accepted as impartial:—"On Christmas day . . . . the Covenanters held armed musters by concert in many parts of the western shires. Each band marched to the nearest manse, and sacked the cellar and larder of the minister, which at that season were probably better stocked than usual. The priest of Baal was reviled and insulted, sometimes beaten, sometimes ducked. His furniture was thrown out of the windows; his wife and children turned out of doors in the snow. He was then carried to the market place and exposed during some time as a malefactor. His gown was torn to shreds over his head: if he had a prayer book in his pocket it was burned; and he was dismissed with a charge, never, as he valued his life, to officiate in the parish again. . . . . In fairness to these men it must be owned that they had suffered such oppression as may excuse, though it cannot justify, their violence; and that, though they were rude even to brutality, they do not appear to have been guilty of any intentional injury to life or limb" ("History", ed. 1858, iii., 250). The details of the persecutions on the other side are worth summing up. Apart from the six or seven hundred killed in battle, those put to death by the royal troops are estimated at about five hundred; 382 are enumerated as executed by form of law; some 750 were banished to the northern islands, and about 1,700 to the Plantations, 200 of the latter perishing by shipwreck; while over 2,800 are calculated to have been imprisoned, and about 7,000 to have fled the country (McCrie's "Sketches", p. 558 and *note*). These figures are probably not far wide of the mark; and they represent the main historic testimony as to the advantage of the establishment of an Episcopalian Church in Scotland.

The effect of these later transactions on the general Scottish character does not fully appear at the time, just as the main influences of the Reformation did not fully assert themselves in the generation which saw it. Under the storm and stress of fanaticism and persecution one can detect certain traces of a popular life which had some of the old freshness, with a fair share of the old savagery. The old genius for commenting on public affairs by nicknames comes out in the name given to the one Presbyterian clergyman left in Edinburgh after the operation of the Abjuration Act. He was popularly called the "nest-egg". Again, there is a curious story (Lauder's "Historical Observes", Bannatyne Club, pp. 55, 303) of how the Heriot schoolboys in 1681, deciding that the dog at the hospital gate held a public office, voted that he must take "the Test" or be hanged. The poor dog refused the paper, and, on its being presented in a buttered state, licked off the butter: whereupon the boys, by way of ridiculing the case for the Crown in the trial of the Earl of Argyll, tried him at great length for *leasing making* or treason, and would have hanged him if he had not contrived to escape. This is at least not quite so bad as the exploit of killing a baillie, achieved by some boys of the Edinburgh grammar-school in 1595 ("Historie of James the Sext", Bannatyne Club, p. 352). But on the side of general culture, as represented by literature, the effect of over a century of more or less Puritan Protestantism becomes now direfully apparent. The consensus of testimony on this point, as Buckle notes, is overwhelming. Principal Robertson, writing his History of Scotland in the middle of last century, sums up (Book viii., ed. 1806, iii., 199): "Thus during the whole seventeenth century the English were gradually refining their language and their taste; in Scotland the former was much debased and the latter almost entirely lost. In the beginning of that period both nations were emerging out of barbarity, but the distance between them, which was then inconsiderable, became, before the end of it, immense. Even after science had once dawned upon them, the Scots seemed to be sinking back into ignorance and obscurity; and, active and intelligent as they naturally are, they continued, while other nations were eager in the pursuit of fame and knowledge, in a state of languor." Laing, writing at the end of last century, is equally emphatic: "The taste and science, the genius and the learning of the age, were absorbed in the gulf of religious controversy. At a time when the learning of Selden and the genius of Milton conspired to adorn England, the Scots were reduced to such writers as Baillie, Rutherford, Guthrie, and the two Gillespies" (History, 2nd ed., iii., 479–80). Again: "From the Restoration down to the Union, the only author of eminence whom Scotland produced was Burnet" (*Ib.*, iv., 390). The scholar Pinkerton, writing in the same generation as Laing, declared that "not one writer who does the least credit to the nation flourished during the century from 1615 to 1715, excepting Burnet..... By a singular fatality, the century which stands highest in English history and genius, is one of the darkest in those of Scotland" ("Ancient Scotish Poems", i., p. iv.). The last great name in Scottish intellectual life had been that of Napier, the inventor of logarithms, and Napier was born in 1550, ten years before the Reformation—and, it may be added, gained nothing from it but a useless theology. "It might have been expected", observes Robert Chambers, ("Annals," ii., 444), "that the country of Napier, seventy years after his time [he died in 1617], would have had many sons capable of applying his key to such mysteries of nature" as the phænomena of comets, concerning which the period yields only a collection of superstitious fancies. "But no one had arisen—nor did arise for fifty years onward, when at length Colin Maclaurin unfolded in the Edinburgh University the sublime philosophy of Newton. There could not be a more expressive signification of the character of the seventeenth century in Scotland. Our unhappy contentions about external religious matters had absorbed the whole genius of the people, rendering to us the age of Cowley, of Waller, and of Milton, as barren of elegant literature, as that of Horrocks, of Halley, and of Newton, was of science." Finally, Dr. Burton, who was willing to credit the Reformation with "bringing forth" the classical scholarship of the few distinguished Latinists connected with it, and who was able to take satisfaction in the literary powers of such men as Baillie, Dickson, and Rutherford, admits that at the Revolution of 1688 "all this glory was departed, and Scots Presbyterianism had scarcely a representative in the world of letters. . . . . There was no theologian", even, "alive in Scotland at the era of the Revolution, whose writings have been admitted into the current theological literature of the world" (vii., 405–6). As Buckle points out (iii., 286, *note*) such a writer as Dickson protested against even so much biblical criticism as would go to ascertaining the date and authorship of any of the Hebrew books. All this obviously implies the sterilising of general culture, and we know in point of fact that the clergy kept a tenacious hold of all means of education. We have seen (*ante*, p. 143; compare Buckle iii., 288, *note*) how at the Reformation they assumed control of all the schools and universities; and in 1648 the Fifeshire brethren are found ordering "all young students, who waittes on noblemen or gentlemen within thir bounds, aither to teach ther children, or catechise and pray in ther families, to frequent the Presbyterie, that the brether may cognosce what they ar reading, and what proficiencie they make in ther studies, and to know also ther behaviour in the said families and of ther affectione to the Covenant and present religione" (extract in Buckle, as above). Thus not only in parish school and university, but in private houses, was education superintended by the class who saw in all notable natural phœnomena instances of miraculous divine action; who regarded disease as amenable only to prayer; who were constantly engaged in impeaching, ferreting out, torturing, and killing, unhappy women on suspicion of an impossible crime; who preached intolerance as the mandate of the creator of the universe, and who regarded the spinning of theological ropes of sand as the noblest exercise of the human mind. So much had the State establishment of the Protestant religion done for Scotland by the time of the fall of the Stewart line.

But there is one more historical fact of perhaps still more salient importance as bearing on the received theory that State Protestantism has always promoted freedom. It is the little noted circumstance that in the seventeenth century the institution of slavery had grown up in Scotland, in connexion with the working of collieries and saltworks. The laborers who dug coal and made salt—they were chiefly located in East Lothian—"went to those who bought or succeeded to the property of the works, and they could be sold, bartered, or pawned. What is peculiar and revolting in this institution is, that it was no relic of ancient serfdom, but a growth of the seventeenth century. We have seen, indeed, that serfdom had a feebler hold on Scotland than on England. We have also seen how astonished and enraged the French auxiliaries of the Scots in the wars with England were at the insolent independence of the common people, impoverished as they were. The oldest trace we have of the bondage of the colliers and salt-workers is an Act of the year 1606, passed, as it would seem, to strengthen somewhat as to them the laws so common at the time for restricting the pursuit of all occupations to those embarked in them. By interpretations of this Act, but more by the tyrannous power of the strong owners of the soil over a weak and unfriended community, slavery had been as amply established [in Scotland] as ever it had been in Rome, Sparta, or Virginia" (Burton, viii., 7, 8). It subsisted all through the war for "religious liberty"; it was left untouched at the "glorious revolution" of 1688. The Church of Rome had at least sought to free all slaves but its own: there is no trace that the Protestant clergy of Scotland ever raised a voice against the slavery which grew up before their eyes. And it was not till 1799, after republican and irreligious France had set the example, that it was legally abolished (Cockburn's "Memorials", ed. 1856, p. 79).

The final establishment of Presbyterianism under William and Mary brings us within plain prospect of modern times—the ecclesiastical history of the subsequent period having practically run in one groove—and it may be convenient here to indicate concisely the ups and downs of the previous century and a half.

1535. Act of Parliament, following up an earlier, prohibiting the importation of the works of "the grete heretik luther", ordering destruction of copies in hand, and sternly forbidding discussion of his "dampnable opinionis". (See Tytler, ii., 357; Acts ii., 342.)
1560. Catholic Church overthrown by Act of Parliament. Hierarchy left an open question.
1572. "Tulchan" bishops appointed by Government—at that time an aristocratic Regency.
1580. Bishops repudiated by General Assembly.
1592. Episcopacy abolished by Parliament.
1597. Episcopacy as a political function re-established by Parliament. 1598. This acceded to by General Assembly. 1600. Act of Assembly ratifying the arrangement, and defining the episcopal office as parliamentary.
1606. King obtains control of Assemblies. Parliament (nominally) confers the old revenues on bishops. 1610. This ratified by a packed and bribed Assembly, which still stipulated that bishops should be subject to Assembly. 1612. Parliament finally ratifies, ignoring that stipulation.
1617. Acts for the recovery of the minor Catholic temporalities, and for better payment of ministers.
1618. James carries ceremonial innovations.
1626. Attempt by Charles I. to recover the tithes for the Church, by way of strengthening episcopacy.
1638-9. Episcopacy repudiated by Covenanting Assembly. Charles yielding; and Parliament ratifying in 1640.
1653. Cromwell suppresses the Assembly, having already suppressed the Parliament.
1660-1. Episcopacy fully re-established; Sharp, the Presbyterian delegate to court, turning his coat and becoming Archbishop of St. Andrews. 350 clergymen expelled under Abjuration Act in 1662; the majority returning under Indulgence Act in 1669. The others persecuted.

1679. Murder of Sharp, followed by second unsuccessful insurrection. Persecution heightened.

1688. Fall of James II. Expulsion of curates in the Cameronian districts. 1689. 184 non-juring clergymen deposed by Privy Council. Act abolishing episcopacy. 1690. Act abolishing civil pains of excommunication. Act establishing Presbyterianism.

It was in 1696 that the Scottish Parliament passed an Act for "settling of schools", which adjusted the famous system of parochial schools, already partly established by the first Protestants, and by Acts of Charles I. and of the Covenanters' Parliament in 1646. It was in the same year of 1696 that the Scottish Presbyterian clergy committed one of the blackest acts of cruelty in the annals of religious persecution. A boy of eighteen, Thomas Aikenhead, a student in Edinburgh, had come to the conclusion that the doctrine of the Trinity was an absurdity, that pantheism was a more philosophic doctrine than theism, and that the authorship of the Old Testament books was otherwise than was commonly stated; and expressed himself accordingly, in a fashion which Macaulay—in what I cannot but suspect to be a disingenuous passage (iv., 784) —says he would probably have been ashamed of if he had lived to maturity. There was no pretence that he had "obtruded his views", as the bigots of to-day would say; the witnesses against him being with one exception the young companions to whom he unburdened himself. At the instigation of the clergy, this boy was tried before the High Court of Justiciary for blasphemy, under an Act of the devout Restoration period, and though there was no proper proof of his guilt in the terms of the statute he was sentenced to death. The boy not unnaturally broke down, professing both penitence and orthodoxy, and pleading his youth in extenuation; but the clergy, having been able to carry matters thus far, would hear of no pardon. Just as La Barre was later given up to the priests in France, this weeping boy was given up to the Presbyterian bigots of Scotland by the Privy Council there—the decision being carried by the casting vote of the Chancellor. This was Sir Patrick Hume, one of the heroes of the Covenanting party, who thus, says Macaulay, accomplished "the worst action of his bad life"; and the prosecuting Crown lawyer was a worthless political time-server. An attempt to get the boy off came to nothing, the execution being hastened as if to prevent the interposition of the king, who was known to be averse to persecution (Burton, viii., 77; Macaulay, iv., 785). It is on record—by a personage who believed in demoniac possession—that the ministers "spok and preached for cutting him off" (State Trials, xiii., 930).

Ten years after the Revolution, Scotland is found to be sufficiently far from moral regeneration under the auspices of the now triumphant Presbyterian Church. Fletcher of Saltoun, republican as he was, could see no means, short of the general establishment of domestic slavery, by which the vast pauperism of the country could be grappled with. Here is a part of his testimony:—"There are at this day in Scotland (besides a great many poor families very meanly provided for by the church-boxes, with others who by living upon bad food fall into various diseases) *two hundred thousand people begging from door to door*. . . . And although the number of them be perhaps double to what it was formerly, by reason of this present great distress, yet in all times there have been about one hundred thousand of those vagabonds, who have lived without any regard or subjection either to the laws of the land, or even those of God and nature; fathers incestuously accompanying with their own daughters, the son with the mother, and the brother with the sister. . . . Many murders have been discovered among them; and they are not only an unspeakable oppression to poor tenants (who if they give not bread or some kind of provision to perhaps forty such villains in one day, are sure to be insulted by them), but they rob many poor people who live in houses distant from any neighbourhood. In years of plenty many thousands of them meet together in the mountains, where they feast and riot for many days; and at country weddings, markets, burials, and other the like publick occasions, they are to be seen, both men and women, perpetually drunk, cursing, blaspheming, and fighting together" (Fletcher's Works, ed. 1732, pp. 144—6).

And this savage pauperism remained a salient feature in Scottish life for many generations. "Before the general establishment of poor's rates", writes Dr. Thomas Somerville in 1813, "the country was overrun with vagrant beggars. They had access to every house, and received their alms in meal and bread. . . . . Strolling beggars often travelled in companies, and used to take up their night quarters at the houses of the tenant farmers" ("My Own Life and Times," p. 370). And Gibson, the historian of Glasgow, writes that in 1707 "the body of the people were but a degree above want; the streets were crowded with beggars, both old and young, who were willing to work, could they have found employment" ("History of Glasgow", p. 106, cited in *Scottish Review*, Sept., 1883, p. 250). Such poverty, it need hardly be said, meant vice and degradation; and the case against the Established Church, regarded as a claimant to credit for promoting civilisation, is not merely that it did not check such demoralisation, but that it on the whole resisted those influences which made for better things. To begin with, the clergy habitually represented dearth and distress as a divine punishment for national sin; never as an evil to be got rid of by strenuous effort; and such a calamity as the collapse of the Darien Scheme was singled out with special emphasis as the work of a chastising Providence. (See Chambers' "Domestic Annals", iii., 221, 241.) There could hardly be a stronger implicit discouragement to enterprise; but there was explicit discouragement likewise. Wodrow, who typifies the clerical mind of the time, writes in 1709 of "the sin of our too great fondness for trade, to the neglecting of our more valuable interests" (Wodrow's "Correspondence", ed. 1842, i., 67; cited by Buckle, iii., 160; also "Analecta", i., 218). This in a country on which the sword of famine had fallen every few years, as far back as living memory went; a country whose poverty was not to be paralleled among the northern states of Europe; and whose largest trading city even then had its streets "crowded with beggars, willing to work, could they have found employment".

The retardation of material progress might have been forgiven, if any enlightenment had been gained by the loss; but poverty of mind went with poverty of body. The killing of the boy Aikenhead is an index to the clerical capacity for tolerance at the beginning of the 18th century. When the Act of Toleration was passed for the benefit of Scottish Episcopalians in 1712, it met with the bitterest clerical opposition. Dr. Burton (viii., 224, *et seq.*)

charitably finds reasons outside of mere intolerance for their outcry, but even such a champion of the Church as the late Dr. Tulloch was unable to shelter himself behind such excuses. "The Toleration Act of 1712," he writes, "was a statute of freedom, obnoxious as it was to the great body of the Presbyterians. It confined the ecclesiastical power to its own sphere; and, while it left the Church its anathemas against schism and 'innovations in the worship of God', protected all who chose to put themselves voluntarily beyond its pale from all forcible interference. It is melancholy to think that even the Church of Carstares did what it could to oppose such a law, and that it can be said with truth by the modern historian that the Scottish Parliament would never have ventured to pass it" ("The Church of the Eighteenth Century", St. Giles Lectures, 1881, p. 260). Dr. Somerville, again, expressly confesses that "many of the members of the Established Church, of . . . . education and of unquestionable piety, regarded the indulgence of Episcopacy as a crime on the part of the legislature" ("Life and Times", p. 375). And official documents of the time unambiguously spoke of the "grievances of the Church of Scotland, ... as the Act granting so large and almost boundles Tolleration to those of the Episcopal persuasion in Scotland" (Spalding Club Miscellany, i., 229). It is hardly necessary to add that when punishment for witchcraft was abolished in 1736, the Scotch clergy were among the bitterest protesters.

It is sometimes contended that the remarkable literary revival which took place in Scotland in the middle and latter part of the eighteenth century should go to the credit of the Church, some of the distinguished writers of the period having been in its ministry. Stout old Dr. Alexander Carlyle, of Inveresk, known in his day as "Jupiter Carlyle", has an eloquent passage implying such a claim, though he was little in sympathy with the devout Presbyterianism of his day. "We have men", he declared, "who have successfully enlightened the world on almost every branch of knowledge and of Christian doctrine and morals. Who have written the best histories, ancient and modern? It has been clergymen of this Church. Who has written the clearest delineation of the human understanding and all its powers? A clergyman of this Church. Who wrote a tragedy that has been deemed perfect? A clergyman of this Church. Who was the most profound mathematician of the age he lived in? A clergyman of this Church" ("Autobiography", p. 561). But it happens that an analysis of that panegyric yields the most crushing refutation of the pretence that the Church had any merit in the matter. Not one of the luminaries mentioned is representative of its true inwardness and practical influence; indeed, some of them came in collision with it. Adam Ferguson, who wrote the History of the Roman Republic, never took a parish charge, though he had been licensed to preach. Reid, the friend of Gregory and Dugald Stewart, was utterly outside the spirit of the Scottish Church of his day. Principal Robertson, while, like Carstares, he was the leader of a Church of which the prevailing temper was so widely different from his own, was in reality so alien to its tendencies that when in 1779 he advocated the repeal of the laws against Catholics, he was in danger of his life from the raving populace, which was countenanced in its bigotry by the majority of the clergy (Stewart's "Life of Robertson", Works, ed. 1817, i., 122). Home, the author of the tragedy "deemed perfect"—the once famous "Douglas", now, alas! utterly forgotten—had to leave the ministry because of the outcry against him by his brethren for writing that very tragedy; and "Jupiter" himself was menaced with a prosecution for countenancing his friend and the theatre in general. But there is no need to pile up evidence: Dr. Tulloch has admitted that "the popular and the moderate clergy of the eighteenth century stand apart" (St. Giles Lectures, p. 285); and the men Dr. Carlyle praised were, I believe, without an exception "moderates", as he was himself. And, what is extremely significant, Dr. Tulloch could not lecture even in 1881 without apologising to his fellow-churchmen for the very "moderation" of these men—precisely the quality in respect of which they attained intellectual distinction.

But there is a further refutation, even more conclusive than the direct disproof above given. For the true explanation of the Scottish literary revival of last century let us turn to the other and greater Carlyle, who, though not a Churchman, was not at all hostilely disposed to the Puritan tradition:—"For a long period after Scotland became British we had no literature; at the date when

Addison and Steele were writing their *Spectators*, our good John Boston was writing, with the noblest intent, but alike in defiance of grammar and philosophy, his *Fourfold State of Man*. Then came the schisms in our National Church, and the fiercer schisms in our Body Politic; Theologic ink and Jacobite blood, with gall enough in both cases, it seemed, to have blotted out the intellect of the country. . . . . Lord Kames made nearly the first attempt at writing English; and ere long Hume, Robertson, Smith, and a whole host of followers, attracted hither the eyes of all Europe. And yet in this brilliant resuscitation of our 'fervid genius' there was nothing truly Scottish, nothing indigenous; except, perhaps, the national impetuosity of intellect, which we sometimes claim, and are sometimes upbraided with, as a characteristic of our nation. It is curious to remark that Scotland, so full of writers, had no Scottish culture, nor indeed any English; our culture was exclusively French. It was by studying Racine and Voltaire, Batteux and Boileau, that Kames had trained himself to be a critic and philosopher: it was the light of Montesquieu and Mably that guided Robertson in his political speculations; Quesnay's lamp that kindled the lamp of Adam Smith. Hume was too rich to borrow, and perhaps he reacted on the French more than he was acted on by them; but neither had he aught to do with Scotland; Edinburgh, equally with La Flèche, was but the lodging and laboratory, in which he not so much morally *lived*, as metaphysically *investigated*" (Essay on Burns, ed. 1840, p. 361).

That passage, despite Carlyle's aversion—which comes out in the context—to the rationalism of the writers he mentions, seems to me substantially sound, if we take "indigenous" to imply those intellectual qualities chiefly conspicuous in Scotland from the Reformation to the Union. Truly the group round Hume got nothing from their predecessors; there was simply nothing for such minds to get in the Puritan period, and they were too far removed in every way from the præ-Puritan period to take up the broken strands of the old national literature. At the Union, as we have seen, Scottish literature was a blank, and it was, as Carlyle says, French seed that raised the great crop in the latter half of the century. And Carlyle indirectly, and perhaps unconsciously, points the moral when he says that the state of things he describes is "unexampled, so far as we know, *except perhaps at Geneva, where the same state of matters appears still to continue*". Geneva was from the first Scotland's ecclesiastical model; and the coincidence in the matter of literary paralysis is indeed significant. The intimate union of democracy and hierocracy obviously does not engender literary genius. It is worth noticing, by the way, that in the England of the period above scanned, where the State Church was then at its most unchallenged supremacy, and there was no French school of culture as in Scotland, there was no intellectual product comparable to the Scotch, if we exclude Gibbon, who again, as Buckle has remarked, was a Frenchman in his culture.

If we change the line of investigation and ask what the Scottish Church specifically did last century to promote culture of any sort, we find no evidence whatever beyond the item of the introduction of the Bible into the Gaelic districts. It may indeed have some doubtful credit for what it indirectly did by keeping up the parish schools, though the object of these was primarily to strengthen itself by inculcating its dogmas; but its failure to promote even ecclesiastical culture effectively is notorious. "When I was a student of divinity", writes Dr. Somerville, who studied at Edinburgh about the middle of the century, "Hebrew was little cultivated, or altogether omitted, by the great number of the theological students" ("Life and Times", p. 18). And Greek, there is good reason to believe, was only a little less unfamiliar. There would be, of course, no very serious weight in the old lamentations over the scarcity of classical culture in Scotland if such scarcity had been balanced by an enlightened promotion of culture of a more vital and valuable kind. An irrational estimate of the value of an academic command of Greek and Latin has notoriously been a serious bar to intellectual advance in England till quite recently, if it is not so still. Apart, however, from the non-ecclesiastical, France-derived culture already spoken of, it is quite impossible to detect in the Scotland of last century any official diffusion of sound knowledge equal in value to the classical cultus of the English universities. The great mass of the clergy had neither Greek nor science, neither philosophy nor art, neither belles-lettres nor general knowledge; and all the evidence goes to show that the spirit of clericalism as developed by the country's religious history was responsible for this general destitution. There is a comic story preserved by Lord Cockburn, of how Sidney Smith in the street one dark night overheard old Dalzel, the distinguished Grecian, muttering to himself on his way home, with regard to the inferiority of Scotland to England in classicism, that "If it had not been for that confounded Solemn League and Covenant, we would have made as good longs and shorts as they" ("Memorials," p. 20). And yet Dalzel was clerk to the General Assembly—another proof of the aloofness of Scottish culture from the spirit of the Church. It is only right to say that while "longs and shorts" were never very successfully cultivated in Scotland, the intellectual movement above sketched included a more methodic treatment of the literature and history of Rome than had yet taken place in England; Ruddiman and Hunter, for instance, being admittedly among the ablest Latinists of their age; while the first good English manual of Roman antiquities was that of Adams. But here again, no thanks are due to the Church. Most of us could forgive Covenanterism the most complete dearth of native Latin verses if it had done anything to foster even such a partial organisation of human knowledge as the good Adams aimed at, or such a reconstruction of the past as was represented by the work of the Scottish historians of the century.

As for the direct and indirect intellectual influence of the Church in other directions, it is only too palpable in a negative fashion. Painting and sculpture could scarcely be said to exist in Scotland last century (Burton, viii., 536–7). Of music, beyond the primitive airs, there was none; the tabooing of the organ in worship keeping the country far behind even England in that regard. "The Earl of Kelly, a man of yesterday, was the first Scotsman who ever composed music for an orchestra" (Chambers' "Traditions of Edinburgh", ed. 1869, p. 279). And in a matter which many will think rather more important, there is a still more direct indictment standing against the Protestant State Church. "The ancient church [*i.e.* the Catholic] was honorably distinguished by its charity towards the poor, and more especially the diseased poor; and it was a dreary interval of nearly two centuries which intervened between the extinction of its lazar-houses and leper-houses, and the time when merely a civilised humanity dictated the establishment of a regulated means of succor for the sickness-stricken of the humble classes. The date here affixed [August 6, 1729] is an interesting one, as that *when a hospital of the modern type was first opened in Scotland for the reception of poor patients*" (Chambers' "Domestic Annals", iii., 557). And for this first hospital, it should further be noted, the funds were raised "chiefly by the activity of the medical profession" (p. 559).

In dealing with the condition of Scotland for a generation after the Reformation, we saw reason to reject the view of Buckle—hastily adopted by him, I observe, from Dr. McCrie—that the Presbyterian clergy had the merit of so stimulating the spirit of independence among the people as to extend their liberties and their political power. In point of fact, the self-assertion of the Scottish democracy, as such, had been more marked and more effectual before the Reformation than after. We saw, again, how the outcome of the Covenant movement was an effacement of national institutions under Cromwell, followed by an all-penetrating oppression under Charles II. It has now further to be noted that, though under William and Mary the Presbyterian clergy showed something of the old Covenanting turbulence, the political history of Scotland from the beginning to the end of the eighteenth century was one of progressive political retrogression; till at the opening of the nineteenth century the country could make no more pretence to be governed on genuinely constitutional principles than any State on the Continent. After the repression of the Jacobite rising of 1745, it seemed as if the nation had lost the faculty of political initiative. Not that it was governed with actual cruelty: the harm lay rather in the suppression of every democratic aspiration, and of the all-important instinct of self-government in every direction save that of the mere domestic economy of the Kirk. But in the long run, when the example of the French Revolution bore its full fruit among us in aristocratic reaction, the tyranny became gross and brutal. Everyone who has read the memoirs of the times is aware of the completeness of the repression. "Public political meetings," says Cockburn ("Memorials," p. 88), "did not arise, for the elements did not exist. I doubt if there was

one during the twenty-five years that succeeded the year
1795 ". That was the period of his own adult experience,
up to the beginnings of political reform; and I cannot
discover that matters were different in the previous generation, which was one of considerable political activity in
England. "With the people put down and the Whigs
powerless," he says again (p. 86), "Government was the
master of nearly every individual in Scotland, but especially
in Edinburgh, which was the chief seat of its influence;"
and he even testifies (pp. 89-90) that in the matter of
Church management the principle of democracy was so
entirely discarded that the expression of a wish by an
Edinburgh congregation in regard to the appointment of
a pastor was made by the Government a reason for
appointing someone else.

Now, this state of things is certainly not in itself an
argument against the national Church, but it is a crushing
disproof of the common assertion that that Church has all
along kept alive the spirit of democracy. That is one
more ecclesiastical myth. If there was anything that a
liberty-loving Church might be expected to be emphatic
about, it was the slavery of the colliers and salters. Yet
not only did the clergy never agitate in the matter, but
they took positively no notice of the Act of liberation in
1799; and their flocks generally were so indifferent that
there is no record of the event in the Scots Magazine of
that year, or of the year 1775, when the first legislative
step was taken. "People cared nothing about colliers on
their own account, and the taste for improving the lower
orders had not then began to dawn" (Cockburn's "Memorials", p. 79). In the days of Tory supremacy, those
who ventured to attend the annual dinner on Fox's birth-
day had their names taken down at the door of the meeting-
place by sheriff's officers, by way of menace (*Ibid*. p. 91).
Ecclesiastical democratism did not meddle with outrages of
that kind—to say nothing of the iniquitous trials and
infamous sentences for so-called sedition.

Printed by ANNIE BESANT and CHARLES BRADLAUGH, 63, Fleet St., E.C.—1886.

XIV.

THE PERVERSION OF SCOTLAND.
By JOHN ROBERTSON.
(VI.)

COCKBURN's testimony as to the political inaction of the Church is decisive. The Whig advocates, as he points out, were the real movers in the cause of political liberty among the educated classes. "The profession of these men armed them with better qualities than any other could supply in a country without a Parliament..... It was among them accordingly that independence found its only asylum. It had a few silent though devoted worshippers elsewhere, but the Whig counsel were its only open champions. The Church can boast of Sir Henry Moncreiff alone as its contribution to the cause; but he was *too faithful to his sacred functions to act as a political partisan.* John Allen and John Thomson, of the medical profession, were active and fearless. And the College gave Dugald Stewart, John Playfair, and Andrew Dalzel" ("Memorials," pp. 84–5).

In all directions, then, a search for proofs of the service so often alleged to have been done for Scotland by the national Church, leads to a demonstration that its influence has on the contrary been substantially for evil. We have found, to begin with, that the Reformation was the outcome not of high-minded religious fervor, but of aristocratic greed; and we have seen that wherever the ecclesiastical spirit proper came into play, the result was, with hardly an exception, disaster to the nation's best interests. The new superstitions were darker and deadlier than the old. The Church never raised morals and manners by being, in its practice, ahead of the average ethics of the day. It not only blighted every form of art, but absolutely suspended the evolution of Scottish literature for some two hundred years; so that when a new growth commenced, the inspiration had perforce to come from other countries. The vaunted services of the Church to the cause of political liberty are found to be sheer delusion and imposture, inasmuch as, within its own sphere, it all along laid on the people burdens grievous to be borne, while latterly failing to touch political tyranny so much as with the tips of its fingers.

It is never an easy matter to generalise soundly on the origin and explanation of national characteristics; but I submit that the case is tolerably clear as to the net effect of the establishment of the national Presbyterian Church on the character of the people of Scotland. Before the Reformation they were vivacious, art-loving, full of healthy life: since then they have become "Museless", as Mr. Ruskin would say; and the darkness cast over their life by clericalism has marked them out as the most fanatical of Protestant peoples, with the nominal exception of the Presbyterians of Ulster, who are, indeed mostly of Scotch descent. England, too, has been blighted by Puritanism, as Mr. Arnold has so often told his countrymen; but the shadow is darker on Scotland. Nowhere, probably, is life made so little of, in the way of all-round enjoyment, proportionately to the means available. Cultured Scotchmen have born ample witness to the sinister results of the hierocracy in individual as well as in public life. Take Professor Masson. His view of the history of the Kirk is to a large extent the conventional one, tinctured with a flavor of Carlyle, but this is his feeling about the general effect of Presbyterian discipline in his native land:—"In no country does one see more manly, courageous, and strongly-original faces; but it might be a fair speculation whether in the 'pawky' type of physiognomy which is often to be marked in Scottish streets, conjoined with the soft walk, the sleek black gloves touching each other in front, and the evasive or sidelong glance, there is not a relic of that old ecclesiastical tyranny which drilled a considerable percentage of Scotsmen through several generations into a look of acquiescence in propositions known to be untenable" ("Drummond of Hawthornden", p. 375). The portrait is somewhat crude, but every Scotchman can recall the type Dr. Masson is thinking of. It is not so much that the rule of the Kirk forced men to pretend to accept "propositions known to be untenable": unhappily it taught them to believe its worst incredibilities, and crippled their very faculty of thinking for themselves; but it made hypocrites and fanatics by the thousand. Scotland is not, in a general way, more hypocritical than England: that is impossible: but in matters of religious dissimulation, formalism, and lip-service, it makes up for any falling short of English attainment in other forms of insincerity.

Did the Church effect anything in the way of promoting good morals? The one species of immorality on which it laid anything like the stress it put on witchcraft and Sabbath-breaking was sexual licence; and what has been the result of its interference? Only the other day a London journal which makes it its business to be "moral" in the English sense, was congratulating England on having such a very much lower rate of illegitimate births than Scotland. I do not share the conception of morality which looks on the illegitimate birth-rate as the test of a nation's general moral position; but there is no disputing that it is the index of a large amount of unhappiness, hardship, and degradation; and all Churches agree in deploring its existence. Why then is "Bible-loving", Kirk-governed Scotland such a sinner in this regard? This is not the place to go into the whole question, but here too the policy of the Church is arraigned by competent Scotchmen. Dr. Burton (viii., 388–9), sums up in these terms:

"It does not follow that because the clerical inquisition [*i.e.*, the general presbyterial and sessional discipline] displayed scenes of revolting licentiousness, it created them. But, on the other hand, it is very obvious to those who read the session records, and otherwise trace the manners of the age, that it did little, if anything, towards their suppression. . . . . The more vice was dragged from the dark, the more seemed to be left behind to be dragged forth, and the inquisition went on, ceaseless and ineffective. The people became familiar with the sight—sometimes too familiar with its cause. If the degradation on one Sunday were insufficient, it should be followed by another and another. It became matter of boast that a parish had risen so much higher in rigidity than its neighbors as to demand more appearances in the place of scorn. A frail victim was sometimes compelled to appear on nine or ten successive Sundays, exposed to the congregation in the seat of shame. The most noticeable effect often produced by the exhibition was in the gibes and indecorous talk of the young peasants, who, after a few significant glances during the admonition, and a few words at the church door, adjourned the general question for discussion in the change-house. Sometimes it was noticed that the young Jacobite lairds, who would not be otherwise induced to enter a Presbyterian place of worship, strayed to the parish church to have an opportunity of seeing the latest addition to the frail sisterhood of the neighbourhood. The exposure sometimes hardened hearts otherwise redeemable; or drove the erring to deeper crimes for the concealment of their guilt. Thus this rigid system, however highly it may have purified the virtue of the select few who were the patterns and leaders of the flock, doubtless deserved the reproach often cast upon it, of driving weaker brethren either into hypocrisy or recklessness, by compelling the people to be either puritans or reprobates."

The historian's judgment seems to me to be absolutely just—or rather to err only on the side of under-statement. It points to a fact in Scottish life which has misled many observers—the coexistence, even in the same circles, of real or assumed fanaticism and more or less demoralising riot. And Dr. Burton's summing-up indicates the explanation—that the one thing implies the other. Asceticism always has a foil of coarseness; witness the offensive fact that John Knox, when a decrepit old widower of fifty-nine, with grown-up children, married a girl of at most seventeen years, affianced to him at about sixteen—a fact probably not known to one person in a hundred in Scotland, so industriously have his biographers suppressed it. (See Burton, v., 86, and Laing's Knox, vi., 532, 533. Dr. McCrie shirks the truth.) The life of Burns has brought before English readers the chequered aspect of popular Scottish morality. Austerity and joyless gloom on the one hand produce their natural corrective in dissolute mirth and defiant licence on the other; and the poet, only too able to see the element of hypocrisy in the austerity, brands the picture of it all in his vividest verse; triumphantly impeaching the Kirk before posterity in the "Holy Fair", and impaling a typical hypocrite, drawn from the life, on the barbs of a murderous satire. Better than any service the hapless singer could render to culture by any beauty of his song was the moral shock of the breeze and the lightning of his mockery and his human protest, blowing and flashing through the world of Pharisaism and shamefaced good fellowship around him. But his genius could not make an end of cant and bigotry, any more than it could transform debauchery at once into healthy joy.

A moral duality, so to speak, runs through past Scottish life in a way that becomes at times perplexing. Burton notes (vii., 425) that "the higher order have always in Scotland but scantily partaken in the religious fervor so abundant among the humbler body of the people"; and this divergence ramified in many directions. Thus we find that when in 1723 a dancing assembly was established in Edinburgh it was almost wholly supported by "Tories and Episcopalians" (Chambers' "Domestic Annals", iii., 480). Cruel as the Episcopal Church had been in its period of supremacy, it was certainly more human in its later social influence than the Presbyterian; the persecution through which it in turn passed after its marked association of itself with Jacobitism having perhaps a salutary effect. It of necessity had affinities for art; and its adherents appear to have been the main patrons of what music and painting existed in the country. To its ranks, too, seem to have belonged most of those delightful old ladies immortalised for us by Dean Ramsay, with their bracing originality, their vigorous wit, their keen understandings, and their delicious profanity. The incomparable old lady, widow of a clergyman, told of by Cockburn ("Memorials," p. 58)—who, on hearing her granddaughter read a newspaper paragraph telling how the "first gentleman in Europe" had compromised a lady's reputation, rose to her feet with the startling exclamation, "The dawmed villain, does he kiss and tell!"—that chivalrous moralist of four-score clearly inherited the Cavalier tradition, and not the Covenanting. Beside that estimable dame and her kind, it happens, we have to set a brotherhood not so estimable, of hard-drinking lairds, frantic Jacobites, and brutal judges, all exhibiting the riotous and bibulous national strain as opposed to the fanatical, whether or not all Episcopalian; but perhaps they in their way were not wholly without redeeming merit as correcting in some degree the blanching gloom and cold constriction of the reigning cult.

One of the plainest marks of the Church's hold on Scottish life—one of the strongest evidences of its social influence for harm—is the national Sabbatarianism. That is emphatically a social condition of Church manufacture. As early as the twelfth century, it appears, Queen Margaret of sainted memory sought to impose strict Sabbatical restraints on the people; but during the Stewart period, down to the Reformation, Scotland enjoyed the same freedom in that particular matter as the rest of Catholic Europe. Even the first Reformers, like Calvin, were partly free from the Sabbatarian superstition; Knox having no objection to feast his friends on preaching day (Burton, v., 86). It was the Judaizing of the later Presbyterians that made the Scotch Sunday the gazing-stock of civilised Europe. The clergy resisted the really sensible attempts of James VI. to liberalise Sabbath observance; in 1640 the Covenanting Parliament is found legislating according to their wishes (*Ib*., vi., 287); and practically ever since they have kept their clutch on the first day of the week. In 1693 the Edinburgh Town Council passed an Act prohibiting all standing or strolling on Sundays in the streets or on the Castle Hill—the only open space then within the city walls (Chambers' "Annals", iii., 342); and in 1709 clerical complaint is made that nevertheless the Sabbath is "profaned by people standing on the streets", "*also by idle gazing out at windows*" (*Ib*., p. 344).

The superstition got hold of the clear heads as well as the cloudy. Sir John Dick Lauder, the careful lawyer, perpends thus judicially in 1686: "This winter ther happened three fyres at Edinburgh, and all on the Sabbath day, to signify God's displeasure at the profanation of his day: tho ther is no certain conclusion can be drawn from thesse providentiall accidents, for a Jew would draw just the contrare conclusion, that God was dissatisfyed with our worshipping him on that day; so thesse providences may be variously interpreted" ("Historical Observes", p. 246). The faint vestige of common sense here apparent soon faded from the discussion of the subject.

And yet Cockburn, looking back about 1825 to his own young days, declares that he "could mention many practices of our old pious which would horrify modern zealots. . . . . In nothing do these differences appear more strikingly than in matters connected with the observance of Sunday. Hearing what is often confidently prescribed now as the only proper mode of keeping the Christian Sabbath, and then recollecting how it was recently kept by Christian men, ought to teach us charity in the enforcement of observances" ("Memorials," p. 43). The explanation is twofold. For one thing, Cockburn had lived in the Episcopalian stratum; but apart from that there had really taken place during his lifetime a change for the worse in the intellectual atmosphere of Scotch society—the inevitable result of the steady pressure of the sinister ecclesiastical influence against that culture which, as Carlyle has shown us, had been imported into Scotland from France in the eighteenth century. The writer of the ecclesiastical chapter at the end of Wright's "History of Scotland" (iii., 607) briefly describes the transition from the restricted and non-popular reign of "moderatism", after Robertson's day, to the "evangelicalism" of later times:—"Towards the end of the century . . . . the current began to turn, and, partly from the returning favor of Government, and partly through the earnest and able advocacy of men like Dr. Erskine, Sir Henry Moncrieff, and Dr. Andrew Thomson, the evangelical party gradually gained the upper hand in the Assembly, and finally a new life was given to it, after 1815, by the energy and talents of the celebrated Dr. Thomas Chalmers, while people's attention was extensively carried back again and fixed on the examples and doctrines of the earlier Scottish reformers by the writings of Dr. McCrie and others." In other words, the inherent reactionary bias of the ecclesiastical system had turned back the hands of the social clock. We have sufficiently seen what was the bearing and value of the "examples and doctrines of the earlier Scottish reformers".

To do Chalmers justice, he was more than a mere past-worshipping ecclesiastic. He was almost the only Scotch clergyman who has had at once the intelligence and the courage to openly proclaim the vital importance of the principle of population worked out by Malthus; and he did other service to economic science. But here again the Church has been true to its mission. In all the clerical eulogy of the memory of Chalmers, not a solitary voice dwells on his social philosophy; and the great majority of Scotchmen now do not even know that he was a Malthusian.

I have gone through two biographies of him without lighting on a single allusion to the fact.

It will perhaps be argued that, seeing the "evangelical" movement of the present century was synchronous with the beginnings of political liberty, the inner spirit of the Church was thus after all influential for democracy. But the facts will not square with such a theory. That movement was independent of the political awakening, of which the active spirits were such men as Jeffrey and Cockburn, who—though not unbelievers—were in favor of the exclusion of religion from the public schools, in view of the irreconcilable dissensions of the sects. This last social feature is one of the things for which we have to thank the institution of State religion. As Cockburn notes in his Journal (ed. 1874, i., pp. 236, 238-9), Churchmen endeavored to prevent the endowment of the education of Dissenters, while Dissenters similarly sought to foil Churchmen. Lord-Advocate Rutherford writes Cockburn in 1839 that "when it is proposed to extend the benefit of education [by giving the Privy Council power to apply £10,000 to the education of Dissenters], there is a cry, responded to in shouts by the House of Commons, that you are undermining and ruining the Church". But Cockburn, a Scotchman who lived his life in Scotland, has a more sweeping indictment against the Church in connexion with the common claim that it has promoted popular education. "It is clear to my mind", he writes ("Journal", ii., 305) "that keeping the popular education any longer in the hands of the Church is nonsense. *The Church has not performed this duty even decently for above a hundred years.*" How much the clerical influence had availed towards spreading that "passion for education" with which the Scottish people is sometimes credited, may be gathered from the same writer's remarks ("Memorials", p. 186) on the Schoolmasters' Act of 1803, which compelled heritors to provide houses for schoolmasters, "but prescribes that the house need not contain more than two rooms, *including the kitchen*. This shabbiness was abused at the time, and seems incredible now [twenty years later]. But Hope [the Lord Advocate] told me that he had considerable difficulty in getting even the two rooms, and that a great majority of the lairds and Scotch members were indignant at being obliged to 'erect palaces for dominies'."

On this matter of popular education, it may be well to point out finally that Scotland stood relatively high in that regard long before the Reformation. "In almost all the periods of the history of Scotland, whatever documents deal with the social condition of the country, reveal a machinery for education always abundant, when compared with any traces of art, or the other elements of education. . . . In documents much older than the War of Independence, the school and the schoolmaster are familiar objects of reference. They chiefly occur in the chartularies of the religious houses; and there is little doubt that the earliest schools were supported out of the superfluous wealth of these houses [ref. to Innes's 'Sketches of Early Scottish History', 134, *et seq*]. . . . In later times, schools are found attached to the burgh corporations. They got the name of grammar-schools, and . . . . Latin was taught in them. . . . . We hear, at the commencement of the sixteenth century, of men acquiring distinction as mere schoolmasters—a sure sign of the respect in which the teacher's mission was held" (Burton, iii., 399-401).

If Scotch Protestants were half as ready to give credit to the Romish Church for what it did for civilization, as they are to magnify the scanty achievement of Presbyterianism, the former body would have a very different reputation from that which it has at present. Those who lay stress on the fancied services of the Presbyterian Church as a reason for keeping up its endowments, never think of mentioning that it was the reviled monks of old who alone fostered agriculture in early feudal times; and that they were far the best landlords of their age (Burton, i., 107-9; citing Innes, "Scotland in the Middle Ages", 138-140, 147). The truth is, that the Catholic Church in Scotland was in the main favorable to general culture, interfering only with religious thought; while its Presbyterian successor was and is hostile to general science and all popular art. To this day it is good for nothing but the propagation of its own dogmas. The series of clerical lectures which have of late years been given in Edinburgh with the professed purpose of spreading a knowledge of the nation's past, and of its distinguished sons, are purely ecclesiastical. The "worthies" they introduce to the public are the otherwise deservedly forgotten fanatics and rhapsodists of the Kirk's early days, extinct volcanoes, whose remains offer no healthy pabulum for any sound mind. Bigots who taught that unbaptized children would eternally burn in hell are extolled for their spiritual graces; and the whole dust-heap of their polemics is turned over by way of edifying the nineteenth century. Such is "education" as the Church affects it. On the other hand, I have no hesitation in saying that Scotchmen, with all their nationalism, are more generally ignorant of the bygone scientific achievements of men of their own nation than are the general public of almost any other country in the world; and this clearly by reason of their past clericalism. Let any of my Scotch freethinking readers cast about for any popular acquaintance with the lives and doings, or even the names, of Black, Leslie, Hutton, Cullen, and Hunter; and they will see cause to endorse my statement. The first generally accessible account—the first worthy estimate —of these great men collectively is in the work of Buckle. The name of James Watt did indeed get into the books for boys; and Scotchmen know something of Adam Smith, simply because Political Economy fell so largely into Scotch hands, and because Smith's name has been kept in the public eye by newspapers and politicians in connexion with Free Trade; but at this moment there is no popular Scotch edition of the philosophical works of Hume, the greatest thinker Scotland has produced; while the cheap English edition in one volume—the only one obtainable by the average purchaser—though professing to be complete, is actually castrated of the essays on miracles and a future state: a scandal calling for redress, by the way, apart from the issues above discussed. Those of us who have noted these and other facts in connexion with Scotch culture, have our misgivings about the compliments sometimes paid to it.

Enough has been already said to show how deadly has been the power of the Kirk as regards what are at once the most subtle and among the most potent influences of civilisation — the arts. The notorious and barbarous Presbyterian prejudice against church music has suppressed a means of musical culture which has flourished everywhere else throughout the world; so that the undoubted national musical faculty remained till practically the present generation pretty much in the state it had attained in the Middle Ages; otherwise educated people still seeing the highest musical possibilities in the early ballads. In the matter of the theatre, the Church is not merely guilty of extinguishing the vigorous præ-Reformation drama; she has done her best to starve and stunt it in its modern revival. As soon as the clergy were able, they obtained the suppression of the small theatre established by Allan Ramsay in Edinburgh about the middle of last century; and a noted Presbyterian *Tartufe* of the time even sought to put down Ramsay's venture of a circulating library (Burton, viii., 551; compare Tulloch, St. Giles Lectures, p. 282). And I believe that as regards the position of the drama in the provinces generally, Scotland is, relatively speaking, more backward than she was a hundred years ago, when Burns wrote prologues for companies who performed at Dumfries. I could lay my finger at this moment on half-a-dozen small Scotch towns in which, for sheer lack of a theatre or any other recreation, a large proportion of the youths become unintellectual, sottish, and dissolute. The more ambitious eagerly flock to the large towns; those left behind have no resource but the tap-room. But every attempt made to establish theatres in these towns is met by shrieks from the clergy, predictive of untold contingent demoralisation—in blatant disregard of the demoralisation actually taking place.

This darkening and worsening of life at the behest of bigotry is to-day the main net outcome of clerical influence in Scotland. If the English people has not yet learned how to enjoy itself, the Scotch is still further behind. In 1838, commenting on the Scottish observance of Coronation Day, Cockburn could say of the Scotchman of the people: "The tippling-house is his natural refuge against a system of moral Calvinism which considers the social and public recreation of whole families as dangerous or shameful" ("Journal" i., 187). A slow improvement is going on, but whatever advance may be suggested—whether the Sunday opening of museums or picture galleries, Sunday secular lectures, or Sunday picnics—finds a certain and strenuous opponent in the Kirk. It is the nature of the ecclesiastical mind to make no advance of its own will: its every modification is the result of outside pressure. As Cockburn said at the Disruption time (*Ibid.*, ii., 43),

"Two centuries have not changed the Presbyterian intellect one inch". While educated opinion has progressed immeasurably from the mediæval positions, the Church nominally stands on its old creed; the only denomination which has made the slightest official change being the United Presbyterian—that in which lay influence is strongest. The spirit of the Church goes back rather than forward. Till quite recent times the ecclesiastical tone and practice of rural districts—whatever might go on at Edinburgh—were exactly what they were at the time of the Civil War. We saw how a clergyman was then rebuked by his colleagues for going about his business on *Saturday*—the clerical mind, not content with Sabbatarianism, extending the sacredness of the Sabbath over the day before and the day after; and I can testify that among my own "forbears" of a generation back the same doctrine was in force; the Sabbath gloom being caused to set in on the Saturday afternoon. The whole cult was a petrifaction of life and mind.

After all, perhaps no Scotchman can fully appreciate how far the work of the Kirk has gone—how completely it has taken his race as it were by the throat and choked down its genial impulses. The impulses are certainly there. The people had once cause for their phrase "a kindly Scot": we see it in that antithesis of conviviality which has lived cheek-by-jowl with the fanaticism. Every Scotchman knows the intensity of the strain of good-fellowship in the national character. It comes out in that curious avowal of Cockburn ("Memorials," p. 41): "I doubt if from the year 1811, when I married, I have closed above one day in the month of my town life, at home and alone. It is always some scene of domestic conviviality either in my own house or in a friend's. And this is the habit of all my best friends." It comes out in the almost hysterical good-will and mirth of the New Year time—a manifestation which is now year by year toning down just as the general emotional life of the people is becoming broader and freer. But strangers can perhaps best see the force of the contrary element in the national character, though their judgment may not always be quite intelligent. Foreign observation of any people rarely is. In the comments of the young Niebuhr, during his stay in Edinburgh at the end of last century, there is a certain priggishness, and indeed a certain bald stupidity, as when he writes ("Life and Letters," English ed., 1852, i., 132) that Scotch people have no deep affection for each other; and that though they are "much more ready and obliging in undertaking trouble for their acquaintance" than Germans are, it is "no great merit in them", seeing that "bodily activity is an enjoyment to them". Still, we must allow some weight to his declaration, "I have never witnessed nor heard of family life full of deep and tender affection, nor of a hearty, enthusiastic, mutual confidence between young men"; and even to his exaggerated statement that he finds among young Englishmen [here meaning Scotchmen in particular] a "universal licentiousness", which he ascribes to a dearth of the better emotional life. He saw the strength of the race as well as its weakness. "The number of vigorous, thinking minds", he writes (*Ibid.*), "is incontestably much larger in this than in most other countries, but the bonds which hold them together are just as much weaker and slighter"—a judgment which is not confuted by any exhibition of national sentiment commonly so-called.

I have seen a curious story of how a Scotch father, dying in the prime of life, said a gentle "Ta-ta" to his young children as he kissed them farewell, and sent them out to play while he breathed his last with his hand in his wife's. There is something in that idiosyncrasy which a Niebuhr could not very well appreciate; but it must be confessed that even such Puritan stoicism in the long run means an extinction of those impulses and faculties which constitute genius. It is an eminently significant fact that the line of Scotchmen of high literary, intellectual, and artistic faculty contains hardly a name that is in friendly association with the national ecclesiasticism. Hume was infidel; Smith was a deist; the clerical historians Robertson and Henry were "moderates"; Adam Ferguson evaded the gown. The other Fergusson, the poet, Burns's predecessor, was obnoxious to the cloth; so was Burns in an eminent degree; Scott's treatment of Presbyterianism, which he never loved, offended most of his countrymen, and brought on him the assault of Dr. McCrie. Even Carlyle, Puritan in blood as he was, could not rub along with the doctrines of the Kirk; Mr. Ruskin's Scotch blood could not reconcile him to the "deadly Muselessness" of Presbyterianism; and

Macaulay's Scotch strain is not appreciable in his character or in his relations with his Edinburgh constituency. To take minor men, Wilson was no Calvinist, and Jeffrey nothing of an evangelical. Dr. John Brown and Hugh Miller are the only Scotchmen of genius I can remember to have been in sympathy with the Kirk; and we knew that in Brown the sympathy was in hereditary alliance with a tendency to insanity; while Miller seems to have broken his heart because he could not reconcile Genesis with geology. And to-day? It is a singular fact that at this moment there is no Scottish writer or artist of European distinction—if we except such a *littérateur* as Professor Masson—resident in Scotland. Our best men, in art, letters, and science, seem to gravitate to England. Even Professor Flint, who has contrived to be heard-of in France and Germany by his questionable compilation on the "Philosophy of History", has publicly lamented the inglorious position of his clerical colleagues in their own pursuit of theology. As Renan has said: "Tedium, stupidity, and mediocrity are the punishment of certain Protestant countries, where, under pretext of good sense and Christian sentiment, art has been suppressed and science treated as something ignoble" ("Les Apôtres," Introd., ed. 1866, p. lxiv.).

I have not sought in these sketches to deal with the question, so often raised in connexion with the disestablishment movement in England, as to the right of the State to meddle with the endowments of the Church. In Scotland the denial of such a right would be too preposterous to be worth a churchman's while. There the entire institution is notoriously on a basis of State legislation and systematic fiscal endowment; and the pleas for the retention of the establishment take perforce a different shape. With the commonest—the formula as to the deep and beneficent union of the Church with the nation's history—I have dealt at large in the foregoing pages; and it need only be said further that if the Church had really done good where we have seen it has only done evil, the fact would be quite pointless in regard to the question of disendowment. A Church, politically speaking, is only a name for the men and women who constitute its membership; and it is with the endowments and privileges of these fellow citizens that we have to do. The rest is abstraction. If there is good reason to strip the Church's members of undeserved emoluments, no supposed rights or merits of "the Church" can avail a tittle to the contrary.

There is, however, one *quasi*-practical plea sometimes urged on behalf of the Church by such of its members as are Liberal in politics and friendly to liberalism of thought —the claim, namely, that whereas the Dissenting Presbyterian churches must needs be narrow in their doctrine, being subject to the rule of the ignorant, the clergy of the Established Church tend to be broader in their views and more tolerant in their teaching and practice, as being comparatively untrammelled. There is a certain speciousness in this reasoning, and it influences not a few minds in Scotland. It is, however, curiously ill-supported by specific facts. Those who look only at the cases of heresy-hunting in the Free Church reason precipitately that it is the less tolerant of the two, because there seem to be fewer such cases in the Establishment. In point of fact the preponderance is chiefly in respect of the famous case of Professor Robertson Smith; and no Scotchman can well doubt that that distinguished heretic would have been prosecuted just the same if he had been a member of the Establishment. What is true in regard to the latter body is that even its most bigoted clergy are somewhat averse to ventilating questions of heresy for sheer fear of helping the disestablishment movement. Its ministers are sworn to teach certain doctrines, which many of them do not believe; and the more generally this is realised the more widely would it be asked, by Liberals and by bigots alike, on what grounds their endowments should be maintained. But there is a more conclusive answer than this to the contention before us.

During the last few years there have come before the public two politico-religious questions, one of enduring character and interest, the other more transient, but still important—I allude to the case of Mr. Bradlaugh in Parliament and the appointment of Lord Ripon, a Roman Catholic, as Viceroy of India. These questions constituted fair tests of the enlightenment and friendliness to liberty of those parties and individuals who expressed opinions in regard to them. Both, as it happened, came before the assemblies of the Established and Free Churches in Scotland—probably also, though on this head I am uncertain, before the United Presbyterian Synod. Whatever may in that case have been the vote of the latter body, it is found that "the Established Church Assembly protested against Lord Ripon's appointment, and the proposal to make affirmation free to all members of Parliament, by much larger majorities than were obtained in the Free Assembly" (article in *Edinburgh Evening News*, February 13th, 1882). That is decisive. Whatever measure of light may be possessed by a few clergymen of the Establishment, the great majority, like their brethren of the Church of England, are foes to reasonable freedom, whether of thought, word, or deed.

It cannot, of course, be hoped that the mere turning of the Church's endowments to educational purposes will speedily impair the influence for harm which we have seen that the Church possesses. The Establishment at this moment pretends to much the same "spiritual position" as the Free Church—as shown by the puerile annual mummery of the Royal Commissioner proroguing the Assembly in the name of the Queen while the Moderator prorogues it in the name of Jesus Christ. Its clergy are chosen by popular election, after a preaching match, just as are those of the Dissenting bodies; and while the Free Church, whatever may be the diplomacy of its leaders, is nominally committed to the principle of Establishment, it follows that when the Establishment is made an end of, there will be plenty of the typical clerical spirit left to cramp and confine the national intelligence, to retard art, to resist freedom, and to disseminate a paralysing superstition. Still, the transfer of the endowments will be one positive gain; and we have seen enough to conclude that while an Established Church may have periods of "Moderatism" which partly make for culture and light, the mere presence of its endowments is a constant opportunity for the aggrandisement of that spirit of fanaticism which has never been long asleep in Scotland in modern times. On the whole, that spirit will do less harm when left to itself than when fed and fostered by national funds.

ROYALISM:

A NOTE ON THE QUEEN'S JUBILEE.

BY

JOHN ROBERTSON.

LONDON:
FREETHOUGHT PUBLISHING COMPANY,
63, FLEET STREET, E.C.

1886.

LONDON:
PRINTED BY ANNIE BESANT AND CHARLES BRADLAUGH,
63, FLEET STREET, E.C.

ROYALISM.

In the early part of 1886, shortly after the fall of the Salisbury ministry—the first of that year—it began to be noticed that the Queen of England was unusually active in the discharge of such of her functions as brought her before the public eye; that is, in the laying of foundation-stones, opening hospitals, witnessing military reviews, and so on. It had already been remarked that Her Majesty had done a most unusual thing—for her—in presiding at the opening of Parliament; but that had been generally set down to her known wish to strengthen the Conservative Government by every means in her power. The subsequent activity, however, had obviously some other purpose; and, looked at in connexion with the coming jubilee and with certain admonitions addressed to Her Majesty by London journalists, the new departure was intelligible enough. The journalists in question had told their Queen that they regarded her with inexpressible respect, but that they were not at all satisfied with the manner in which she had lately performed her duties. She had not laid foundation-stones enough, had not been seen enough, had not been sufficiently talked about; hence hisses on the day of the opening of Parliament, and a certain general coldness towards the institution of the throne. Her Majesty, it now became apparent from her conduct, graciously accepted the rebuke; and her now frequent public appearances represented her determination to consolidate the monarchy. The crown, like other old-established houses, had acknowledged the virtue of advertising, so long the specialty of younger concerns.

To the people who had prescribed the policy, its adoption naturally gave entire satisfaction. It has come to this with the institution of monarchy in England, that those who profess to believe in it are yet not ashamed to represent the sovereignty as having its *raison d'être* in the expediency of providing a certain kind of vulgar attraction in connexion with public celebrations. If it were seriously believed that royalty possessed any political value or importance, its active adherents could hardly thus liken it to a brass band or the procession of a travelling circus. At all times, doubtless, shrewd monarchs have seen in show-making a means of fortifying their dynasty and filling their coffers with a saving of friction; but in the England of to-day, where dynastic rivalry is an impossible conception, and where the royal stipend and State expenditure are alike controlled by the legislature, the counsel to royalty to make itself a gazing-stock would appear to imply either that there is nothing else of importance for royalty to do, or that the institution, however otherwise advantageous, depends for its continuance on the industrious fulfilment of that particular function. It will perhaps be worth while, in the season of jubilee, to look into the merits alike of such an institution and of its upholders.

Sir Henry Maine, little as he desires to aid, either directly or indirectly, the spread of democratic notions, has probably done as much as most men to undermine the symmetrical theory with which Sir Robert Filmer established in their faith the monarchists of two hundred years ago. Whether or not Sir Robert's circle believed in a patriarchal succession, meandering from Adam by way of Abraham down to Charles II., it is not now fashionable to point to such an explanation of the monarchies of modern Europe. The envy of surrounding nations has now for a hundred years been the recognised after-dinner vindication of the English throne, as of the rest of the constitution; and if it is felt to be losing its edge from tear and wear, there is still not the least hurry about getting a solider pretext. In short, of rational justification of the monarchy among us there is none. The average Englishman no more seeks to defend it than he—or an Ashantee—would "defend" the existence of his deity. It is there, and that is enough for him. Like the Ashantee with his fetish, he may grumble against his sovereign, but the idea of doing without one, or of analysing the fact of the sovereignty, never of his own will crosses his mind. And, what is more to the point, the suggestion of such an idea from outside moves the passive royalist to something like fright, while those of the active type—the anonymous journalist and the tribe who aspire to " shape the whisper of the throne "—reserve for such a suggestion the most solemn invective in their venerable vocabulary. It is the Conservative's last impeachment of the Liberal—an impeachment which he reserves for special crises, as Napoleon did the Old Guard—that the tendencies of Liberalism point to the abolition of royalty; that if the House of Lords goes there will be no security for the throne. What *is* the thing thus spoken of as Romans might speak of the republic—this national palladium and fountain of honor?

I have not the slightest wish to make the present an occasion for a personal attack on any member of the royal family. Neither her Majesty nor any of her house can conceivably be less deserving of ordinary respect than the individualities which prosternate before them in court and in press; and to abuse the royalty instead of the royalism would in the circumstances be to fall into crass fallacy, not to say downright injustice. For people educated enough and magnanimous enough to govern themselves, either politically or privately, at this time of day, it cannot matter a whit, politically speaking, what is the character or the capacity of the sovereign or the heir to the throne. A well-conducted or estimable king is no fitter to hold the regal position than an immoral or foolish one. In Britain, above all existing or bygone monarchies, that is an irrelevant issue from the point of view of practical politics. But inasmuch as we are here looking into the nature of royalism as a cult or opinion, it is necessary to set forth what the royalist worships, if we would fully realise his place in the scale of humanity.

Now, it is a matter too notorious to be gainsaid, except by anonymous journalists and after-dinner speakers, that the British royal family, with perhaps one or two partial exceptions, does not include one lady or gentleman of more than average intellectual gifts, and that it does include several who fall below the average. The latter fact is not the fault of those concerned; I do not even say that it is their misfortune: it is simply a datum. Nor can it greatly matter whether the most prominent members of the family belong to the last indicated order of minds. It would, however, be an affectation not to note here that the lady whose jubilee is at hand must be so classed; and we can hardly look at the matter without having our sensations qualified by that fact. Her Majesty has written certain books, the briefest perusal of which makes it clear that they would never have been published—or even written—if she were not the Queen of England. No other English lady would have been allowed by her domestic circle, if it had any control over her actions, to put such matter together as constitutes these volumes. That being so, the occasion becomes one for compassion rather than for blame. A woman whose lot is laid in a position in which she is loudly flattered on the score of her worst imbecilities, and lured to virtual moral humiliation by the united voices of the morally and mentally worthless of all classes in her nation, is not happily placed, from the point of view of those who keep any dignified ideal of human life before themselves. No one of us can have the least right to assume that he or she would not be morally unbalanced by such conditions; and if Queen Victoria happens to have made a rather egregious exhibition of defective powers as beside crowned heads generally, the fact only comes under the previous datum as to intellectual averages. She being the personality she is, her appearance in the sphere of the intellectual life follows of necessity. Candid people admit that a monarch who should write a really good book would give proof of natural gifts and judgment higher than those which might produce such a work in ordinary society; and it follows that even the issue of an extravagantly weak book by a queen should not be made a special ground for impugning her mental calibre.

But what is to be said of those who, whether by personal adulation and encouragement or by printed praise, fooled to the top of her bent the royal lady they professed to revere? To jest over the newspaper part of the process would be like satirising a farce; so gross was the laudation, so brazen the pretence; and the spectacle of the typical journalist writing with his tongue in his check has in it too much suggestion of moral disease to call forth simple indignation. This sort of corruption, like certain forms of vice, makes one grow hopeless rather than angry. It is bad enough that there should be well-intentioned people by the hundred thousand to whom the Queen's compositions are matter of reverential interest; bad enough that, apart from the chorus of fashion, the average middle-class family should make the purchase of these volumes the largest part of its scanty expenditure on books for the year, and should exhibit them on the drawing-room table with unaffected pride. These things point to an amount of *banal* sentiment, intellectual destitution, and sheer uncivilisedness, which, existing in such a society as ours, promises badly enough for the early future of culture. But the hypocrisy, the puffery, the cant—are these not still worse and stronger forces of frustration to the assumed upward tendency of things? The gods, according to Schiller and Carlyle, fight in vain against stupidity; how then against stupidity with a guiding and inspiring Asmodeus that can out-Grundy Mrs. Grundy and out-roar Caliban?

To be sure, the "guide of public opinion" is not always entirely insincere. Even the man who writes up any cause for hire cannot escape having a bias or sentiment of some sort; and his sentiment of course tends to be worthy of his trade—something cheap and coarsely convenient; so that there are many prestidigitators who believe in and applaud monarchy *per se* as honestly as it is possible for them to do anything. And then there is always a strong force of instructors of the public who are providentially fitted to it, as the parodist's fat driver to his fat oxen. This type of oracle it is who anticipates and eclipses the flattest platitudes of the fattest heads in the commonwealth at any given juncture; and the changes he can ring on the themes of loyalty and royalty give the crowning proof of his powers. He is the genius of fustian. To the bankrupt claptrap of the primæval toast-speech he gives a new gloss and an undreamt-of unctuousness; till the simple citizen, seeing his vague ineptitudes of floating sentiment thus fulmined across the realm with front and throat of brass, learns to respect his most abject instincts, and to see in the clanging vacuity of his echo-fetish the witness of his own sagacity. The self-styled leader actually does lead his public—to the very Utopia of fatuous make-believe, to the uttermost limbo of buncombe.

History warns us, memorably enough, not to suppose that the devoutest worshipper of the squalidest idol in its motley pantheon must needs be either base or small. At the junction of Pall Mall and Cockspur Street, London, there stands an equestrian statue of a microcephalous man, which is probably not to be equalled in the carved-work of the civilised world for meanness. The head, seen up there, seems the very model of the ignoble, so trivial is it, so beggarly, so graceless. It is the effigy of George the Third, to whom, in his day, many a good and true English gentleman did homage, as did Walter Scott to his successor, with an unfaltering enthusiasm that would have cherished as a priceless thing the cup from which that paltry mouth had drunk. Such worthlessness of breed as is proclaimed by this statue, shamelessly salient in the heart of the empire city, stirs an observer to that kind of uncalculating aversion which, in the case of meritless human deformity, is analogous to the instinct that moves the rearer of animals to destroy the hopelessly puny. It is unjust to contemn the unworthy organism as such; but just that monstrous elevation of it makes it almost odious. Yet there can be no question that, just as Walter Scott was entirely sincere in his strangest homage to his king, many a manly and generous soul in those generations took delight as he did in honouring as regal the man who held the regal place, never dreaming of his unworthiness. So Bishop Ken could kneel by the bedside of Charles the Second as reverently as could any disciple by his dying master. Such things in his own day might have made intelligible to Milton the worship of stocks and stones.

Not mean and not small, surely, was Sir Walter Scott; but you do not worship stocks and stones for nothing. "Whoever meanly worships a mean thing," was Thackeray's account of a snob. But even when the worship is not mean, but merely childlike, it cannot well fail to bring about some resemblance in the worshipper to the thing worshipped. The most notable aspect of Scott for us to-day is, to put it briefly, that with the imagination and the impulses of a man of genius he had the political and social ideals of a schoolboy; and it is mainly because so many honest men among us are schoolboys in his fashion, and because so many others can only rise above the schoolboy ideal to attain that of the pedant, that the throne of Queen

Victoria can be said to be "broad based upon her people's will". Now, the schoolboys and the pedants must needs, so far as their collective will is concerned, have a polity in keeping with their notions: no people can long have any other. The question is whether these citizens are in the line of progress; whether their walk and conversation promises anything for an advance of the community in health and strength; and there is only one answer. In its best type, that of Scott, the loyalist class is seen to be void of upward political impulse; fit only, whatever be its own virtue in the way of sincerity, to bring to pass a Chinese millennium of mindless convention, a stucco Paradise of all starched and gilded things, with who knows what vile underworld of rottenness and bruteward-verging woe. One sometimes feels as if the foolishest Republican were in one way a more hopeful spectacle than the soberest convinced monarchist, in that the first has at least the sense for and the yearning towards an ideal of human things in which man shall not of necessity be despicable, while the other has willingly embraced the ideal of the slave, giving his vote for a perpetual session of indignity; fixed in the faith that mankind has none but low destinies, because himself well pleased with such. Surely the last are the true vulgar.

I should expect competent minds to admit this. I should expect the really cultured people to agree that the level of life and mind indicated by the crush to a royal *levée*, the thronging to a theatre where royalty will appear, the doing of things because the Prince of Wales does them, and going to places because he goes there, and the wheezy bombast in connexion with his and the Queen's public appearances—that all this is rather further away from human dignity and upward social evolution than even the rant of the pot-house. The life of the upper mob is not merely sterile, socially speaking; it is already realised decay—the decay that history whispers-of in the places of Babylon and Nineveh, and reveals in the grimy vestiges of Rome. On the other hand, the outcry of discontent, however cheap and frothy, is, in the terms of the case, a struggle for better things, hinting of all the race's immemorial aspiration and life-giving unrest.

There are among us, however, able men with a very keen eye for the alloy in all aspiration, who take much pains to insist on its presence, and to save us from being taken in by it. So far as it goes, theirs is a perfectly proper work, there being no more good, and indeed worse harm, in democratic pinchbeck than in any other. Inasmuch, however, as these critics of democracy are in many cases seen to desire not so much its purification as its discredit, it becomes at least interesting to know what state of things, what political practice, it is that does or would satisfy them. One can understand distrust and disesteem of republican morals and mouthing as they are to be seen in contemporary republics: what one has a difficulty in understanding is a quite contented civility towards our own domestic drama. On the one hand, the written and other performances of her Majesty; the comedy of her political functions; the chronic marrying of her descendants to princely but accommodating Germans, and the accompanying dignified appeal to the British taxpayer, with the always resulting popular protest that the Queen is well known to have immense accumulations of her own: on the other hand the devotion, unalterable by any scandal, with which the upper classes fix their eyes on the Prince of Wales as a divine ensample in all things; and the edifying national custom of producing one or other member of the family, if possible, at the inauguration of every new public building; the royal performer on such occasions being felt to combine, as it were, the functions of the ark of God in Israel and of the Tichborne claimant or a champion sculler at a London music-hall. Just as the critics of democracy overlook a myriad items of iniquity in their praise of the strong governments of the past, so do they stedfastly ignore the whole question of the influence of the royalist cult on the mental and moral tone of nations, treating the problem of government as if it were solely one of the maintenance of a permanent executive.

Much has been heard among us, and rightly, of the political corruption of the United States. That cannot be too well remembered by democrats, for whom it is more important to keep the fact in view than to point out that their critics have a convenient way of forgetting alike the corruption that filled monarchic England only a few generations ago and the unique conditions lately existing in the States. But there is one more question worth keeping before the public mind, and that is whether the presence of any of the special vices of the United States polity has had a more degrading effect on the American people than the fashion of royalism has had on the English. One of Sir Henry Maine's weighty objections to the democratic formulas of the past is that they have "enervated the human intellect". That is a serious matter, and in so far as the statement is true it is entirely cogent—so cogent that I could wish Sir Henry Maine would bring his tests to bear on other branches of thought than politics. But—to stick to politics—if enervation of the human intellect is a crass vice in a political theory, what is to be said of the influence of British monarchism?

It is a very puzzling business to go back in history a few centuries, say to the time of the Tudors or the præ-Revolution Stuarts, and ask oneself what was the effect of a reverence for Henry VIII. or Elizabeth or James I. on the mind of the average Englishman, and what would have been the effect on his character of some other political system. These inquiries belong to the obscurest departments of that science of "Hypothetics" for which Sir Henry Maine has such a passion that, even while describing it as futile, he repeatedly resorts to it, on the pretext of queries as to whether we should have had the Gregorian calendar or the steam engine under universal suffrage, and so forth. But "Hypothetics" so-called, like other forms of speculation, has points of direct connexion with practical life, as when we ask whether the substitution of a republic for a monarchy in England now would raise or lower the national character; and it is an almost necessary prelude or rider to such a question as this last, to ask whether in recent times the habit of regarding the monarchy with devotion has not been degrading.

"What seems to us baseness," says Sir Henry Maine, speaking of the old flattery of kings, "passed two hundred years ago at Versailles for gentleness and courtliness; and many people have every day before them a monument of what was once thought suitable language to use to a King of England, in the Dedication of the English Bible to James I." It is a curious thing that a writer of Sir Henry's sagacity, with such a thought in his mind, should be only concerned to append to it a reflexion on the existing fashion of flattering the populace. Does he suppose that the last is a new development? and, above all, does he think the conventional attitude towards sovereigns to-day is greatly changed from what it was at the times he mentions? He is perfectly right in calling notice to the one evil; but it gives his teaching a certain air of partisanship that he should so completely avoid the other considerations of the case. Flattery of the people must more or less lower both the people—if they swallow it—and the flatterers; and sincere but unwise eulogy may do similar harm. But if there be any value in the principles on which all such judgments proceed, this period of jubilee in particular, and the worship of royalty in general, is corrupting, lowering, and enervating. Most of us have some sympathetic shame at the spectacle of a Scott at the feet of a Guelph: Thackeray, if no one else, has stung us into a sense of the abasement implied in the nation's homage to the "first gentleman in Europe". Even the shuffling protest of Trollope, one hopes, has done little to restore that utter deadness of moral sense which permitted not merely the payment of respect to the regal function, but fulsome and debasing adulation of the known man, gross, treacherous, foolish: one hopes, that is, that Englishmen have generally got past the stage of cherishing the memory of George the Fourth; whether or not they feel as hotly about him as Thackeray did. They wince at the thought of the state of things in which a man of letters could be put in jail for cracking a joke at the expense of such a personage, and in which the attention of the country could be fastened on the band of loose fish and demoralised wits who shared his society; while what was best in the nation—brave endeavor, patient science, eager philanthropy, fine faculty, and wise thought—went its obscure way as best it might, and what tolerable performance had any recognition was held as honored in being associated with such a reign. These things suggest that while England was ostensibly covered with glory it was in the main besotted and unworthy, wedded to base ideals, and for the time positively going downwards in its moral and mental pitch, much as it had sunk in some respects during the century and a half before.

There always forces itself the question, however, whether we are much better to-day; granted that our moral level —or at least our taste—is on the whole more creditable than that of our fathers. To keep the issue quite free from doubtful personal matters, let us take the case of the late Prince Consort, generally allowed to have been an estimable and cultured gentleman. In his case we have no worship of naked unworthiness, but only a quasi-reverential homage to a quite ordinary personality. What was or is the effect? Certainly a lowering of ideals and an enormous cultivation of mediocrity. All the arts have here combined to treat as an immortal a well-meaning gentleman because, being the Queen's husband, he took some intelligent interest in national progress, and in his way sought to promote it. A great poet hymns his memory as he might do that of a great man, and British taste does its villanous worst in his monumental commemoration. It is with the moral side of the process as with the artistic —standards of judgment are vitiated; facts are falsified; the small is made to seem the great and the cheap the precious. What can more "enervate the human intellect" than this vast perversion of all the instincts of admiration through a whole age and a whole people? The very function of the laureate here stamps his art with the stigma of the mercenary and the commonplace. Poetry in his hands here becomes but one more of the world's venalities; one more procuress for the lords of Vanity Fair.

The cult is carried on, one sees, just as easily without any pretext of personal worth as with it. The sovereign's son's son—possibly a good lad enough, though he must find it hard work to stay so—goes to Edinburgh when there is an exhibition to open; and straightway the fountains of civic drivel are broken-up; the incense is burned; the local muse is invoked, and the elders of the people abase themselves—just the same for a raw unknowing boy as for his sire or his sire's sire. And in the land where leal once meant good and bravely true, this serf-like subserviency is known as loyalty; a vulgar vice here as everywhere taking the name of a virtue. Despite all' literary pretence, there is no country with a duller public sense of humor than England. The Mayor and Corporation of Eastbourne, like others, thought fit to humbly felicitate the newly adult prince on his coming of age, and the answer went throughout the empire: "Whatever the future may have in store, the kindly care of my parents will never be forgotten by me." The good youth! The inanity is too flat for a smile; but is the heart of

England—that fat-encumbered organ—aught but well pleased?

Turn Elizabethan phraseology into modern, and you have in the dedication of the Bible just the kind of sycophancy that flourishes round the throne to-day. That the old sample happens to be printed on a fly-leaf of the national sacred-book is neither here nor there. What more of abjection is implied in that than in the unspeakable fact of a national thanksgiving to the gods, after pagan precedent, for the recovery of the Prince of Wales from a fever? What interval is there between the eternal singing of "God save the Queen" by assemblies of her subjects—that simple summary of the national religion—and the panegyric of Elizabeth and James by the translating bishops? The fact that any one should miss seeing the perfect correspondence simply proves how the habit of royalism stupefies. A few years ago, when a lunatic fired at the Queen, a priest came forward with a freshly inspired stanza-and-a-half for the national "anthem", as the royalist song is very fitly termed, by way of embodying the feelings supposed to be stirred up by the lunatic's procedure. Remarkable verses they were.

"Angels around her [Majesty's] way
Watch, while by night and day,
Millions with fervor pray
God save the Queen!"

was part of the reverend bard's contribution to the body of revealed religious truth; and instead of that poetic adjuration so dear to loyalty—

"*Con*-found their pauly-ticks,
Frustrate their knavish tricks"

—sentiments which, as the *Rock* thoughtfully observed at the time, "touch so nearly on secular questions,"—the servant of God and the Queen, always apropos of the lunatic, proposed the more devotional prayer:

"Break thou rebellious wings,
Smite when dark treason springs."

Perhaps impressed by the celerity with which the reverend innovator's curse had come home to roost on the wings of his Pegasus, the respectable British public did not take to the revised psalm; but they went about breathing fire and slaughter against the lunatic in such a way as to suggest how much he and they had in common. It is always the same. Nobody but a madman ever did shoot at the Queen, but every fresh fiasco elicits the same blatant execration, the same shrieks for blood. And the gentlemen of the *Saturday Review*, with that genteel blackguardism which seems to be maintained among them by the laying on of hands, take such an opportunity to compare the crazy culprit with the "average Northampton elector"; while the otherwise inspired *Tablet* announces that the madman's attempt may "fairly be referred" to men of Atheistic opinions. So do bigotry and royalism join hands on the common ground of native brutality.

> "Dummheit und Bosheit buhlten hier
> Gleich Hunden auf freier Gasse."

There is, perhaps, no clearer proof of the vicious influence of the whole royalist gospel than the fashion in which the Prince of Wales is at once flocked after and vilified by London society. Even in those society journals which are wont to dog him with fœtid flattery and snobbish gossip, he is liable at any moment to insolent attack; but in the world at large his name is found at one season the centre of an offensive scandal, and at another the watchword of fashion. He is told by journalists of the backstairs that he is the "social sovereign" of England; that it was he who taught his countrymen to smoke cigarettes; that to him men owe the modification of the dress-suit by a white waistcoat; that he is a profound judge of character; that when he was absent "the season was a failure, and the entire social system (!) was dislocated. Society, in fact, went to pieces. Nobody knew what to be at or what to do, because the Marlborough House ideal was not visible in their midst." In him at length, in short, the valet had found his hero. But of all the mindless mob thus represented as looking to him for an "ideal" of life, how many are there who have not chuckled or tittered over every story told to his shame?

With these unclean records, in detail, I have here nothing to do, whether by way of founding on them or examining them. The point is that again and again since his early manhood, England has resounded with a scandal in which he figures disgracefully; that the great majority of his countrymen affect to believe each infamy in turn; and that he yet retains his precious "social" prestige unimpaired. If he is in the main innocent—as may well be—no man is better deserving of sympathy; and if he were guilty, followed as he has been from his youth up by a herd of sycophants mean enough to laud him for any vileness, he would at least be no worse a personality than the people who make him their "ideal", to say nothing of his actual corrupters. But whatever his life may have been, there can be neither mistake nor doubt about the moral spectacle presented by the "society" which makes him its lawgiver. Purposeless as that of the Restoration, and tasteless as that of the first Georges; frivolous as ever was that of France, and undignified as ever was that of a German principality; it is the most unwholesome limb of the English race; a danger to civilisation and a confusion to all high hopes of human things.

II.

To turn from the intimate study of royalism as it flourishes among us to the tracing of its natural history, is to change our outlook without greatly altering our sensations; though the latter inquiry has the saving quality of generalness. Sociologically considered, the royalist cultus has the interest of standing alone among human superstitions, in that it has up till now obeyed none of the laws of decay which affect all the rest. It is a remarkable fact that there is no case in all history of a State getting rid of the monarchic form of government by a peaceful process, as it might get rid of any other institution which its members had deliberately decided to make an end of. All suspensions of monarchy have been by revolution. The American habit of talking of the monarchies of to-day as "effete", and of assuming that thrones are now less secure than in the middle or early ages, is quite fallacious. Kings in those days were unseated by rebellion and revolution just as often as now— nay, much oftener; and the supposed spread of Republican principles is made far too much of when it is pointed to as involving the euthanasia of kingship. Such an euthanasia

—that is, a peaceful ending as opposed to a violent—may be in store, but there are no very good grounds for predicting it. Whatever might be the measure of freedom existing in the old democracies, there was at least plenty of Republican intelligence and enthusiasm at various times in the antique world; but it never led to the orderly removal of one sovereignty by affecting the intelligence of any nation that had a different polity. Men could rebel against a tyranny rather more easily in the past than at present: what reason is there to infer that, either in the case of a despotism or in that of a dummy monarchy, they will in future abolish thrones on the sheer impulse of progressive common sense? For that there would need some movement at once strenuous and dignified, serious without violence and yet really forcible, and where is there such a movement? If there were one in England, these particular pages need not have been written.

In keeping with the blindness of the critics of democracy to the moral bearings of royalism is their complete omission to analyse its intellectual basis. Of late years we have had any number of demonstrations of the "metaphysical" and "abstract" character of many democratic formulas; but what could be more essentially metaphysical than the sentiment of monarchism? The only doubt is whether, according to Comte's categories, it is not rather of the "theological" order—that is, belonging to the fetishistic line of thought instead of the idealising, as commonly understood. The early savage saw deities in things: the later man explained things in terms of deity: the royalist may be held to do either of these things. But in any view his habit of mind is far enough away from the scientific methods professedly followed by the critics in question. The reasoning which dismisses as baseless the plea that men are naturally equal, or possessed of "rights", must have hard work to find a solid place in the mirage of blind emotion that has surrounded kings and dynasties from the dawn of history. The curious thing is—it is another way of putting the uniqueness of the royalist delusion—that men were nearer a positive or rational notion of the matter in barbaric times than in modern. Even after the establishment of the hereditary principle had introduced metaphysical obscurity, a rebellious baron very nearly saw his king for what, biologically speaking, he really was—a feudal superior putting on airs; and there was generally an appreciable crop of rebellious barons. And even for the non-rebellious there was nothing outlandish in the idea of putting down one king and making another. Here there was a certain hold on facts and forces, on matter and motion. But the history of monarchic civilisation is a record of the passing of such a positive and factual way of thinking into one partaking largely of the nature of hallucination. Certain it is that for many a century kings have been as truly hedged by divinity as ever were any claimants of supernatural powers. The feeling towards them has been on precisely the same psychological plane as that of the devout towards idols and consecrated things. It is mere idle pedantry[1] to explain it as a sense of respect for the holder of the highest office in the State. It is unreasoning, unreflecting, rising in obscure hereditary sensations, in all likelihood deriving from præ-human conditions, but certainly much developed in late times; and it is only by a conscious effort of reasoning that one bred in a monarchic country makes his first step to a saner state of mind.

It is clearly a superstition, or something strictly of that nature, that makes men insist on keeping the crown in the line of family succession. It may be superficially compared to the ordinary principle of inheritance, or to the early custom of keeping handicrafts in particular families; but a glance at history shows that the hereditary principle is adhered to in royalism where it is discarded in other affairs. The property of a traitor or a convicted felon escheated to the crown, his children's rights falling to the ground; and in the case of hereditary offices we do not find that a son was held to be entitled to a post from which his father was summarily dismissed. But the regal right of a deposed king's son has been almost invariably held to subsist despite the deposition—so held even by those

---

[1] Professor Freeman, whose historic generalisations are invariably either second-hand or worthless, and are frequently both, has laid it down that the spirit of Christianity is fundamentally opposed to the recognition of any pre-eminence in a person or a family as such. If that were the fact, it would be one more proof of the supernatural failure of Christianity to carry its supposed spirit into practice. But the Professor's further statement that kings to-day are appointed for reasons of political expediency, serves as a measure of the value of his opinion. The solemn elevation of one maniac to the throne vacated by another in Bavaria, is only a rather picturesque instance of the rooted practice of modern Christendom.

who deposed the father. Thus in Scotland those who rebelled against James III. did it by way of setting up his son; similarly Mary's subjects professed to be fighting against her on behalf of her infant; and indeed there seems to have been no time of life at which a Scotch monarch's crown was so absolutely undisputed as in his childhood; his person at that stage, instead of being menaced, being fought for by all factions as a sort of talisman. No conjunction of events could break down this instinct of the heredity of royalty. Rebellion against Charles I., for that matter, never meant to anyone in Scotland, and seems to have meant to no one in England up to the last complications, any design against the King's kingship; and there can be little doubt that but for the dominance of the army, England would have followed Scotland in declaring for Charles II. as soon as his father was beheaded. Sir Henry Maine very truly says that the popular enthusiasm was only for the Restoration, never for the Commonwealth. Royalism is a cult, not a conviction.

The Revolution of 1688 proved this once for all. A king was exiled as being intolerable to the greater part of the nation; but, it being no more possible for them to abandon all at once the royalist superstition than for a tribe of savages suddenly to become scientific Agnostics, the next step was to crown a new king whose claim consisted in his being the husband of the daughter of the exile. If the transaction had been carried through by men who were free from the superstition, they would undoubtedly have taken the most politic course open to them in the situation; but the diplomatists were in point of fact as devout in their reverence for the sacred descent as the mass of their countrymen. The faith has never dwindled since. Through a line of sovereigns which has not included one respectable intelligence, and whose lives, in the case of the males, have without exception defied the morality which English cant has always claimed for English society, the average run of English men and women have stood fast in what they call their "loyalty". Such loyalty inspires the sheep which leaps an open space where the bell-wether jumped a gate. The one supportable figure in the list is that of the man who got into it by the chance of his having married the daughter of a king declared unfit to rule. After him comes another daughter, in whose life we have the spectacle of a nation's destinies hanging on the forlorn decisions of a worried woman who could by no chance have changed places with one of her chambermaids without putting a clearer head under the crown than her own. Then in succession two ignorant boors; then a mischievous cretin, beside whose twilight intelligence the blundering prejudice of his ancestors seems actual sagacity; and here loyalty touches its high-water mark. Descending in the scale of religions, we find the least human-looking idol receiving the intensest adoration: so, in the royalism of England, the king who began with a nutshell of mind and died insane has obtained the most reverential devotion. And in his case history has come within living memory. It was patriotic of Sir Henry Maine to cast in the direction of France for a case of base flattery of a king; and only to hint that in the far-off times of James the Sixth English royalism might tend to hyperbole. But it happens that Louis XIV. and Louis XV. were competent minds in comparison with our Hanoverian kings; that they were tolerable company for fairly clever men; and that the malignant idiocy of George the Third did not prevent his being exalted as highly in the moribund rhetoric of the churchmen of his day as was James in the tropes of the bishops.

Next to George the Third came George the Fourth, whom Mr. Trollope thought Mr. Thackeray ought to have spoken of with respect because the people whom Mr. Thackeray called snobs were well pleased to have him as their king. Here, almost in Sir Henry Maine's own time, were English aristocracy and English respectability at the feet of one of the shamefullest specimens of kinghood that modern mankind has seen; and Sir Henry, making evil cheer over the risk of his countrymen's getting into rough water in the attempt to sail their own boat, cannot find a word of comfort on their having contrived to drift out of that putrid sea. For whom then is Sir Hubert Stanley's praise reserved? What is that condition of the human intellect, that bearing of a nation's forehead, that seems to him manly?

Coming again to our own time, I again disclaim all desire to make a personal attack; though it has to be pointed out that the right to protest against such an attack is forfeited by those who thrust on the world a list of the sovereign's personal virtues, and compel criticism by their measureless eulogies. On this head I will just say that there are details in the domestic conduct of the reigning sovereign which can call forth nothing but reprobation from men and women with anything like a rounded ethical code; and that in view of these details the all-round laudation now going on is a corruption of practical morals. In the case of a private person, it would be improper to make such items of conduct the ground for a public censure; and were the sovereign treated by the champions of the throne as strictly a political functionary there would be no fair warrant for challenging them with details of her personal action, any more than for commenting on the private life of a Cabinet Minister; though, as it happens, nobody ever scruples to pass judgment on a public man who has figured in the Divorce Court. But when the country is flooded with a literature of venal panegyric on the score of the royal jubilee, it would, I submit, be perfectly justifiable to confute certain of its figments with specific facts. Let us, however, concede that the royal position is in itself a demoralising and perverting one, and accordingly put all particular acts in the background. There remains more than enough in the general and impersonal statement of the situation to provoke grave question.

The situation is, then, that while the country is said to be progressing in culture, it has shown itself, as a whole, no whit nearer getting rid of the central superstition of royalism than it was a generation ago. Monarchism today is as unreasoning, as undignified, as backward as ever. It is still essentially a worship of a sacred family, unqualified by any criticism of the merits of its members. Neither character nor *quasi*-political function having anything to do with the general mental attitude, the appearance of a child of the royal line will make more sensation than that of any celebrity whatever, short of a political party-leader. As the royal *gens* multiplies year by year, it is as scrupulously provided for by the nation as ever was that of Confucius in China, though the chronic grumbling suggests that, like other species, that of royalty in England may one day be found to have pressed too heavily on its means of subsistence. As it is, the random discontent is only one more testimony to the lowering influence of the cult, representing as it does the mere ill-temper of taxpayers at increased outlay on an institution whose moral demerits would be the same, however many thousands it might cost per annum. In time, doubtless, the mere cost, at the present rate of increase, may bring the demerit home to the general mind. In that case the royalist instinct would be held to have died outright of those irritants which in past times have spoilt the chances of some individual sovereigns. But if the house of Guelph would but pay some heed to Malthus, there seems no reason, as things go, why it should outlive the delusion on which dynasties have hitherto flourished; so potent still is the habit of homage, so scanty the general self-respect, so feeble the reasoning impulse in the average mind, and so far-reaching the forces of perversion. Men of some education can apparently be found in any number to write in good set terms, for the public's reading, of the satisfaction and the good fortune of Britons in having a sovereign and a royal family to love, while some States have none, and of the likelihood of France coming one day to covet similar privileges. Such writers have their audience—the people who call themselves "loyal subjects", drink the Queen's health at public dinners, and cheer when she is seen in the streets. In two English households out of three the coming of the Prince of Wales to the throne of his parent seems as much a matter of course as the daily rising of the sun. The conception of the royal succession is at this moment as strictly a doctrine of divine right as it ever was in history.

III.

As has been said, there is no weighty movement in England for the abolition of the monarchy, and it becomes important to realise what that means. We of these islands have never been lacking in self-complacence; and we have long been wont to regard our national condition, whatever may be the political troubles of the hour, as something peculiarly healthful and majestic in comparison with that of any State of antiquity or of the Middle Ages, except, perhaps, the England of Elizabeth. Our tutors, as Sir Henry Maine, point to the hollowness of French society in past centuries, and exhort us to take joy in and maintain our present—or at least recent—superiority. Yet a resort to the methods of comparison employed by some of these very authorities would, as we have seen, lead us to conclude that modern England has never been one whit less morally or intellectually unsound, relatively speaking, than any of the so-called corrupt States of the past. At this moment not a writer of standing raises his voice in protest against a *régime* which, as is here contended, is as trivial and despicable as any history records. Its vices are, of course, in keeping with the surroundings. We do not affect gladiatorial shows, and royalty, accordingly, does not promote them. It takes up pigeon-shooting and horse-racing instead. We are little given to murder, and our monarchism is therefore free of such associations. But we contrive that the upper strata in our society shall do as little credit to contemporary civilisation as did the similar strata of the world of Nero, or of Sardanapalus. We in England speak of ours as the age of the telegraph and the electric light, of steam, parliamentary government, and evolution: it does not occur to us that history will write us down also the age of the worship of George the Fourth, of the adulation of the author of the "Journal of Our Life in the Highlands"—the age in which, even as he of the backstairs proclaims, the Prince of Wales gives its "ideal" to "society".

I cannot see that, all things considered, we have any cause to hold ourselves better than our ancestors of Charles the Second's time. The best thinking and teaching of the day, brought beside our performance, reveals us no less unworthy than they, no less false to our best instincts, no less meanly acquiescent in the reign of the tawdry and the vulgar. With our ethics and our philosophy, we are about as poor creatures in our civic life as ever lived. Nay, there was in the Restoration period some remnant of Puritan conscience which, if fanatical, was honorably high-minded: but who to-day, whether in the name of religion or of any national memory, protests against the prostration of the mind of England before enshrined commonplace, transfigured incompetence, and deified inanity? The jubilee is one *banal* chorus of shoddy sentiment, in which all orders of "loyal" intelligence fraternise on the broad ground of bathos. "A bagman's millennium" is the title said to have been given to Cobden's political ideal by an English lady, who had doubtless been presented at court. The year of jubilee, on that scale, should be the millennium of the scullery-maid and the pot-man. And the better sort

are implicated by their consenting silence. If the men of
mind and culture in England are to be held to have any
share in the national life at all, they are accountable for
their utter failure to hold up any better standard to their
fellows than that now in force.

Poor Mr. Ruskin has for this many a year been denouncing the unworthiness of the life around him; and
what has he had to say on this typical and national
vice? Once, that he and Carlyle alone in England at the
moment " stood for God and the Queen "—an announcement which must have given great comfort to the pair of
powers in question, whatever effect it had on Carlyle.
The latter moralist, if incapable of such superlative rant,
never once raised his voice against the royalist sham.
There has been, in fact, all along a conspiracy of silence
on this subject among those writers who were not in a
conspiracy of cant. The reception of the Queen's last
book is a proof. A Macaulay could perhaps again be
found to chastise a second Montgomery, if need were; but
Macaulay was not the man to speak out about the Queen's
diaries; and the literary class does not appear to include
one who will, or an editor who would let him. Only
among men who have set their faces against imposture in
general—among Freethinkers—has there been more than
a whisper of dispraise. The nearest approach to honest
speech in ordinary current literature was in the most advanced of the reviews, and there the protest was so absurdly
ceremonious and diffident as to make the obsession of the
national mind only the more obvious. It was as if the
Times should regretfully and respectfully but firmly demur
to the fatuities of an after-dinner speech by an elderly
officer, unaccustomed to public speaking. One thought of
the clerical criticism of " the extraordinary conduct of
Judas Iscariot ".

Now while it is difficult to suppose that the absence of
any avowed utterance on such a matter from the leading
literary men of the day arises from a general acquiescence
on their part in the common tone, it is almost equally
difficult to understand their thus keeping silence if they
at all deplored what was going on. A particular habit of
public speech really cannot go on unchallenged for generations without getting into minds of the better order as well
as the worse. And nearly every other species of public
folly has been derided more or less extensively. The

platitudes and absurdities of mere patriotism, the claptrap of parties, the commonplaces of political argument and newspaper rhetoric—all these have been held up to the light by writers of authority; but the same critics stedfastly hold aloof from the topic of royalism. What, then, are we to infer? Sir Henry Maine, noting how in the generation after Rousseau it was the fashion in France to talk of a past golden age, says of the "countless" essays written on that theme before 1789, that "they furnish very disagreeable proof that the intellectual flower of a cultivated nation may be brought, by fanatical admiration of a social and political theory, into a condition of downright mental imbecility". This is extravagant enough, in all conscience, as a description of the intellect of France before the revolution; but here again one's uppermost sensation is curiosity as to what Sir Henry's line of criticism would lead to if applied impartially. Is a literary belief in a bygone golden age really more imbecile than the adoration of a Prince Albert or a Queen Victoria by the mass of a nation, whether by way of countless ambitious and costly monuments—much more durable, unhappily, than essays—or of a year of jubilee? We have heard a good deal of the blind hysterics of the Celt, from poets and others not quite undistinguished for hysteria; but can Gaul point to any kind of national demonstration more significant of brainless sentiment than that made in England over the Prince of Wales's recovery from an illness? Yet the intellectual flower of the nation have never done aught but countenance these doings.

To see the bearings of the literary complaisance towards the throne, let us make a list of some of the best known writers on questions of public morals—the writers who are accustomed to comment on our social and intellectual conditions, to hold up ideals, and to condemn shortcomings. Take the names of Mr. Spencer, Mr. Arnold, Mr. Harrison, Mr. John Morley, Mr. Leslie Stephen, Mr. Hutton, Mr. Goldwin Smith. These gentlemen are accustomed, with varying emphasis, frequency, and accuracy, to point out the weak points in our manners and morals; and one can scarcely conceive their entirely ignoring a particular public vice, recognised by them as such, provided there were nothing "unsavory", as Mrs. Grundy's phrase goes, in the discussion of it. Seeing therefore that none of them have ever dwelt explicitly on the phænomena of royalism, we are shut up to one of two conclusions—either that they do not see anything ignoble or vulgar or demoralising in the matter, or that they are deterred by the force of the reigning convention from speaking their minds. It would be difficult to say which of these conclusions is the more unwelcome. The first would imply that all that has been said in the foregoing pages of the unworthiness of the royalist superstition applies in some measure to these writers; the second, plainly by far the more probable, implies that, while professing to act as serious and responsible critics of the national life, to rebuke fearlessly and to counsel earnestly, they have timorously or weakly held their tongues where it much behoved them to speak out.

What, for instance, does Mr. Arnold think of the question before us? He has claimed—not loudly, but with some right—to have set before his countrymen warnings as to their failings and their follies; and he evidently has their higher welfare at heart. He believes in equality, and points to that as a condition of national well-being. Does he then suppose that men in general are going to attain intellectual maturity and dignity while continuing to kiss the steps of the throne as they have done? Supposing the marrying of one's deceased wife's sister to be really as tasteless a proceeding as he represents, is there much good in hammering away at an idiosyncrasy of that sort while the collective taste and tone of the nation are perpetually being vulgarised and degraded by the worship of the "ideals", and the personalities, presented to it by royalty? And the Queen's books? Mr. Arnold would perhaps reason that monarchism cannot be attacked without some reflexions on living royal personages; and that such criticism is to be deprecated; but I cannot find that he has acted on such scruples in other cases where personal matters were bound up with broad questions. I cannot see why the Queen's book should escape judgment any more than Bishop Colenso's. If Mr. Arnold is simply deterred by his official position from saying anything about royalism whatever, I can only say that it is very unfortunate that he should have so gagged himself. And it is a curious official gag which leaves him free to write down Mr. Gladstone, and the policy of any Government, but keeps him silent as to the institution of the sovereignty.

To Mr. Spencer, again, applies the general objection which lies against Sir Henry Maine on this issue. The philosopher complains, rightly enough, of the looseness and inconsistency of the bulk of political thinking; and he has commented weightily on various anti-social tendencies. Almost alone among public men he has condemned military immorality. Yet, whatever he may suggest as to the development of political institutions, he has no passage that I can recall on the general aspect and influence of the royalist cult among us. He, too, would seem to count on getting men to advance while keeping their minds on one important point in a state of paralysis or abasement. All schools are alike in this regard. Mill and Carlyle, from their different standpoints, touched royalism as gingerly as they were emphatic on other themes. Nobody with literary authority will speak, and John Bull goes on unweariedly bellowing his loyalty.

But it is to Sir Henry Maine in particular, after all, that the appeal for consistency may most fitly be addressed. Nobody has been more distinct in insisting on the necessity of a lucid and dignified cast of mind to a nation which seeks to govern itself, and nothing could exceed the rigor of his criticisms, unless it be the eccentricity with which he applies his canons. On his view, popular folly and lack of self-respect is the most serious danger to democratic or semi-democratic States; and it is surely impossible to believe that such an acute critic can really look with satisfaction on the *rôle* now played in England by the royal family, or on the response made by the people. Such a keen analyst of claptrap cannot reasonably be conceived as throwing up his hat for the family virtues of the Queen, and for the blessedness of a nation which has such a royal house as ours to love and honor for so benignly presiding over its destinies. To think of Sir Henry Maine as an average courtier or "loyal subject" would be to class his last book as the product of spleen and prejudice, and himself as a partisan instead of a philosophic political thinker. We all, on the contrary, whether we agree with him or not, regard his as an efficient and vigorous mind, incapable of the mere inherited imbecilities of aristocrats and snobs. Why then is he so absolutely silent on what is, to say the least, the worst weakness, the most enfeebling intellectual vice of this community, regarded as a political whole? Again, if we are not to class the moralist with the mob, there is but one answer—that, however, he may denounce particular shams and delusions, there is one sham he winks at, one delusion before which he smugly dissembles.

Once more—and now the inquiry becomes more than ever practical—what is the notion as to royalism in the minds of those who declare that social conditions will not be tolerable before they are utterly revolutionised? Of all the extravagances of the Socialists of what may be called, for want of a better term, the Slap-Bang school, none is more glaring than this, that they vociferously demand the speedy adoption of that social system which most emphatically requires a high standard of citizenship, without even proposing to get along without an institution which, as here contended, is the negation of such a standard. The only Socialist programme before the British public makes no specific mention whatever of royalism. It can hardly be supposed that this means attachment to the throne, or even a willingness to retain the monarchy as part of the constitution; it can only signify a feeling that to agitate for the abolition of the monarchy at present would be useless, though it is far from clear on what grounds it is held that certain other suggestions in the same programme are more immediately practicable. What then does this imply? That the programme-makers count on, or hope for, the realisation of a polity of enlightened altruism in a society which is unable to rise to such a point of self-respect as to give over adoring the members of a particular family because they are of royal descent. Inconsequence could no further go. It was bad enough—mad enough—to imagine that Socialism could be accomplished off-hand in a society in which—as regards its commerce—the self-regarding impulses are relatively about as deeply-rooted as those of a herd of wolves. But to suppose that the revolution would be effected without even a beginning of upward political progress in the substitution of a true democratic spirit for the ignoble temper which cherishes monarchy—this was to attain the very topmost degree of forethoughtlessness, the sublimity of political unwisdom.

Where, then, are we to look for better things? I can offer but one answer, and that is conditional. The one quarter in which there has ever appeared any marked feeling of healthy aversion to the monarchy as such, apart from incidental grievances as to its operation, is that of the working classes, chiefly those of London. There may be plenty of room for criticism as to the fashion in which the feeling at times manifests itself; but it is inconceivable to me that it can ever be so foolish or so gross as the fashion to which it is opposed; and at worst these Republicans of the populace have kept on record an honorable protest when, save for one or two democratic politicians—latterly, I believe, only one—the whole of the rest of England hugged humiliation. To the people, then, if anywhere, the Republican has to look for his party.

IV.

From the point of view here taken, what is first to be desired in a movement for the abolition of the monarchy is that it shall be deliberate and persistent. It may or may not be that the actual abolition, supposed to be in store, will take an orderly shape: there is indeed, as Sir Henry Maine has sought to show, and as has been above urged, no such decisive reason for counting on the peaceful abolition, as some democratic writers have assumed. It may be that the present era of civilisation will spend itself without our reaching even that much of democratic fruition in the countries now monarchic. That, however, would mean that our civilisation is already rotting towards collapse; in which case it would matter nothing what forecasts we now make; so that the only practical course is to reason on the assumption that the removal of all thrones is not only feasible but likely; and that it behoves us to be active in preparing the way. Now, one of the most obvious weaknesses of democratism[1] among us is the tendency to make important reforms turn on accidents. The late furore about the House of Lords is an instance. That movement, controlled as it was by a statesman whose policy is above all things opportunist, rose and fell in such a way as to imply the condemnation of most of those concerned. The attack on the House of Lords for fulfilling its ostensible function was a mere partisan immorality if the assailants did not believe that the function ought not to exist; and if such was their belief they wrote themselves down shufflers, in so far as they willingly gave over

---

[1] "Democracy", as its latest critic feelingly insists, "is a form of Government". I use the term "democratism" to designate democratic tendencies and impulses in general.

the campaign. To judge from the result, the talk of "mending or ending" was mainly braggadocio, and none the less so because it terrorised the enemy. The Upper House is neither mended nor ended; and the gentlemen who threatened these alternatives appear to go on their way without chagrin. Even the "People's League", formed for the express purpose of carrying on the movement, visibly declined in its zeal when the immediate pretext was removed; some of the leading politicians who joined it being found to discourage the idea of a steady and strenuous activity towards the purpose in view, and to recommend instead a lying in wait until the House of Lords should again do something to irritate the majority. It is not the people who are unwilling to respond; it is their ostensible leaders who fail to keep any principle, as such, steadily before them, and make legislation a game of campaigns and stratagems, panics, spurts, intrigues, and revivals. These are not the methods of principled politics; and if Republicanism is thus to make headway merely by turning to account the indiscretions or misdeeds of members of the royal family, half the moral gain that might accrue from the process will be lost. In so far as it might make capital in that fashion, indeed, it would be no worse than other political movements in general; but one hopes that it will spread rather by means of a simple perception of the essential unmanliness and unworthiness of the monarchic cult as such—of the incurable discord between its whole phænomena and the profession of self-government.

Much, indeed, might be said as to the mere financial burden represented by the monarchy. It is one of the demoralising elements in the royal position that it involves, over and above the pressure of social conditions as they are, a further grinding of the faces of the poor, and a fleecing of the merest paupers, to maintain the idle splendors of the throne and its domestic appendages. But still one would rather that the people should look at the central evil, and not merely at the minor consequence. The real harm of royalism lies not nearly so much in the wasting of some million sterling per annum as in the sapping of the nation's self-respect, and in the partial paralysis of the impulses which make for political advance. Worse than the intensifying of material poverty—bad enough as that may be—is that poverty of the spirit which is in no sense blessed. A movement for the abolition of monarchy, then, should be above all things a moral movement, and would come even more fitly from the ranks of culture than from those of the poor.

The survey of the situation, however, goes to show, as we have seen, that the ranks of culture are standing very much at ease under the *régime* of shoddy and inanity, thinking much less about their own vulgar compromises and mean conformities than about the dangers arising from the misguided sincerities of the lower orders. Consequently the chances are that it will be left to the rank and file of Radicalism to bring the question to the front in its own way, with what of uproar and asperity belongs to a cause denied a hearing in high places. And this process, be it remembered, involves certain risks. If we are not entitled to assume with Mr. Bancroft that there is going on an obvious evolution towards democracy, equally little have we the right to suppose that the long spell of peaceful transition we have had in England will never be broken by a crash. To say nothing of the spectacle in Germany and Russia, we can see in Denmark at this moment a distinct possibility of a collision between a patient people and a foolishly obstinate king; and history shows that these collisions tend to communicate their impulses. Now, there is a certain amount of inflammable material in England at this moment, and it is not very difficult to conceive that the apparent complicity of the upper and educated classes in such a flagrant abuse as the monarchy, with its futility, its cost, its hollowness, and its greed, may at a critical moment be interpreted by discontent as a proof that these classes are as unfit to survive as the monarchy itself. What such a view might lead to is a matter for speculation.

In any case, this much is clear, that those who now try to remove the central blot from our system of self-government are striving to purify the state; while those who would callously leave it, or who deny that it is a blot at all, are promoters of social corruption. It is idle for the Conservative moralist to prate of the dangers of popular ignorance and demagoguism while he constitutes a living proof that culture can tolerate and even champion the grossest political impostures. He is himself the worst of charlatans, the type noted by Carlyle—and perhaps in part exemplified by him—in which the traffic in empty phrases leads in the long run to sheer hallucination. The restive proletarian has some hold on fact; his own discontent is a leading political fact of the time; and the demagogue is dealing with solid things even if he be insincere—that, indeed, is the Conservative's complaint. But, once more, what shall we say of the political ideal in which loyalty to the throne is a constant quantity; and a vista of reigns such as the present, with starry points of jubilee, constitutes the historic future? What of "God Save the Queen" as a marching-song for civilised humanity? Let the demagogue do his worst, his claptrap is at a discount while his royalist critic keeps the field.

This, then, is the upshot, that if the "men of light and leading" will do nothing to purge the commonweal of a cult which is at once a superstition and a vice, the movement must come from the people, where its germs have so long lain—that is, if it is ever to come to vigorous growth at all. And the alternative, I repeat, is a spreading moral paralysis, which means a great failure of civilisation. On the one hand a consummation of the national life in all ignobleness, on the other a forward movement towards a real democracy. For not only does the democratic principle theoretically exclude the form as well as the substance of monarchy, but democracy remains a mere formula while men are capable of supposing that the shell of monarchy subserves any political good. If we are unable to carry on our Parliamentary Government without a pretended centre of authority and fountain of honor in a sacred family, then the fact that the sovereign is a political nullity both in theory and in practice, does not hinder us from being far below the point of democratic efficiency. The phænomena of the throne and the second chamber jointly constitute a proof that we do not really trust the principle of self-government. While that is so we are clearly not self-governing at all; and it is equally clear that we never shall be until we actually take the step of removing our sham safeguards. Not till the nation deliberately exercises its political will without that abject avowal of fear of itself which is the formula of the second chamber, will it cease to have need to fear itself. Its fear and its danger are correlatives. And just so it is with the throne. We shall never be fit to be Republicans until we are ashamed of being Monarchists. We shall always be fit to crawl before and kiss the feet of clay until we bury the image.

THOMAS PAINE:

An Investigation.

BY

JOHN M. ROBERTSON.

LONDON:
FREETHOUGHT PUBLISHING COMPANY,
63 FLEET STREET, E.C.
1888.

PRICE SIXPENCE.

LONDON:
PRINTED BY ANNIE BESANT AND CHARLES BRADLAUGH,
63 FLEET STREET, E.C.

THOMAS PAINE: AN INVESTIGATION.

In Mr. Leslie Stephen's "History of English Thought in the Eighteenth Century" there occur a number of allusions to Thomas Paine, and in particular two passages in which the historian discusses Paine's work as an anti-theologian and as a politician, prefacing the second with what purports to be a brief sketch of his later life and an estimate of his character. Mr. Stephen's work is in two volumes; and his account of the "Age of Reason", without biographic elucidation, occurs in the first; the criticism of the "Rights of Man" coming separately, with the elucidation, in the second, where it was necessary to contrast Paine with Burke. The biographical notice, which is extremely brief, presents the markedly hostile version given of Paine's life and character in the professed biography of him by Cheetham, Mr. Stephen making no reference to any other authority, though he shows he is aware of the existence of other Lives. The falsity of Cheetham's and Mr. Stephen's account has been pointed out before now; several subsequent biographies having exposed Cheetham's, and Mr. Stephen's paragraph being indirectly answered for English readers by Mr. Moncure Conway's valuable article in the *Fortnightly Review* of March, 1879. A direct and explicit answer to Mr. Stephen's statements and criticism as a whole, however, seems still awanting; and as his book continues to be a standard source of information on Paine for English readers, such an examination seems worth attempting in the interests of truth and justice.

I quote first Mr. Stephen's biographical paragraph as it appears in his first edition:

"We have already encountered Paine as an assailant of the

religious belief of the day. No ingenuity of hero-worship can represent him as an altogether edifying phænomenon. Indeed, he is commonly made to serve the purpose of a scarecrow in religious tracts. One of his biographers describes his first interviews with the old reprobate after his final flight to America. Paine appeared shabbily dressed, with a beard of a week's growth, and a 'face well carbuncled, fiery as the setting sun'. Sitting over a table loaded with *beer*, brandy, and *a beefsteak* he repeated the introduction of his reply to Watson; a process which occupied half an hour, and was *performed with perfect clearness, in spite of the speaker's intoxication*. The details of his habits during the few remaining years of his life are simply disgusting; he was constantly drunk, filthy beyond all powers of decent expression, brutal to the woman he had seduced from her husband, constantly engaged in the meanest squabbles, and, in short, as disreputable an old wretch as was at that time to be found in New York. Two or three well-meaning persons tried to extort some sort of confession from the dying infidel; but he died in a state of surly adherence to his principles. The wretched carcase, about which he seems to have felt some anxiety was buried in his farm" ("History of English Thought in the Eighteenth Century," ii. 261).

The "one of his biographers" here cited is Cheetham, whose relations with Paine before he composed Paine's "Life" were those of open and violent enmity; and it is to Cheetham that Mr. Stephen owes his statements as to filthiness and drunkenness. On the points as to whether Paine, immediately after landing from a long voyage, undertaken in a weak state of health—for it was then that Cheetham professes to have first met him—may really have appeared shabbily dressed and unshaven, it seems scarcely necessary to spend inquiry. It is enough to point out that the devotion of one-third of the paragraph of biography in Mr. Stephen's "History" to an enemy's description of Paine, made up of such details as these, is more suggestive of unthinking prejudice than of literary judgment. The "face well carbuncled" I pass over for the moment; and the clause on the "table loaded with *beer*, brandy, and *a beefsteak*" might perhaps be left to dispose of itself, with the slight help of italics. Mr. Stephen is evidently trying to create the impression that Paine's way of life was brutal and disgusting, and to that end he catches at the items in question. Beer and a beefsteak, it will probably be admitted, might innocently appear on any man's table; and even brandy is not unknown in respectable households in our own time, to say nothing of the drinking usages of Paine's. But the alliterative effect got by coupling it with the beer and the beefsteak is calculated to convey the requisite idea to readers who combine sensitiveness with carelessness, and so the description is produced. Of readers who possess only the former quality I have to ask pardon for pausing over such topics, a passing comment being necessitated by Mr. Stephen's having thought them fit garniture for a " History of English Thought in the Eighteenth Century ".

To come to more important matters, I would ask the reader first to notice the rare verisimilitude of the statement that Paine while in a state of intoxication repeated with "perfect clearness", at half-an-hour's length, the "introduction" of his reply to Watson.[1] Most unprejudiced inquirers would pronounce the story an unplausible falsehood; and a falsehood, I think, it will finally be pronounced when the evidence as to Paine's way of life has been set forth. But by way of prefatory indication of the value of Cheetham's testimony, and of the general trustworthiness of Mr. Stephen's paragraph, it will be expedient to state the facts as to the allegation of Paine's having seduced a woman from her husband and then behaved brutally to her.

There is, I think, only one such story current concerning Paine, and the allusion is doubtless to Madame Bonneville, the wife of one Nicholas Bonneville of Paris, who with her children came to America with Paine when the latter finally returned to his adopted country. Paine had boarded with Bonneville during part of his stay in Paris, and is said to have been "much indebted" to his hospitality. Bonneville had often declared his intention to emigrate to the United States as soon as he could, and when Paine was able to leave France he invited the Bonnevilles to accompany him, which they promptly agreed to do.

"But", says Sherwin, "as Mr. Bonneville could not get ready by the time appointed, it was agreed that his wife and three sons should embark with Mr. Paine, and that their father

---

[1] All that has been published of Paine's reply to the Bishop of Llandaff might be recited in about half-an-hour, and there is no part that can be marked off as introductory. If Paine recited all or part of what is published, he was recapitulating a close and detailed argument. Mr. Stephen of course attempts no investigation on the point.

should follow them as soon as he conveniently could. Whether this was a design on the part of Bonneville to rid himself of his wife is more than I can say, but it is certain that he never troubled himself about her or the children for some years afterwards, and they were entirely abandoned to the generosity of Mr. Paine. In addition to his estate at New Rochelle, Mr. Paine had likewise a small house with some land attached to it, at Bordentown: these he offered to Mrs. Bonneville, and proposed to establish her as a schoolmistress, but this she declined. Mr. Paine was therefore charged with her entire maintenance, and that of the children, an act of kindness which he cheerfully performed. . . . It is a fact that they scarcely ever lived together after our author's return to America" (W. T. Sherwin's "Life of Thomas Paine", 1819, pp. 208-210).

Sherwin is partly in error as to the "entire maintenance", since it appears that Madame Bonneville gave lessons in French to help to maintain herself. But as to the substantial truth of his story there can be no reasonable doubt. Taken by itself, it might stand as an unsupported testimony by a friend of Paine; but it is sufficiently made good by the result of the legal proceedings instituted by Madame Bonneville against Cheetham when the latter published his slanderous work after Paine's death. Cheetham declared Madame Bonneville to be Paine's mistress, offering no proof save an angry letter from one Carver, written after a quarrel with Paine. On the action for slander being raised, Cheetham's counsel admitted the falsehood of the charge, and pleaded simply that Carver's letter justified Cheetham, as a historian, in repeating the statement. At first it was pleaded that the statement was true, but when "several ladies of the first distinction, whose daughters had been entrusted to the care of Madame Bonneville to learn the French language, appeared in court, and attested to the unblemished character of this much-injured female", this plea was abandoned, Carver besides backing out of his statement under examination. Further, Carver later published the avowal that his letter had been written in anger, and that it was "first printed by Cheetham without my consent for base purposes, after he became a tory and political turncoat"; also printing a letter of reconciliation he had addressed to Paine when the latter was on his deathbed, with the remark: "This shows what opinion I had of him; I think he was one of the greatest men that ever lived". (See the documents in the preface to G. Vale's "Life of Thomas Paine", New York, 1841.) The judge in the libel case, in summing up for the jury, took occasion to remind them that Cheetham's book was calculated to aid the cause of Christianity. The jury, however, brought in a verdict against him with £100 damages; and Cheetham, who had admitted the falsity of his statement, was ordered to expunge it from later editions of his book. (See "Refutation of the Calumnies on the Character of Thomas Paine", Providence, R. I. 1830, p. 2.) Thus a wholly or partly Christian jury pronounced the story a slander; Cheetham and his informant alike withdrew from it; and it is left for Mr. Stephen to revive it in an important work without a word of qualification or an attempt at inquiry.

It is worth noting, finally, as to the Bonneville episode, that Paine left some money by his will to Nicolas Bonneville, and the bulk of his property to Madame Bonneville, in trust for her and her children, "in order that she may bring them well up, give them good and useful learning, and instruct them in their duty to God and the practice of morality". The aspersion thrown out by Mr. Stephen as to Paine's "brutality" to Madame Bonneville rests partly on Carver's letter, in which Paine appears as disputing a payment on Madame Bonneville's account, partly on other statements of Cheetham. We have seen something of that authority's trustworthiness; but there is yet further evidence to be taken.

Cheetham's Life of Paine is not only thus discredited on one important point by explicit proofs: it was recognised and proclaimed as collectively untrustworthy by orthodox American writers in Paine's own time and later. I quote first from Mr. Conway:

"It is important . . . . to state that the most eminent Christian writers in America were not deceived by these libels [as to Madame Bonneville]. Thus, the Rev. Solomon Southwick, editor of the *Christian Visitor* when Cheetham's book appeared, wrote: 'Had Thomas Paine been guilty of any crime, we should be the last to eulogise his memory. But we cannot find that he was ever guilty of any other crime than that of advancing his opinions freely upon all subjects connected with public liberty and happiness . . . . We may safely affirm that Paine's conduct in America was that of a real patriot. In the French Convention he displayed the same pure and disinterested spirit.... His life, it is true, was written by a ministerial hireling, who strove in vain to blacken his moral character. The late James Cheetham likewise wrote his life, and we have no hesitation in saying that we knew perfectly well at the time the motives of that author for writing and publishing a work which, we have every reason to believe, is a libel almost from beginning to end. In fact, Cheetham had become tired of this country, and had formed a plan to return to England and become a ministerial editor in opposition to Cobbett, and his *Life of Paine* was written to pave his way back again.'" (Art. on "Thomas Paine", in *Fortnightly Review*, March, 1879, p. 400, citing the "Testimonials to Thomas Paine", compiled by J. N. Moreau, 1861—an American pamphlet, not in the British Museum).

The impartial judgment of Paine's own generation is endorsed by that of the next. An unsigned article on "Thomas Paine's Second Appearance in the United States" appears in the *Atlantic Monthly* for July, 1859. Its author thinks (p. 16) that "The 'Age of Reason' is a shallow deistical essay, in which the author's opinions are set forth .... in a most offensive and irreverend style"; that he "drank more brandy than was good for him"; and (p. 13) that he "was no exception to the general rule, that we find no persons so intolerant and illiberal as men professing Liberal principles". There is here small prejudice in Paine's favor. But the same unfriendly critic says: "We suspect that most of our readers, if they cannot date back to the first decade of the century, will find, when they sift their information, that they have only a speaking acquaintance with Thomas Paine, and can give no good reason for their dislike of him" (p. 15). And this is how he comments on the biography by Cheetham:

"This libellous performance was written shortly after Paine's death. It was intended as a peace offering to the English Government. The ex-hatter had made up his mind to return home, and he wished to prove the sincerity of his conversion from Radicalism by trampling on the remains of its high-priest. So long as Cheetham remained in good standing with the Democrats, Paine and he were fast friends; but when he became heretical and schismatic on the Embargo question, some three or four years later, and was formally read out of the party, Paine laid the rod across his back with all his remaining strength. He had vigor enough left, it seems, to make the *Citizen* [edited by Cheetham] smart, for Cheetham cuts and stabs with a spite which shows that the work was as agreeable to his feelings as useful to his plans. His reminiscences must be read *multis cum granis*" (*Id.*, p. 12).

The reader will now probably not hesitate to accept the statement made by Mr. Vale in his "Life of of Paine" (p. 2) that it "was the opinion of the intimate friend of Cheetham, Mr. Charles Christian, who gave this relation to Mr. John Fellows and others whom we have seen, and from whom we have learned this fact", that Cheetham meant his book "as a passport to the British treasury favor."

I have thus far dealt with Mr. Stephen's account of Paine as it appears in the first edition of his book, for the moment excluding considerations of certain alterations which he has silently made in his second edition. And I have taken this course on two grounds; first, that the former version is still in the hands of many readers, whose attention has not been publicly called to the partial retractations Mr. Stephen makes; second, that he has made his qualifications in a manner that only aggravates the offence of his first misstatement. Let the reader judge. The alterations are as follows: (1) For "one of his biographers" we now read "a hostile biographer", the rest of the passage being left unaltered down to and including the word "principles". Then we have these sentences:

"The portrait is drawn by an enemy, and *represents what we may call the orthodox version* of the last days of a notorious infidel. Paine was *not likely to receive full justice from his adversaries*, and his admirers *urge* that his career was sincere and disinterested."

Yet while these qualifications are introduced, the "enemy's" picture is left as it was at first drawn; the expressions which were first used with the most grossly opprobrious intent are left unchanged, and the reader is left to settle for himself how much he will believe of the disgusting charges made, Mr. Stephen simply suggesting that an enemy was "not likely" to do "full justice"! I do not know a more extraordinary piece of procedure in literary history. If the story first told was an enemy's, and is only "what we may call the orthodox version" of a Freethinker's life, why, in the name of common decency, was it allowed to stand? Does Mr. Stephen, like the average Christian bigot, owe neither truth nor justice to an infidel? His first paragraph was bad enough in all conscience. His discovery that Cheetham was Paine's enemy would have been arrived at by most men in his place at the first glance through Cheetham's book; but he apparently only reached it after the publication of Mr. Conway's article. Yet though that article not only revealed this fact, but showed Cheetham's absolute untrustworthiness all round, Mr. Stephen has gone to no other source for his facts, has left his pages befouled with half-admitted falsehoods, neither standing to them nor withdrawing them, and has made no overt avowal that his first edition has at this point undergone alteration. Such a course only adds to the need for exposing the baselessness of the whole story. He who would defend Paine must still furnish the full disproof just as if the first were the only edition of Mr. Stephen's book; and in view of the fashion in which the matter is handled in the second, it is very meet that Mr. Stephen should receive in full what discredit attaches to his production of both versions. It is difficult to say which shows the less readiness to deal justly by the memory of a man held in common odium.

Evidence has been led at length as to the notorious untrustworthiness of Cheetham's book, the venality of his general motives, and his bitter enmity to Paine, though it is not easy to understand how any critic of ordinary fairness of mind, after reading (or even dipping into) Cheetham's book, could require much evidence of its worthlessness. It is on the very face of it a bitter attack on a dead man's memory by his enemy, an attack exceptionally scurrilous even for that time, in which unscrupulous slander went perhaps further than it has ever done in England before or since. Of a previous American "Life" of Paine, nominally by "Francis Oldys", Mr. Edward Smith has observed in his Life of Cobbett (ii. 210, *note*) that it was "one of the most horrible collections of abuse which even that venal day produced". That book was written in reality by George Chalmers, then one of the clerks of the Board of Plantation, to the order of Lord Hawksbury, afterwards Lord Liverpool, who paid or at least promised him £500 for the work (Sherwin, *pref.*). Such transactions were not uncommon in the period, and a historian of English

Thought might have been expected as a matter of course to be on his guard, accordingly, in reading any Life of such a man as Paine. And Cheetham's book, I repeat, is so gross in its aspersions, so patently malignant in its general drift, that no reader of average judgment, unless much swayed by prejudice, can well suppose it to be a true record. Its slander is the slander of the slums; obscene falsehood retailed with the zest of prostitutes in their cups. To a healthy mind, I should think, some of Cheetham's hearsay and other stories would be a decisive proof, not that Paine was drunken or dirty, but that Cheetham was an offensive blackguard. But since Mr. Stephen, even after remonstrance, declines to make up his mind on this head, and as he is a writer of distinction, I will cite some further evidence to show that Paine was not what he still half-insinuates him to be.

It is often assumed even by Freethinkers who esteem Paine's memory that in his latter years he sometimes "drank more than was good for him". Mr. Conway, like Sherwin, has accepted the tradition to that effect, sensibly pointing out, however, its small virtual importance in the eyes of just-minded people. There are, nevertheless, very strong reasons for doubting whether there is any more positive truth in this tradition than in any of the other stories to Paine's discredit. I quote the temperate and impressive summing-up of Mr. Vale:

"In commencing our inquiries we really thought the fact that Mr. Paine was a drunkard in old age was well established. In seeking, however, for the proofs of this we arrive at a very different conclusion." "It is by [Cheetham] that the public have been informed that Paine was drunken and dirty in his person; and so industriously and faithfully have the clergy preached and circulated these calumnies, that we shall scarcely be believed in contradicting them on the very best evidence, that of his companions now alive, and in some cases the very men whom Cheetham impudently names as sources of his information. Thus Mr. Jarvis, the celebrated painter, with whom Mr. Paine lived, informs us distinctly that Mr. Paine was neither dirty in his habits nor drunken; nay, he goodhumoredly added that *he* always drank a great deal more than ever Paine did. Mr. John Fellows lived in the same house with Mr. Paine above a twelvemonth, and was his intimate friend for many years after his return to this country, and never saw him but once even elevated with liquor, and then he had been to a dinner party. We know more than twenty persons who are more or less acquainted with Mr. Paine, and not one of whom ever saw him in liquor. His habit appears to have been to take one glass of rum and water with sugar in it, after dinner, and another after supper. His limit at one period, when at Rochelle, was one quart of rum a week, for himself and friends, for Mr. Paine was rather penurious in his old age. This, and this alone, is the only moral fault we find in his character, and we wish to be his impartial historian. His manner of life at this time we get from Mr. Burger, a respectable watchmaker in New York, but then a clerk in the only store at Rochelle, who served Mr. Paine with his liquor, and waited upon him when sick, and drove him about the neighborhood at the request of his employer, and thus saw much of his social habits. This gentleman never saw, Mr. Paine intoxicated. Carver, with whom Paine lived, but from whom he parted in anger, is the only man we know who has not spoken distinctly on the subject; and he remarks that 'Paine was like other men [at that period] he would sometimes take too much'! But Carver had unfortunately committed himself on this subject in an angry letter, the same on which Cheetham based his libel. In fact, this letter is the groundwork for all Cheetham's calumnies" (Vale's Life of Paine, pref. pp. 12—14: cf. pp. 142, 163).

People who are scrupulous in weighing testimony may feel that even this is not decisive proof that Paine never in his life drank to excess; but it will probably satisfy even the majority of Christians as to the untruth of Cheetham's assertion, reproduced by Mr. Stephen, that Paine was a habitual drunkard. Is it necessary, further, to disprove the slander as to the habits "filthy beyond all powers of decent expression"? I will not quote the beastly gossip on which the decent Mr. Stephen founds his phrase, but I will quote again from Mr. Conway :

"Paine was described by Aaron Burr, hypercritical in such matters, as a gentleman; and the sense in which he was so may be understood from a passage in one of Lord Edward Fitzgerald's letters from Paris to his mother:. 'I lodge with my friend Paine; we breakfast, dine, and sup together. The more I see of his interior the more I like and respect him. I cannot express how kind he has been to me. There is a simplicity of manner, a goodness of heart, and a strength of mind in him that I never knew a man before to possess'" (*Art. cited*, p. 409).

It is not for a vindicator of Paine, answering Mr. Stephen, to conceal any known facts; and I will mention that in the literature of the subject there is one piece of evidence as to Paine's having been in one short period of his life somewhat careless of his domestic amenities. A Mr. Yorke, who knew Paine in England, published in 1802 a volume of "Letters from France", in which he tells how he visited his friend after he had been released from imprisonment. He was received by Paine in a room, not a bedroom, which he describes as exceedingly dirty, the only details given being, however, that

"the chimney hearth was an heap of dirt; there was not a speck of cleanliness to be seen; three shelves were filled with pasteboard boxes, each labelled after the manner of a Minister of Foreign Affairs, *Correspondance Americaine, Brittannique, Française; Notices Politiques; Le citoyen Français*, etc. In one corner of the room stood several huge bars of iron, curiously shaped, and two large trunks; opposite the fireplace, a board covered with pamphlets and journals, having more the appearance of a dresser in a scullery. Such was the wretched habitation", etc. ("Letters from France in 1802", by Henry Redhead York, 1804, ii. 339-340. See the passage also in Sherwin's "Life", pp. 188-9).

Mr. Yorke states that he "never sat down in such a filthy apartment in the whole course of his life", which is perfectly credible, he being a person of means; but the reader will see that even this statement does not make out Paine to have been generally offensive in his habits. Paine was at that moment preparing to return to America, as Mr. Yorke goes on to intimate; the "bars of iron" were parts of his model iron bridge; and his trunks and papers were presumably packed for transport. The room was not Paine's living-room, and in the circumstances it will be intelligible to most people that without becoming demoralised he should let such an apartment remain unswept. Beyond this Mr. York has not a word to say against the habits of his old acquaintance, though like many other Englishmen at the time he had become conservative in his opinions, and was a good deal worried by Paine's freethinking. He makes an explanation, however, which would decently account for worse carelessness than he tells of. "I was forcibly struck", he says, "with his altered appearance. Time seemed to have made dreadful ravages with his whole frame, and a settled melancholy was visible on his countenance." And this recalls a circumstance of importance which is not disclosed by Mr. Stephen's biographic notice.

Paine, it will be remembered, after being eagerly welcomed in France and made a member of the National Convention, came under the displeasure of the extreme Jacobin party by strongly opposing the execution of Louis XVI., such a step being repugnant to his essentially humane cast of mind. Like so many others, he was cast in prison at the order of Robespierre's Committee of Public Safety. The accident by which, on one occasion, he escaped execution—a mark being made on the inside instead of the outside of his cell door—is well known. But it is less well known that during his imprisonment of eleven months he not only had a violent and almost fatal fever (which again preserved him from execution) but became permanently affected with an abscess in the side, which during the remainder of his life caused him much pain. Now, if a man thus afflicted had really fallen into a habit of drinking too much, or of neglecting appearances, or of even worse slovenliness, a fair-minded critic would have felt it only just to mention the fact of his painful disease. And if, further, a man so situated labored under Paine's grief of feeling that the great cause in which he believed had utterly wrecked itself in France, such a critic would further have recognised that a resort to strong drink on the sufferer's part was a pathetic and painful, rather than a crudely disgraceful proceeding. And if, finally, such a sufferer, on returning to his adopted country, of whose freedom he was one of the most influential founders, saw himself shunned and vilified by old associates on account of his conscientious religious opinions, the same hypothetic just-minded critic would have seen in the fact a very adequate apology for indulgence in stimulants. But Mr. Stephen, while believing in the story of Paine's intemperance, hints at none of these circumstances; and after all, as has been pointed out, the alleged indulgence did not really take place.

We have seen evidence that Paine's habits were not drunken in America even in his last darkened and lonely days. There is equally good proof that his habits were sober in Paris. Joel Barlow, the author of that defunct epic "The Columbiad", was applied to by Cheetham for evidence as to Paine's habits in Paris, where Barlow had been one of his intimates. "He was a great drunkard here", wrote Cheetham from New York, "and Mr. M——, a merchant of this city, who lived with him when he was arrested by order of Robespierre, tells me he was intoxicated when that event happened" (Sherwin, Appendix, p. xxxiii). This letter, as Mr. Vale has pointed out, with similar hearsays, misled Barlow, who had never been in Paine's neighborhood after leaving Paris, into believing that the latter had really become latterly intemperate, and he expresses this belief in his answer. But he is explicit as to Paine's sobriety in Paris:

"I never heard before that Paine was intoxicated that night. Indeed, the officers brought him directly to my house, which was two miles from his lodgings, and about as much from the place where he had been dining. He was not intoxicated when they came to me. . . . . You ask what company he kept—he always kept the best, both in England and France, till . . . . he conceived himself neglected and despised by his former friends in the United States. . . . . Thomas Paine, *as a visiting acquaintance and as a literary friend, the only points of view in which I knew him*, was one of the most instructive men I ever have known. . . . . He was always charitable to the poor beyond his means . . . ." (Sherwin, Appendix, pp. xxxvii-viii).

The remaining items in Mr. Stephen's biographical paragraph are the phrases as to "the meanest squabbles", the "surly adherence to his principles", and the "wretched carcase, about which he seems to have felt some anxiety". The first I will let pass in the present connexion, admitting simply that Paine, broken in health and disordered in nerves, had some quarrels. The "constantly" is Mr. Stephen's own characteristic touch. The "surliness" consisted in this, that Paine, vexed in his last painful hours by the indecent intrusion of Mr. Stephen's "well-meaning persons", sharply dismissed one of the most brutally offensive, and finally gave orders that they should all be excluded. One old lady he had previously turned away with a grimly humorous comment which even Mr. Stephen would hardly call surly. One other lady there was to whom he was indeed stern. She had once been his intimate friend and correspondent, but during his stay in France she had married, and when he returned to America she and her husband were among those who refused to resume his acquaintance. During his last illness she was moved to visit him; but when he saw her he refused to shake hands, saying, "You have neglected me, and I beg you will leave the room". She went out into the garden, the story goes, and wept bitterly; and we may believe, I think, that had the life-weary Paine seen her tears he would have relented.

It is true, as Mr. Stephen puts it in his first edition, that Paine's "wretched carcase" was buried in his farm. But the "anxiety", as to which the historian offers no particulars, had merely consisted in a wish to be buried in the graveyard of the Quakers, in whose denomination Paine had been brought up, his father having been of that persuasion. "Though he did not think well of any Christian sect, he thought better of the Quakers than of any other." The Quakers refused the request, and Paine, who in his dying state was "affected considerably" by the refusal, was buried in his own ground. I can hardly trust myself to characterise the kind of criticism which can only describe this as showing "anxiety" about a "miserable carcase", withdrawing the statement later, evidently not with regret for having made it, but simply to make room in the page for a few lines necessarily added. One has a difficulty, indeed, in passing fitting judgment on Mr. Stephen's two accounts of Paine as wholes. One recalls the story of the Duke of Wellington's attitude towards the performance of a careless officer who, by disobeying an important order, placed the army for a time in dire jeopardy. "What did you say?" asked a friend to whom he afterwards related the episode. "Oh, by God, I said nothing!" was his Grace's answer. That were perhaps the best course with Mr. Stephen. But I believe I shall have the support of any unbiassed literary man who examines the matter, in saying that the biographical paragraph I have dealt with in Mr. Stephen's book, alike in its original and in its amended form, is a disgrace to literature.

It is hardly necessary, of course, to express the belief that Mr. Stephen would not have written what he did at first if he had properly investigated the matter. One does not for a moment compare him to Cheetham, whose slanders he so recklessly retailed. One simply says that, having erred first through culpable prejudice, and still more culpable carelessness, he had not the candor later to make righteous amends even when his error had been made fairly plain. It would seem as if, having once judged unjustly on insufficient knowledge, he cannot disabuse his mind of his first impressions. But in our further examination of his non-biographical observations on Paine we shall, I fear, see cause to deny him credit for dealing fairly even with matters which were all along fully before him. His remaining criticisms not only commit that kind of injustice which is disputable as turning on matters of opinion, but once more, and this time with no qualifications, injustice which is indisputable, as consisting of flat misrepresentation of matters of fact. The latter I will first deal with.

Though it is only in contrasting Paine with Burke that Mr. Stephen avails himself of the help of Cheetham, his earlier notices betray no tendency to show fair play to the unpopular infidel. The following is from the passage which introduces Paine in the theological section:

"Good Englishmen expressed their disgust for the irreverent infidel by calling him Tom, and the name still warns all men that its proprietor does not deserve even posthumous civility. Paine indeed is, in a sense, but the echo of Collins and Woolston; but the tone of the speaker is altered. . . . . . The early deists wrote for educated men. Paine is appealing to the mob. . . . . His ignorance was vast, and his language brutal; but he had the gift of a true demagogue, the power of wielding a fine vigorous English, a fit vehicle for fanatical passion. His tracts may be set without too (*sic*) much disadvantage beside the attack upon Wood's half-pence, or the best pieces of Cobbett" ("History of English Thought in the Eighteenth Century", i. 458).

It was thus presumably by way of showing he was a "good Englishman" that Mr. Stephen himself repeatedly names Paine "Tom" in his incidental allusions; and if scrupulous incivility to the dead unbeliever will suffice, he certainly ought to stand well with his orthodox countrymen. It will be noticed that where, as in the foregoing paragraph, he has occasion to accord such praise as it is impossible for a rationalist decently to withhold, Mr. Stephen is careful to so phrase it that it shall have a certain flavor of detraction. Thus Paine's fine vigorous English must needs be further labelled as a "fit vehicle for fanatical passion". Now, if fanatical passion be an offset to a man's literary power, there is no case in which more deduction must be made than in that of Burke, who in his later utterances on the French Revolution carried such passion to an extent hardly attained in any important composition of the period, and certainly not by Paine. Yet it never occurs to Mr. Stephen in criticising Burke, for whom he has an extreme admiration, to make such a qualification concerning him. Again, if Paine be a demagogue in that he wrote like Swift in the Drapier Letters, Swift is properly to be termed a demagogue in the same connexion. But I do not recall that Mr. Stephen, in his book on Swift, ever thought it necessary to bestow on the Dean the epithet in question. On the contrary, even in admitting that the Drapier Letters contained many falsehoods, Mr. Stephen puts it that the Dean "went to work with unscrupulous *audacity of statement*, guided by the *keenest strategical instinct*" ("Swift", p. 154). These are small matters, but they are illustrative of Mr. Stephen's critical practice.

Paine, says Mr. Stephen, wrote for the mob. He did indeed appeal to the general population, who were habitually appealed to by the Church he wished to overthrow; but anyone not bent on casting epithets at him would see, I think, that he never appealed to "the mob" in the sense of striving to stir the passions of the unreasoning. I should say there is at least as much appeal to reason in any one of Paine's chief works as in Burke's "Reflections on the French Revolution", though the latter certainly appealed more to upper-class sentiment. And Wesley and Whitefield daily appealed to "the mob" in the true sense of the term, since they addressed those who could not read, and those on whom sheer argument would have been lost. But Mr. Stephen never uses the word in connexion with Methodism. In that regard we are told that "all *warmth of sentiment* had passed to the side of Wesley and Whitefield" as compared with preachers like Blair (ii. 346); Whitefield, the great mob orator of evangelicalism, is classed as an "enthusiast" (378), and his power is "dramatic rather than .... intellectual"—but not demagogic or fanatical; and while Wesley's writing is "full of a doctrine which *frequently leads to* an unlovely superstition", yet "as clearly it implies a vivid sentiment, never to be despised for its ugly clothing" (ii. 432). It is only when a man's sentiment is unpopular that it is to be despised for its clothing, in Mr. Stephen's critical system.

Let us come to more precise issues. We are told that Paine is "*in a sense* but the *echo* of Collins and Woolston, but the *tone of the speaker is altered*"—a choice Hibernicism, better worth preserving than most of Mr. Stephen's sayings on Paine. But when the critic asserts that Collins and Woolston wrote for educated men as compared with Paine, we are on another ground. Will the reader believe that Mr. Stephen had already pointed out that Collins had discredited his cause by translating the Latin word *idiotis* in the well-known edict of Anastasius concerning the *idiotis evangelistis*, by the English form "idiotic"; and that the critic had also referred to "poor mad Woolston" as the "most scandalous of the deists" (i. 87)? Chubb he similarly described as "the good Salisbury tallow-chandler, who ingenuously confesses, whilst criticising the Scriptures, that he knows no language but his own". Take Mr. Stephen's detailed criticisms of Woolston:

"The argument [against miracles] was the more offensive because there is no sign that Woolston appreciated the difficulties which may be suggested by criticism, or by *a priori* objections to miracles. His contention is simply that the narratives are on the face of them preposterous. . . . . This strange performance would have been sufficient of itself to raise doubts of its author's sanity." "Through six straggling discourses, Woolston attempts to make fun of the miracles. There are, at intervals, queer gleams of distorted sense, and even of literary power, in the midst of his buffoonery. Occasionally he hits a real blot" [the miracles in general not being blots]; "more frequently he indulges in the most absurd quibbles, and throughout he shows almost as little approximation to a genuine critical capacity as to reverential appreciation of the beauty of many of the narratives. He is a mere buffoon jingling his cap and bells in a sacred shine; and his strange ribaldry is painful even to those for whom the supernatural glory of the temple has long faded away. Even where some straggling shreds of sense obtrude themselves, the language is obtrusively coarse and occasionally degenerates into mere slang" (ii. 229-232).

Observe that whereas Woolston in one set of passages is pronounced mad, in another he is criticised as being sane, so as to leave the most unpleasant impression about freethinking in the reader's mind. Now compare with this one of Mr. Stephen's explicit criticisms of Paine.

"Paine .... reproduces the objections to the Bible which occurred to him on a hasty reading, or which had reached him through the diffused scepticism of the time. It must be added, however, that such arguments might be effective enough with popular readers who regarded every letter of the English version as directly dictated by the Holy Ghost; and *moreover* keen mother-wit supplies many deficiencies, and Paine's reasoning *often hits real blots*, whilst it *loses little* (!) *by not being smothered* in masses of erudition. His reasoning, indeed, though defaced by much ribaldry, is *simply the translation* into popular language of a theory expounded by more accomplished critics. .... He is *apparently ignorant that anything of the kind had been said before*; and makes no reference to the deists, such as Tindal or Morgan, who had put his arguments into more decent language. .... Paine's creed .... is simply the creed of all the deists of the eighteenth century. Paine's peculiarity consists in the freshness with which he comes upon very old discoveries, and the vehemence with which he announces them" (i. 459-461).

Here, contradictions apart, Paine is characterised in terms almost identical with those previously applied to Woolston, except that he is made out much the better reasoner of the two. But, it being necessary to discredit him in the long run, we later learn that the ribald and futile Woolston wrote for educated men, and Paine only for the mob. I need now hardly remark to careful readers that Mr. Stephen's account of any unpopular freethinker is not much more to be trusted, without close enquiry, than his account of Paine.

When Mr. Stephen observes that Paine's "ignorance was vast"—a phrase which might loosely be used of any man—we are forced to assume that he has in view some of the matters on which he himself expressly comments, as this:

"He [Paine] explains .... that his chronology is taken from the dates printed on the margins of the 'larger Bibles', which he apparently supposes to be part of the original documents" (i. 459).

I am here once more in a difficulty as to the proper way of answering Mr. Stephen. The plain truth is that this is a scandalous perversion of the plain fact. So far from there being the slightest reason for believing that Paine made the incredible blunder here wantonly charged on him, the passage itself shows that he did no such thing. It runs thus:

"The chronology that I shall use is the Bible chronology, for I mean not to go out of the Bible for evidence of anything, but to make the Bible itself prove historically and chronologically that Moses is not the author of the books ascribed to him. It is *therefore* proper that I inform the reader (such an one at least as may not have opportunity of knowing it) that in the larger Bibles, and also in some smaller ones, there is a series of chronology printed in the margin of every page, for the purpose of showing how long the historical matters stated in each page *happened, or are supposed to have happened, before Christ*, and consequently the distance of time between one historical circumstance and another."

Will Mr. Stephen next tell us that Paine, in the very act of analysing the biblical books with a view to questions of authorship, held that a pre-Christian scribe wrote in his margin the year B.C. in which the events he narrated were "supposed to have happened"? I doubt whether wilful dishonesty could reach worse results in the way of false witness than Mr. Stephen contrives to get to through mere carelessness and prejudice.

Take next the derisive passage following:

"Wishing to prove that much of [the Bible] is so poetical that even the translation retains 'the air and style of poetry', and remembering that some of his readers may consider that poetry means rhyming, he [Paine] adds to a verse from Isaiah a line of his own composition" (i. 459).

Let me remind the reader that in the passage in question is a footnote, which Paine begins thus: "As there are many readers who do not see that a composition is poetry unless it be in rhyme, it is for their information that I add this note". That is to say, the footnote is expressly added for the benefit of uncultured readers. Is this a proof either of gross ignorance or of fatuity? If Lord Selborne teaches a Bible class, does this prove him unfit to hold the Chancellorship? I am not arguing that Paine was a scholar. On the contrary, we know that he read comparatively little, his power lying in his original faculty of thought and speech. But I observe that it matters nothing to Mr. Stephen whether Paine were well-informed or not: either way he will contrive to belittle him. Take as illustration the following sentences:

"The most remarkable argument in the second part [of the 'Age of Reason'] is a collection of the various passages which, if occurring in the original, show that the so-called books of Moses cannot have been composed by Moses or his contemporaries. . . . . *The remarks are creditable to Paine's shrewdness.* The same difficulties had been suggested long before by Spinoza and by Newton; but those writers were apparently beyond the range of his reading" (i. 461).

Anybody but Mr. Stephen, I think, would have admitted that if Paine detected for himself, without any help, a number of the proofs that Moses could not have written the Pentateuch, he would have given proof of great critical acuteness. Mr. Stephen believes he did so discover them, but will only concede that the discovery showed "shrewdness"; just as elsewhere he follows the impudently absurd academic usage of making out good reasoning to be unworthy of respectful comment when it is arrived at by "mother-wit". Thus can a learned historian arrive at the sage decision that a man's reasoning "loses *little* by not being smothered". Judicious concession! With Mr. Stephen, it is rather better to be obtuse with culture than clear-headed without it. But in the passage before us he contrives to err in his facts in one direction as well as to pervert justice in another. Paine *did* know something of Spinoza's criticism of the Bible. In the second part of the *Age of Reason*, the very section to which Mr. Stephen alludes, he states that he has "seen the opinion of two Hebrew commentators, Abenezra and Spinoza", on the subject of the authorship of the book of Job. It is indeed a small matter, compared with the others, that Mr. Stephen should assume Paine to have had no help from Spinoza, since in any case it is certain he had not much; but it is interesting to have this further light on Mr. Stephen's way of going to work. It now appears that he had not thought it worth while to do more than glance into the book he was criticising.

Take yet another of his imputations:

"The 'Age of Reason' indeed sometimes amuses by the author's impudent avowals of ignorance. In the last part, he mentions a few authorities, and appears to have been dabbling in some inquiries as to the origin of the Jewish and Christian faiths. This, however, was an afterthought. In the first part he avows, with some ostentation, that he has not even a copy of the Bible. Quoting Addison's paraphrase of the nineteenth psalm, he adds, 'I recollect not the prose, and when I write this I have not the opportunity of seeing it'. Before the publication of the second part, he had 'furnished himself with a Bible and a Testament', and found them to be 'much worse books than he had conceived'" (i. 458-9).

Again, what are the facts? The first part of the *Age of Reason* was written by Paine in Paris while in hourly expectation of arrest and consequent death; it being his earnest wish to leave behind him a protest against the irrationality of the popular religion. The manuscript was only finished a few hours before the arrest came. English or any other Bibles were not likely to be very abundant in Paris at that time, and Paine expressly states in the First Part that he "had not the opportunity of seeing one", and again in the preface to the Second Part that he "could not procure any". To call this an impudent avowal of ignorance is just to add one more to Mr. Stephen's sins against literary good morals. Paine knew the Bible in general extremely well: he had been brought up on it, and he had an excellent memory; only it required the later perusal with an emancipated mind to see all its flaws. In any case, the First Part of the *Age of Reason* is a general argument such as any thinker might fitly write in his study without specially consulting the Bible at all. It attacked central principles and not details. And the fact remains, as Paine was entitled to boast, that he had "produced a work that no Bible believer, though writing at his ease, with a library of Church books about him, can refute"; whatever Mr. Stephen may choose to suggest by the safe process of insinuation. One would have thought that a book of such earnestness and force, written under such circumstances, would extort from any critic of repute an admission of the writer's elevation of mind: that the man who wrote such a treatise while in hourly expectation of death on the scaffold would receive at least credit for courage and magnanimity. But no: all that Mr. Stephen can discover is an "impudent avowal of ignorance".

Mr. Stephen's language implies, if words mean anything, that Paine's arguments were weighty mainly as against those who believed in the literal inspiration of the English version of the Scriptures. A criticism so egregiously wide of the mark is really not worth detailed refutation; but as so often happens with him, Mr. Stephen himself supplies the answer. Paine's arguments, deduced from a "hasty" reading of the Bible, while mainly adapted to the most ignorant believers, yet have their defects largely atoned for by "keen mother-wit", and "*moreover*" often "hit real blots". It is inimitable, this blowing hot and cold in the same breath: I know no rival to Mr. Stephen in the art. But the triumph of his method is attained only in this sentence:—

"Paine's book announced a startling fact, against which all the flimsy collection of conclusive proofs were powerless. It amounted to a proclamation that the creed no longer satisfied the instincts of rough common sense any more than the intellects of cultivated scholars" (i. 463).

Here the historian's exquisitely balanced mind contrives to imply at once that the orthodox answers to Paine were one and all flimsy, and yet that Paine's being right was no great proof of his being a competent thinker. It was only "rough common-sense"!

Need I here state that the implication as to the "cultivated scholars" having generally seen the truth before Paine is not true? The general effect of Mr. Stephen's own book is to show that there were cultivated scholars in abundance who could not see what Paine perceived by his deplorably unvarnished common sense. The critic's favorite, Burke, could not see it, remaining a blind and unreasoning believer; the scholarly Horsley had just been showing, in controversy with Priestley, that scholarship could very well be on the side of irrational faith.

When all is said Mr. Stephen is obliged to admit of Paine's "Age of Reason"—and I fear the avowal must have cost him discomfort—that the book made powerfully for righteousness as well as for right reason. In a passage considerably earlier than the detailed notice of the book, he had observed that "Wesley from one side, and Tom Paine from another, forced more serious thoughts upon the age" (i. 273)—this after "the attack and defence" of previous writers had "lowered the general tone of religious feeling", and generally furthered intellectual stagnation. And the admission is once more made later on.

Mr. Stephen is a critic not devoid of conscientiousness; and when' he really feels a truth he does not hesitate to state it. But his idiosyncrasies will not let him reduce his criticism in order even by a methodical balancing of pros and cons: he must needs leave only a distracted series of contradictions. This is the note of his criticism in general, but least of all could he contrive to produce a clear generalisation as to Paine.

"Paine, indeed, deserved moral reprobation for his brutality; and his book has in it an unpleasant flavor. Yet there was a fact which the respectable public tried hard to ignore. Paine's appeal was *not simply* to licentious hatred of religion, but to genuine moral instincts. His 'blasphemy' was not against the Supreme God, but against Jehovah. . . . . Paine, in short, with all his brutalities, had the conscience of his hearers on his side, and we must prefer his rough exposure of popular errors to the unconscious blasphemy of his supporters" (i, 463). [*Sic.* Query "their supporters" or "his opponents".]

It will be necessary in conclusion to examine this reiterated charge of "brutality" against Paine; and the inquiry will bring us to a final decision on Mr. Stephen's fitness for the work of comparative criticism.

No quotations being given by Mr. Stephen in support of his reiterated charge of brutality, we can but assume that he has in view some of those passages in the *Age of Reason* in which Paine attacks some Biblical absurdities with a rough derision that some might call coarse. Were the latter epithet used against him in these cases, I for one should not be much concerned to object, since I have no wish to pretend that Paine's polemic is always of the most refined kind. It could not well be, since he wrote for the people—or, as Mr. Stephen prefers to say, for the mob. It would seem to follow from the latter view that in Mr. Stephen's opinion the mob should have no literature whatever, since he will hardly say that it would have been profitable in Paine's time to write for them in a refined style. Cobbett, who could and did write for them, is admitted to have been tolerably brutal. It would probably stand for little if I were simply to counter Mr. Stephen on this head, and say that Paine was not a brutal writer, especially for his time. Such dicta in matters of taste are unconvincing, and in mere authority Mr. Stephen's dictum of course outweighs mine. I will therefore simply cite one other expression of opinion on the point before resorting to comparative critical tests. Mr. Conway writes as follows :

"I know of no similar investigation in which the writer's mind is so generally fixed upon the simple question of truth and falsehood, and so rarely addicted to ridicule. Few will deny the difficulty, however reverent the reciter, of relating the story of Jonah and the whale without causing a smile. Paine's smile is in two sentences ; in one place he says it would have been nearer to the idea of a miracle if Jonah had swallowed the whale, elsewhere that if credulity could swallow Jonah and the whale it could swallow anything. But after this, for him, unusual approach to the ribaldry of which he is so freely accused, Paine gives over three pages of criticism on the Book of Jonah, not only grave and careful, but presenting perhaps the earliest appreciation of the moral elevation and large aim of the much-neglected legend" (Article on "Thomas Paine", in *Fortnightly Review*, March, 1879, p. 413).

This also, of course, is not conclusive ; but neither I trust is Mr. Stephen's simple epithet ; and the next step is to weigh his characterisation of Paine's tone and method against his treatment of other writers. Let us take one of his own sentences :

"Johnson turns the roughest side of his contempt to anyone suspected of scepticism, and calls Adam Smith a 'son of a bitch'" (ii. 369.)

I am loth to attempt a precise definition of the term "brutal", since I fear it might be difficult to frame one which should not cover some of Mr. Stephen's own language against Paine; but I think it will be generally agreed that the word would apply to this utterance of Johnson[1]. If it is possible for a man of letters to speak brutally, Johnson did it when he thus spoke of Smith. Now, it is a simple matter of fact that there is nothing nearly so coarse in the whole of Paine ; yet Mr. Stephen must needs speak austerely of the latter's "brutalities",

---

[1] I say nothing as to the validity of the story. In his "Johnson" (p. 115) Mr. Stephen tells the other story that Smith applied the same expression to Johnson, to his face. I do not believe the latter version ; but Mr. Stephen thinks "it is too good to allow us to suppose that it was without some (*sic*) foundation". Another sample of Mr. Stephen's critical method. Need I point out that the presumption against both versions of the story being true is enormous ? Mr. Stephen, however, seems to accept both.

while the ruffianism of Johnson is genteelly described in the same book as the "roughest side of his contempt". Again, in his chapter on Warburton, Mr. Stephen quotes, by way of showing some of that divine's tendencies of style, two passages in which indecent words have to be represented by dashes (i. 352). On any theory of critical justice that I can formulate for myself, the term "brutality" should either be applied to such achievements as these of Johnson and Warburton, or else reserved for something still worse. Mr. Stephen never once uses it in regard to the sentences referred to. There is, however, in all Paine's writing, I repeat, nothing coarse enough to be put beside these passages. What is the inference as to Mr. Stephen's critical equity?

The points just dealt with lie on the face of Mr. Stephen's own narrative, but there is a further proof of his bias in the fact that he has entirely suppressed all mention of the frantic violences of Burke against the promoters of the French Revolution. The catalogue lies to the reader's hand in Buckle (3-vol. ed. i. 471–5). Burke in his later years saw fit to speak of the pure-minded Condorcet as a determined villain; to gloat over the sufferings of the imprisoned Lafayette, terming him a "horrid ruffian"; to shriek against France as a "Cannibal Castle", against the National Assembly as the "prostitute outcasts of mankind", and against the French people as the "scum of the earth"; and to urge that the war waged against them by England should be carried on revengefully, bloodily, and for a long space of time. And all these insane ferocities are never once hinted at in a compendium which professes to compare Burke with the thinkers and publicists of his time; while again and again the unenvenomed crudities and coarsenesses of the unsanguinary Paine, who braved death by opposing the execution of the French king, are stigmatised, forsooth, as "brutalities". Thus can history be written.

We come finally to the question of Paine's general calibre, or comparative intellectual standing among the men of his day. Comparative, one says, for it is difficult to imagine any other criterion by which a man's mind is to be finally measured or classified. And Mr. Stephen, though as we have seen he generally leaves the comparative method carefully alone, does fall back upon it here.

It is after his memorable biographical paragraph that he proceeds to draw a comparison between Paine and Burke. In his first edition it began thus:—" And yet Paine, though even his earlier years "—again wanton aspersion, this time without even a biographical reference—" were but too good a preparation for this miserable close, had in him the seeds of something like genius ". The paragraph in the second edition runs:

" Yet Paine, whatever may be the truth " [the discovery of that being modestly left by the historian to the general reader] " as to his private life, or the motives which guided his restless political activity, had in him a dash of genius. Of his chief political writings the tract called 'Common Sense', published in January 1776, had, as was thought at the time, very great influence in promoting the Declaration of Independence; and the 'Rights of Man', published in 1791, in answer to Burke's 'Reflections', had an enormous sale. The attack upon the established creed in politics showed, in fact, the same qualities as his attack upon the established creed in religion. He was confronted, indeed, in his later writings by an opponent of incomparably greater power than the orthodox theologians who shrieked at the blasphemies of the 'Age of Reason'. But though Burke moves in an intellectual sphere altogether superior to that in (*sic*) which Paine was able to rise, and though the richness of Burke's speculative power is as superior to Paine's meagre philosophy as his style is superior in the amplitude of its rhetoric, it is not to be denied that Paine's plain-speaking is more fitted to reach popular passions, and even (! !) that he has certain advantages in point of argument " (ii. 261–2).

Here, despite the syntactical infirmity of the last sentence, there is no difficulty in tracing Mr. Stephen's usual bias. The fact, as stated by almost all other historians, is that "Common Sense" really had a most decisive influence in bringing about the Declaration of Independence: it was not only thought so then; it is known now. In that matter, Paine affected the people of the States just as comprehensively and as powerfully as Burke later affected Englishmen towards the French Revolution: he was not merely appealing to the mob: he stirred a people to fateful action; and he maintained the impulsion by his further writings at critical moments. This, one would say, represented a genius at least for that sort of thing; but Mr. Stephen's measure makes out the faculty involved to be but a "dash" of genius. Wherein then lay the amplitude of the genius of Burke? There is a danger that in defending Paine against Mr. Stephen's special pleading we may be tempted into doing Burke injustice; but I think we shall not be so beguiled when we say that Burke's eminence and merit lay in the breadth and elevation of his social sentiment in his præ-Revolution period, and in the literary and dialectic skill with which he enforced his sentiment at all times, for good or for evil. Alike in his earlier sociology and in his self-expression then and at all times, he was powerful and original. But to say this is not to credit him with an all-round vigor of intellect, or to place him in the front rank of great men. To sum up a man, on the comparative principle, we have to take note of his limitations.

Now, Mr. Stephen is not slack to attribute limitations to Paine: as usual he can furnish the list without being at pains to collect the proofs. Burke is in an "altogether superior" intellectual sphere, revelling in "richness of speculative power"; while Paine's philosophy is "meagre". But what are the data? In what respect is Burke's speculation "rich" as distinguished from his rhetoric? There is really no "speculative" element in Burke's politics whatever: his great characteristic is the vehement and various eloquence with which he enounces his instinctive attitude towards the social tendencies of his time; now resisting what he felt to be blind pedantry and inhumane conservatism; anon finding a wealth of ingenious and imaginative justification for a pedantry and a conservatism in which he shared—as in resisting the claims of the Dissenters; and yet again exhausting the power of words to hurl hatred at those who outraged his habits of emotional attachment to historic institutions. He might be right or he might be wrong, but at least he was not speculative in his philosophy: he was a man of deep and strong sentiments and glowing sympathies, with an incomparable gift of vivid dialectic; a Gladstone raised to a higher power, because more intense, original, and organic in his convictions, endowed with a genius rather than a talent for expression, and carrying passion in his blood and senses, as well as in his brain. Is it not the express statement of all his admirers, Mr. Stephen included, that he hated the speculative men, who thought out schemes of policy without due regard to "prescription"? I cannot see how this squares with richness of speculative power. What Mr. Stephen was really thinking of was just the richness of dialectic, of illustration and figure; of all, in short, that makes Burke really answer to that much abused designation—a prose poet.

Try him by his relation to non-political ideas, and the limitations become clear. He thought freely and freshly on law, history, and language, but what was his cosmogony, what his religion? When Mr. Stephen wishes to discredit Buckle, he asserts that the latter evaded the theological problems of his day; insisting that this proves intellectual restriction. Of Buckle the statement is simply not true: of Burke it is true. He contrived to set aside, by his sheer force of prejudice, all the religious questionings of his time, and to rest in the exulting, blatant orthodoxy of the rural Tories of his and our day. And his science? I cannot recal a trace of proof that he gained anything seminal from the scientific movement of his age: on that side he was at bottom non-receptive. What Paine could see in regard to traditional faith by "rough common-sense", Burke could not see with all his endowment; where Paine was natively alive to the great problem of the physical universe, Burke was wrapped in a husk of literature, book-culture, and every-day human association.

Consider in particular, however, the attitude of the two men towards the French Revolution, the issue on which they can best be weighed against each other in respect of breadth and sanity of mind, as distinguished from brilliance of rhetoric. It is presumably in this connexion, indeed, that Mr. Stephen draws his comparison of the two men; since he does not refer to Burke's bigotry, and appears to know nothing of Paine save as a writer on politics, and against the Bible. It is like Mr. Stephen to say that the "Reflections" are pitched on an intellectual plane "altogether superior" to that represented by the "Rights of Man", but the proposition, like so many others of his, will not bear examination. Burke, after a lifetime of *succès d'estime*, suddenly attained a popular success just because he voiced with incomparable eloquence and energy the sentiments of the average Englishman at the Revolution crisis. To say that the work by which he first caught the upper-class and middle-class mind, and produced a general and enduring reaction, is addressed to intellects of a comparatively high order—this is only a sample of that unreasoning panegyric of Burke which has so long discredited English criticism. To any one who will apply fair tests it is plain that the elevation lies in the style and not in the thought, which is again merely typical Tory sentiment dignified by an uncommon range of association and argument. So to dignify it was assuredly a great feat, which let us duly admire; but let us not pretend that the great rhetorician is a great thinker.

Even Mr. Stephen has a feeling that such a performance as the *Reflections*—of which the sounder elements are not profoundly original, while the unsound are shallow with the shallowness of George the Third—will not survive impartial comparative criticism, much less such arbitrary treatment as he accords to Paine; and he indicates his apprehension in the fashion with which we are now so familiar:

"Paine fully believed, or appeared to believe, in the speedy advent of the millennium. His vanity, it is true, was interested in the assumption. The American Revolution, he thought, had brought about the grand explosion, and the foundation of the American Constitution had given the first example of a government founded on purely reasonable principles. Now the pamphlet 'Common Sense' had led to the Revolution, and therefore Paine had fired the match which blew into ruin the whole existing structure of irrational despotism. Still the belief was *probably not the less genuine, though* thus associated with an excessive estimate of personal merits, and Paine is at times eloquent in expressing the anticipations of universal peace and fraternity destined to such speedy disappointment. His retort upon Burke's sentimentalism about chivalry and Marie Antoinette is *not without dignity* .... A *degraded representative* of the popular sympathies, Paine yet feels for the people, instead of treating their outcry as too (*sic*) much puling jargon. And therefore he gives utterance to sentiments *not to be entirely quenched by Burke's philosophy*" (ii. 263-4).

Like nearly every passage of Mr. Stephen's that we have had under notice, the foregoing would suffice by itself to convict him of a singular incapacity for equity. Assuming that he had made good his point as to Paine's vanity, which again is worded with hostile animus, what becomes of the insinuation of insincerity? Either Paine believed, as he was well entitled to do, that his "Common Sense" had been a main influence in precipitating the Revolution, or he did not. If not, there was no vanity; yet even in that case he might surely be perfectly sincere in the hope at which Mr. Stephen sneers. We know he lost it later; but we (*nous autres*, that is, excluding Mr. Stephen) know him to have been full of it before the collapse in France. But if, as Mr. Stephen is satisfied, Paine vaingloriously believed he had brought about a beneficent revolution in America, where is there any pretext for hinting at insincerity in his words as to the movement of things in Europe? "The belief," our acute historian finally decides, was "probably not the less genuine *though* thus associated" with personal vanity; this just after pointing out that the vanity was "interested in" that very belief. As who should say, Cromwell was probably "not the less" sincere in believing God was with him after he had won Dunbar. One would be inclined to say that explicit absurdity was Mr. Stephen's strong point, were there not so many reminders that he can be worse than absurd. The deduction as to Paine's probable sincerity, despite vanity, in a belief which flourished on vanity, is worthy to be treasured beside that other that an argument "loses little from not being smothered"; but we are not allowed to forget dissatisfaction in amusement. The question in hand is the validity of Paine's answer to Burke, from the point of view of right reason. Mr. Stephen will not say that Burke's defence of "prescription" will stand, or that his attitude towards the Revolution was that of one who rightly appreciated the case. He does not like to defend the treatment of the hoarse cry of a wretched people as "too much puling jargon". He feels that Paine has "even some advantages in point of argument", is not always "without dignity", and utters sentiments "not to be entirely (!) quenched by Burke's philosophy". Partially quenched they may perhaps be (that is for the reader to ascertain) but not entirely. Is Burke's "philosophy" then, after all, left in possession of the field? On the contrary, the conclusion of Mr. Stephen's chapter, after all this unspeakable see-sawing, is that Burke's political philosophy is a mere wreck on the shore of time! But before this was conceded, the man who had the right end of the stick must needs be described as "degraded", as appealing to popular passions, as a meagre intelligence, as excessively vain; and his failure to reach finality of political science must be alleged with contempt before the other's failure could be admitted with reluctance and respect.

A final comparison of Mr. Stephen's dismissals of Paine and Burke respectively will serve to close an examination of which, in that connexion, the reader is perhaps already weary. It is after he has given a "pejorative" account of the drift of the "Rights of Man" that the critic thus pronounces judgment:

"The doctrines thus vigorously laid down [by Paine in politics] have become tolerably threadbare, and every scribbler can expose their fallacy" (ii. 263).

The said doctrines included, even on Mr. Stephen's showing, the proposition that the hereditary principle in Government is an absurdity; that morality consists mainly in doing as we would be done by, and not, as Burke insisted, in reverently regarding all constituted authorities in their order; that the British Constitution was predisposed to corruption; and that the representative system "meets the reason of man"—theses which some of us are fain to maintain still, against even Mr. Stephen and "every scribbler". Nay, Mr. Stephen himself concedes, with his inalienable grace of modification, that Paine spoke "pretty forcibly" when he said that "a body of men holding themselves accountable to nobody ought to be trusted by nobody". But one hastens from such details to a contemplation of the historian's final judgment on Burke, which presents a consummation of dead-lock in antithetic allegation not easily to be paralleled in critical literature.

"Burke's magnificent imagination and true philosophical insight led him more nearly than any of his contemporaries, and even than any of his successors in English political life, to a genuine historical theory. Unluckily his *hatred of unsound metaphysical doctrine* induced him to adopt a view which seems often to amount to a denial of the possibility of basing any general principles upon experience. *Like the cruder empiricists*, he admires the 'rule of thumb' as the ultimate rule, and conservates mere prejudice under the name of prescription. Godwin's title, 'Political Justice', indicates the weak side of his great opponent. Burke had not solved the problem of reconciling expediency with morality, though he indicated the road to a solution" (ii. 280).

That is to say, his true philosophical insight led Burke nearer the truth than any man of his time, or any English politician since; and at the same time his hatred of bad philosophy made him such a bad philosopher that he landed in the philosophy of the "cruder empiricists", *videlicet*, the rule of thumb. And yet, after all, though he attained no solution of his problem, he "indicated the road to a solution". And the solution—which no English politician has yet hit on—? In the very act of coming to a fair conclusion on Burke Mr. Stephen must needs drown decision in contradiction and leave the reader facing blank frustration. It were superfluous to deduce at length the net value of the correlative judgment on Paine; and in any case the task has become too monotonous to be supportable. One grows weary of this suicidal process of vacillating commentary and incoherent prejudice parading as analytical criticism. Turning from counsel darkened to the stage of darkness visible, let the reader attempt fairly to measure Paine by his relation to his age on the main grounds of universal mental activity. There are some further materials for such a judgment, of the existence of which Mr. Stephen does not appear to be aware.

We have seen that, even by the admission of a critic with small gift for fairness, Paine did two very remarkable things in his day. Without political or social influence, he roused the American people to revolution by one stirring manifesto; without learning, he began a new epoch of rationalism by a new and straightforward criticism of the reigning religion. These, be it observed, were not the transient successes of a demagogue; they were performances which gave trend to history, and notably affected the courses of thought and civilisation. Wilkes made more local uproar, but Wilkes did not appreciably influence universal politics, and Wilkes's scepticism bore no fruit in influence on his nation's mind. The constant note of Paine's writing is a commanding and compulsive sincerity, which won for his writings a hearing and a following without precedent in English affairs. In his gift of getting at the heart of any matter he took up he is excelled by no writer of his age; if he could not, like Burke, "wind into a subject like a serpent", he struck into it as with the hammer of Thor. By sheer murderous directness of stroke, his pamphlet on English finance at one blow vanquished and convinced Cobbett, who had hated Paine by repute with all his robust gift of hatred, and assailed him with the ferocity in which he excelled his whole generation; and the bitter enemy was thenceforth the extravagant worshipper and champion of the dead man he had vituperated living. Genius is a word very loosely used, and it is not necessary to commit Paine's case to any definition of it; but if not the note of genius, then certainly the note of power, is felt in Paine's swift exertions of living force; as when, after precipitating the American Revolution and inspiring it till its consummation, he felt convinced that if he could only get quietly to England and issue a pamphlet he could sway the nation to a new purpose, and did so sway it with a rapidity which startled into new fear the holders of power. And to the end his faculty of conquering conviction never left him. In the leaflet he wrote on "Gunboats" shortly before his death, every phrase is a blow.

But this faculty and this achievement, eminent as they are, do not nearly exhaust Paine's intellectual inventory. Let me again quote from the competent and appreciative essay of Mr. Conway, who I believe has been the first to do full justice to the range of ability exhibited in the "Age of Reason":—

"What homage should we have heard if, in any orthodox work of the last century, had occurred the far-seeing astronomic speculations of the *Age of Reason*? It was from the humble man who in early life studied his globes, purchased at cost of many a dinner, and attended the lectures of Martin, Ferguson, and Bevis, that there came twenty-one years before Herschel's famous paper on the Nebulæ, the sentence: 'The probability, therefore, is that each of those fixed stars is also a sun, round which another system of worlds or planets, though too remote for us to discover, performs its revolutions'." (Article on "Thomas Paine", *Fortnightly Review*, March, 1879, p. 413.)

But that is not the only exhibition on Paine's part of an energy and endowment of mind which carried forward human achievement in other directions than politics. In the appendix to Sherwin's Life, and in some other quarters, will be found an account of Paine's invention of an arched iron bridge, which compelled the approval of the scientific men of his day, and which has been the pioneer of the long line of great modern works of bridge-making in metal. The credit for the first use of iron in bridge-building, like so many other first steps in human progress, appears to be due to the unprogressive Chinese; but Paine seems to have had no predecessor's hint or help in his introduction of the idea among his race. I cannot ascertain the date at which, in his first sojourn in the States, he constructed his model of an arched iron bridge to cross the Schuylkill at Philadelphia, and it may be that he was preceded in point of time by the English projector of the iron bridge built over the Severn at Coalbrookdale in 1779; but I believe I am right in saying that this small structure was essentially different from Paine's in its principles. Certainly there is no trace of his having got his idea from it, and the French Academy of Sciences dealt with his as a new invention, furnishing " a new example of the application of a metal of which sufficient use has not hitherto been made on a grand scale". It is in 1789 that we find him superintending the construction of his bridge at Rotheram in England, and his accounts of the work give striking proof of his practical capacity in the walk of engineering, for which he had had no formal training. He had been moved to the task by the difficulty of bridging the Schuylkill, where the periodical passage of vast masses of ice made piers impossible, and the 400 feet span precluded the erection of a stone arch. And coming to the problem of the bridge with the same native vigor of insight which he brought to bear on politics and religion, he " took the idea of constructing it from a spider's web, of which it resembles a section ". I am not competent to speak of the degree of engineering originality implied in this inspiration; but it is, I believe, the fact that he made a very great advance in his perception of the tubular principle, which dates from the same time. " Another idea I have taken from nature ", he writes, " is that of increasing the strength of matter by causing it to act over a larger space than it would occupy in a solid state, as is evidenced in the bones of animals, quills of birds, reeds, canes, etc., which, were they solid with the same quantity of matter, would have the same weight with a much less degree of strength ".

Had Mr. Stephen bethought him to ascertain these matters, which alone would seem to some of us enough to prove Paine a man of uncommon ability, he might perhaps have allowed that they pointed to yet another " dash " of genius. But it never occurs to Mr. Stephen, in writing the history of the English "Thought" of last century, to take any trouble about estimating the nature, amount, and value of the thinking done in connexion with physical science. His critical method is not concerned with these sides of mind. Let me, in exposition of a critical question of some general importance, beg the reader's jaded attentention to the passage in which Mr. Stephen passes general judgment on the intellect of Priestley:

"Priestley . . . . possessed one of those restless intellects which are incapable of confining themselves to any single task, and, unfortunately, incapable in consequence of sounding the depths of any philosophical system. . . . . He gave to the world a numerous series of dissertations which, with the exception of his scientific writings, bear the marks of hasty and superficial thought. As a man of science he has left his mark upon the intellectual history of the century; but, besides being a man of science, he aimed at being a metaphysician, a theologian, a politician, a classical scholar, and a historian. . . . . So discursive a thinker could hardly do much thorough work, nor really work out or co-ordinate his own opinions. Pushing rationalism to conclusions which shocked the orthodox, he yet retained the most puerile superstitions. He disbelieved in the inspiration of the Apostles, and found fault with St. Paul's reasoning, but had full faith in the prophecies, and at a late period of his life expected the coming of Christ within twenty years. . . . . He flashes out at times some quick and instructive estimate of one side of a disputed argument, only to relapse at the next moment into crude dogmas and obsolete superstitions" (i. 430-1).

Did it ever before occur to a historian to sum up a man's performance by enlarging condemnatorily on what are alleged to be his failures, and dismissing in an incidental clause the great successes which have kept his name alive? To see what such a method would lead to if consistently applied, let us just take one of Mr. Stephen's own sentences, concerning Newton:

"Newton himself was unconscious of the bearing of his discoveries upon the traditional theology, and bent his mighty intellect to that process of solving riddles which he called interpreting the prophecies" (i. 82).

This is, by comparison, a sufficiently lenient way of speaking of Newton; seeing that the belief in "prophecy" is, in the eye of pure reason, to the full as puerile a superstition as any of Priestley's, being indeed the very form of superstition which Mr. Stephen specially so characterised in Priestley's case. But anyhow Mr. Stephen admits that Newton was a consummate failure as a rationalist theologian, apart from his Arianism. Yet what in Priestley's case is made the justification of a substantially belittling verdict is in Newton's only made an occasion for a respectful remark on the weaknesses of greatness; and Newton is reverently adjudged "mighty" on the strength of his notorious scientific success, while Priestley's notorious scientific success is barely reckoned as a mentionable offset to his theological weaknesses and inconsistencies. The thing would be ludicrous if it were not so displeasing a violation of the simplest instincts of critical justice. Mr. Stephen undertakes his history of a century's "Thought" without a glimpse of a scientific interpretation of his term; and he passes judgments on men by the score without an attempt to arrive at a reasoned or uniform standard of measurement. He has neither test nor method.

Such criticism is but a formal restatement of the drift of general prejudice, deflected by prejudice that is personal. And to come back finally to the matter in hand, it is just the drift of general prejudice that has settled Paine's place in ordinary history. His singular powers have been in part ignored, in part treated as mere genius for evil, for the simple reason that he was identified with two causes which passed before his death into common odium, the French Revolution and Freethought. In the immense reaction against the evil outcome of the Revolution, all pretence of fair criticism of the men who had incited it disappeared; and in the English imagination Paine was slumped with Robespierre and Marat, who sought to slay him because he boldly resisted them. Burke's to-day is seen to be the really lost cause; but eighty years ago he seemed a kind of archangel assaulting the dragon; and the gradual change of sentiment has left his legend almost intact; while Paine, who became identified with the dragon forthwith, is whelmed in limitless slander. His Freethought was taken as a dispensation for every form of calumny that Christian malignity could devise; and in his adopted country the result was a new revelation of the possibilities of human baseness. No tale of national ingratitude in the annals of antiquity, where they are so plentiful, will eclipse the record of the repudiation of Paine by the Republic he had helped to make, when he recorded his hostility to its superstitions. Others, known to be as unbelieving as he, dissembled, and retained their place on the roll of fame: his name became the chosen target of the great tribe of dastards. "A bust of [Paine], by Jarvis, in the possession of the New York Historical Society, is kept under lock and key because it was defaced and defiled by visitors" (Article in *Atlantic Monthly*, July, 1859, p. 15). And men who are far above the moral plane of the Christian blackguard can still be found to carry on the defilement with pen on paper. Where the known vices of great men are habitually palliated, one falsely imputed vice is made out to be Paine's main characteristic. Addison suffers no diminution of esteem for his confessed intemperance; Lamb is loved no less for his pathetic weakness; the licence of Burns leaves him worshipful to his countrymen; but the disproved charge against Paine is forever iniquitously fastened on his memory, and his unquestioned innocence of life in other regards only stimulated to new fury of obloquy the bigots whose creed he had impeached. The thrice disproved lie as to his death-bed terror and remorse is still part of the stock-in-trade of "Christian Evidence"; and I have just had sent me a copy of a tract entitled "The Inspiration of the Bible", by H. L. Hastings, published by the reputable firm of Bagster and Sons, circulated by the late Lord Shaftesbury, and marked "Fifth Hundred Thousand", in which the lie is retailed with the "circumstance" that it was vouched for in 1876 by a woman of eighty-eight, who at the age of *eleven* was "invited by a distant connexion .... to go and see T. Paine on his death-bed". And this precious story the pietist offers by way of answering, as he says, the statements of "infidels who were *not present*", and who speak of "events which occurred years before they were born". The inspiration of the Bible apparently cannot be defended without false witness against unbelievers, and the story is deliberately told in such a way as to prevent the pious reader from suspecting that the death-bed figment was exposed, after personal investigation, by Cobbett, who was Paine's contemporary. And all the while piety is complacent over the assertion that a child of eleven was taken by a Christian relative to hear, for edification, the delirious blasphemies and shrieks for mercy of an infidel dying in extreme bodily agony.

In the face of these crass mendacities of average Christian controversy, it is but just to mention that Mr. Stephen from the first rejected the death-bed story as a fiction. I am sorry there is so little more to say in praise of his treatment of the subject.

TORYISM AND BARBARISM.

By JOHN ROBERTSON.

"In the involuntary errors of the *understanding* there can be little to excite, or at least to justify, resentment. That which alone, in a manner, calls for rigid censure, is the sinister bias of the *affections*."—*Bentham*.

"The past turns to snakes."—*Emerson*.

"The chief causes of the low morality of savages, as judged by our standard, are, firstly, the confinement of sympathy to the same tribe. Secondly, powers of reasoning insufficient to recognise the bearing of many virtues . . . . on the general welfare of the tribe."—*Darwin*.

No man who has seen anything of the world, be he enthusiast or cynic, will expect to find in any public association or party a complete immunity from any form of personal misconduct. Liberal and Conservative, Christian and Freethinker, Protestant and Catholic, if candid, will alike admit that there are black sheep on their own side of the hedge and white ones on the other; rightness of opinion, from any point of view, being no guarantee of moral merit, any more than ordinary good conduct involves high intelligence. A fair-minded party-man or disputant, therefore, will never urge against any school or set of opinions the fact that specific vices can be charged against certain individuals who adhere to it. The canons of fair impeachment will only allow the contention that if a particular way of thinking is found to be frequently associated with a form of wrong-doing which is markedly less common among those who think differently, the onus of self-vindication lies with the party stigmatised. And as party controversy is usually neither fair nor methodical, it may be set down that a large number of the imputations most usual in politics and polemics are either false or exaggerated; and indeed it is understood to be one of the charms of the higher politics, as prosecuted in Parliament, that you converse amicably with men whom you publicly proclaim to be the allies of assassins; and courteously send to congratulate on his improved health the personage whom you brand as the destroyer of his country's liberties. "The man who loudly denounces," says Goethe, "I always suspect"—of what, is not quite clear, but we may assume insincerity. It is needless to examine in detail, then, the general charges of turpitude brought by rival parties against each other as wholes, and against leaders in particular. Such charges have their foundation, such as it is, in the scattered acts of unfairness, equivocation, dishonesty, and treachery which are committed by a number of individuals under varying circumstances—acts more or less inexcusable, but practically inevitable at the present stage of moral progress. Besides, it lies on the surface that in many cases measure of inconsistency—or tergiversation, as the accuser is pretty sure to call it—is made the measure of imputed criminality; whereas the more a man knows of human nature the more clearly does he see, if he will be candid, that the most striking, the most speedy, and the most extreme changes of view on a particular point may be made in perfect sincerity. Such changes, of course, are proofs of weakness of some sort—weakness of perception, of purpose, or of reasoning power; and are not to be lightly condoned as such. It is difficult to say which of the prominent party leaders of modern times —Peel, Disraeli, Gladstone, or Salisbury—has the most humiliating record of intellectual vacillation, of hasty belief and hasty conversion, thoughtless denial and thoughtless assertion, standing against him in the passionless compilation of "Hansard"; and it will be bad for posterity if these men's successors do not learn something of self-criticism and forethought from a study of their careers. For the rest, however, it is plain that the moral is pointed with nearly equal clearness all round. And something is perhaps to be allowed for the stress of the practical difficulties of statesmanship in such a State as ours, where the traditions and the exigencies of party Government make it so hard for leaders to maintain perfect singleness of purpose. If Mr. Bright has stood almost alone among our great politicians in his character for honesty, it is not improbably because he has had so little to do with actual Ministerial work; for even he is found to incur a charge of inconsistency in connexion with his last tenure of office; his withdrawal, on its merits, being somewhat tardy.

To find a statesman turn his back on himself, then, and to find his party turn with him, is not to convict him or them of any uncommon flagitiousness. If Lord Salisbury took service under a man whom he had denounced as an unscrupulous adventurer, Mr. Gladstone, on the other hand, collaborated with one whom he had accused of mean-mindedness; and Sir William Harcourt has vociferously sung the praises of a leader whom he once bitterly derided. Even the assumption of Lord Randolph Churchill into the Cabinet, if it casts into the shade all previous surrenders of embarrassed statesmen to detested domestic foes, is not a political transaction unique in kind in the annals of either party. In short, the most frequently discussed charges in party warfare are common property and of a common application; and in the present study of Tory morals I shall adopt none of these commonplaces of platform recrimination. There is, indeed, some reason to question whether the recent tactics of the Conservative leaders do not represent an unprecedented lowering of the political standard of morals. The brazen avowal that criticism in opposition is one thing and action in office another; the unabashed concession to and alliance with the Home Rule party after the unmeasured denunciations of the "Kilmainham treaty" and the impassioned demands for coercion in Ireland—these are certainly most conspicuous displays of political improbity. Still, while this is noted, it must be remembered that such a policy is only an extension of the moral licence permitted themselves by party leaders on both sides for generations past. If Mr. Gladstone has not expressly discriminated between his words in opposition and his course in power, it must not be forgotten that in one important particular, to say nothing of others, he has utterly abstained from doing what he easily might to support a profession of principle made by him before his last accession to office. Nothing could be more impressive, more apparently sincere, than his præ-triumphal declaration that the people of these kingdoms ought to have the power of deliberating in Parliament on the expediency of any war in which Ministers desired to embark; and nothing could be more complete than his virtual repudiation of that principle since. He has made war as madly, as mistakenly, as unpardonably as ever did his antagonists; and though his Cabinet has shown some redeeming sensitiveness to just blame, he has perhaps personally carried his policy with as high a hand as the worst of his predecessors. The reminiscence is an evil one for those who have been deceived in him: let it be dismissed with the confession that righteousness in dealings with the inferior races cannot be dwelt on as a virtue which notably distinguishes Liberal from Conservative thus far; and let it at the same time be allowed that Mr. Gladstone's shifty prevarications go some little way to balance the bolder falsities of his rival; though the elder casuist has in fairness to be credited with his recent confession of error—a confession probably not to be paralleled in the history of British statesmanship.

What, then, is to be taken as a test of the comparative development of morality among political parties? Is there any test that can fairly be called crucial? I think there is. First let it be asked what are the special vices that a dispassionate inquirer might reasonably expect to find common among Liberals and Conservatives respectively? If we assume, as we reasonably may, that political sympathies are the result of a certain bias of mind and feeling, it is fair to suppose that they will generally consist with a particular intellectual or moral flaw. Now, it is pretty clear that, comparatively, the special element in Liberalism, historically speaking, is intellectual; while the special element in Conservatism is emotional or affectional; that is to say, the minds which desire change are *ex facto* more speculative, more inquiring, than those which are averse to it. Not that the Liberal is deficient in those sub-rational tendencies which are so strong in the Conservative; but that, in whatever degree he may possess the latter, he has the former in addition; and, keeping this in view, we find it natural that while the Liberal, like the Conservative, has his bad wars to answer for, he is often dead against the other party's wars, while the Conservative is as a rule in favor of any war whatever, and usually condemns the Liberal for not fighting vigorously enough. The element of difference is the intermittent assertion of the Liberal's reasoning faculty, which is obviously and demonstrably the chief factor in all moral progress. The special failing of the Liberal, then, in the terms of the case, is to be looked for on the intellectual side, in that direction in which he constitutionally diverges from his opponent; and it will perhaps be found most philosophic to say that his shortcoming lies in his tendency to believe that his pet set of measures —his "machinery", as Mr. Arnold calls it—will work profound changes in things, or at least will sufficiently modify the world for all practical purposes. Hence the tendency of every generation of Liberals to imagine that their favorite reforms are the consummation of progress. Conservatives may perhaps reject this view, and put it that the Liberal vice is, in the mildest terms, the unreasoning desire for change. As to that, the independent inquirer must be left to decide for himself; as indeed must be the case when we come to diagnose the moral diathesis of the Tory.

On our assumption that the Tory specialty is the supremacy of feeling, commonly so-called, it will follow that his special vices arise from the ebullition of his hereditary impulses. Using the word "defect" in its strict sense, we might say that he is seriously defective in that he entirely lacks the element of mental ferment, so to speak; but it seems hardly fair to blame a man for his entire lack of a particular faculty. Mill struck the right note when he explained that in calling the Conservatives the stupid party he did not mean to say Conservatives were generally stupid, but that stupid people were generally Conservatives—a distinction which will appeal to all accurate thinkers. We do not say, then, that the Tory's vice lies in any defect. It is something positive. In the first place, his lack of speculative turn tends to make him do extreme injustice to the motives of those who have it, and to condone and uphold established injustices; but beyond this he is clearly liable to obey his passions and prejudices to an inordinate degree; which amounts to saying that he is in a serious sense nearer the primitive state than his opponents. I trust the argument is clear thus far, and I challenge a scientific scrutiny of it.

Let it here be granted that the Tory's specialty may at times have its good side—comparatively speaking. While more given to delight in war than the politician of more speculative turn, he may show a generous if ill-judged sympathy where the latter exhibits a somewhat cold caution. If the Tory's taste for intervention is apt to lead to mischief, it is at least not always repugnant to our "better feelings", as they are called; while the prudence of the Manchester School is not always free from a touch of the sordid. On the whole, while bad landlords are only too common, a generous Tory landlord is perhaps as common as a generous Liberal manufacturer. But all this only makes it the clearer that where the Tory's feelings happen to make definitively for evil his wrong-doing will tend to be the more atrocious. If his good feelings tend to outrun judgment, what of his bad? In the terms of the case, he is at his best a species of noble savage, who may do a chivalrous thing on occasion, but who is at any moment capable of working a gross injustice. The question is a scientific one. What is the prominent evil of the barbarous state—the state in which feeling is least trammelled by intellect? Plainly the active injustice of brute force—the sacrifice of every consideration of natural equity to the impulses of dislike and affection. Tyrannous power, lawless hatred, deliberate and complacent injury—these are the salient moral phænomena of barbarism. The barbarian, who is a bundle of emotions controlled by no tribunal of reflection, but swaying him to good or evil as they happen to be stimulated without or within—the out-and-out emotionalist knows nothing of right and wrong beyond the narrowest limits. Towards his enemy he is absolutely unscrupulous; and where he has given his allegiance he is uncritically, brutally obedient. So, *mutatis mutandis*, with the unspeculative political emotionalist of to-day. The history of Liberalism shows no such blind obedience of rank and file to leader as we find in Toryism. Peel might be cold-shouldered, but Disraeli's after-career showed that, if he knows his business, mere change of front need lose no Tory leader a handful of his followers. It was not for a reasoned principle that they joined his flag, and once he has got hold of them by their instincts he may manipulate his and their official creed as he pleases. All party Government tends to develop unconscientious obedience; but it is past all question that Conservatives have carried it to a maximum. It is very idle for them to retort on their opponents the stigma of "mechanical majority" when they seek at the same time to make their chief capital out of the known discordancy of the elements of the Liberal party. Fortunately for themselves, the Liberals' claim to unity of creed falls to the ground before the competing programmes; while the readiness of the antagonist body to follow its leaders *en masse* anywhere is plain to a demonstration. The Churchill scandal is no disproof. That is essentially a transient trouble. A section of "dolphins" there might indeed be who grinningly encouraged Lord 'Arry to discomfit his elders; but there was no schism of opinion whatever; and his absorption into the bosom of the family brings about a delighted fraternisation throughout the ranks. It was with the Churchill sub-faction as with the faction proper—the ruling impulses were personal feeling and the instinct of pugnacity; and the reunion is as purely a matter of temper as the dissension. Lord 'Arry was the natural leader for the more puerile minds of the party, appealing to them as he did with no reasoned doctrine whatever, but tickling their ears with a series of *ad captandum* proposals of various kinds, effectively flavored with invariable vituperation of the other side. That, by the way, is a constant aspect of the Tory specialty. Liberals are not without the faculty of invective, but in practice we find, what in theory we might expect, a much less constant resort to it on their part than on that of their opponents. Mr. Gladstone, with all his serious faults, may be cited as a decisive illustration of the Liberal superiority in that direction; his most impassioned impeachments of, say, Lord Beaconsfield, being amenity itself beside that statesman's attacks on Peel. Beaconsfield, of course, was in no sense either a sincere or a typical Conservative, and owed his success entirely to his clear perception of the nature of the Conservative idiosyncrasy; so that Lord Salisbury is the better antithesis to point to. The contrast in that case becomes decisive; his lordship's every speech, almost, containing some abusive references to one or other of his leading antagonists; while Mr. Gladstone hardly ever flings a personality in return; and even Mr. Chamberlain's attacks are impersonal and dignified in comparison with the angry insolences and unmeasured imputations of the Marquis. The latter is above all things the *beau sabreur*, the wrathful assailant, prone to charge, barbarian-like, without regard to his following. He is the Berserker of politics.

But his supremacy in scurrility is clearly the less serious aspect of the Tory's vice. If that were all, it might be dismissed as amounting to the venomous shrewishness of consciously inferior strength; but there is worse behind. His capacity for brutal injustice, always frightfully prompt of exercise where there is a chance of coercing, is specially at the service of any movement of tyrannous fanaticism that chimes with his prejudices. The worst oppressor of Ireland, the bigoted persecutor of struggling sects, he is in his element when he gets an opportunity of denying an Atheist his constitutional rights; and he adds insult to injury, cowardly slander to gross iniquity, with a zest that sometimes makes it difficult to conceive him as in some respects a civilised personality, with decent habits and some inoffensive tastes. Here, at length, is our crucial test. The authentic mark of the beast, the stamp of the savage, is the shameless assertion of force where passion prompts, in absolute disregard of every appeal to natural right or established law; and precisely such a shameless, lawless, iniquitous denial of an unquestionable civil right has been perpetrated with almost complete unanimity by the Conservative party in the case of Mr. Bradlaugh. It has been said that the blame of that injustice lies with those Liberals who were false to the principles of their party in the matter; but anyone who studies the question dispassionately will see in that defection the last proof of the fundamental connexion between Tory instinct and the worst kind of social wrong-doing.

What are the facts? That Mr. Gladstone, notoriously an eager, emotional Christian, explicitly declared the clear right of the disbarred member to sit. I should be the last person to eulogise the ex-Premier for his slack and reluctant championship of the cause of simple justice in this matter; but though he has stood coldly by while the wrong was being endured, the fact remains that he so far did violence to his religious sympathies as to make even an emphatic declaration on the side of fair-play; and in this he was supported by a majority of his party; while Mr. Bright made a chivalrous demonstration on the same side. On the other hand, there came from the Conservative side not a solitary word of the dictates of justice; not an admission of the hardship that was being inflicted; nothing but a dastardly chorus of boorish contumely and currish hostility—the outcry of a body of upper-class rowdies indecently delighting in the oppression of a man in whom they saw an enemy, and by wronging whom they hoped to strengthen their cause among their fellow barbarians. Now, it lies on the face of the matter that the action of the Conservatives in the House of Commons was not the outcome of religious earnestness. The pretence that it was so, and that the opposite attitude of Messrs. Gladstone and Bright came of sympathy with Atheism, might be pointed to as the crowning achievement in partisan lying, if it were not so entirely ludicrous. Religious belief, no doubt, entered into the matter to a considerable extent. Curious as it may seem, it is perfectly credible to the student of human nature that politicians who make gun-wadding of the decalogue in their wars of aggression may be more or less essentially devout men, with a natural affinity for religious mysteries. To suppose, however, that such men as Beaconsfield, Salisbury, and Iddesleigh have anything like the fervor of religious feeling which is found in Bright and Gladstone, is too absurd. No man of the world, further, will believe for a moment that the Conservative leaders would cast off a follower whom they knew to be an Atheist, supposing he were a libertine into the bargain. That the party includes a few sceptics and a great many libertines is sufficiently notorious; and the party leaders would no more ostracise these than wear the blue ribbon or refuse to meet a Roman Catholic at dinner. A few of their followers have felt so far coerced by these considerations as to avow that they would not have kept out Mr. Bradlaugh if he had dissembled decorously at the start, like so many other members; and the admission is something. It in no way alters the fact, however, that the pretence of piety has been almost unanimously used by the party to justify what is really an act of pure and simple ruffianism. I use that word advisedly, to express the patent spirit of unhesitating, zealous, impish iniquity which has been displayed in the matter. Coleridge has defined wickedness as "egoism designedly unconscientious"; and if that formula overlaps the Tory action in the case before us it at least partly covers it. The element of deliberate infliction of wrong, which is the chief ingredient in wickedness, is present to the full in their conduct; and if egoism, in the ordinary sense, has not been their inspiration, they figure none the better when we reflect that they have shown a spontaneous delight in tyranny which is commonly associated with the state of savagery, or semi-savage militarism. This may perhaps seem to a calm enquirer an extravagant indictment of the action of a political party; but let him see if any less severe construction can be rightfully put on the episode.

I have said that the defection of a number of Liberals from the cause of religious freedom is the last proof of the essential connexion of the spirit of Toryism with that of social wrong-doing of the kind under consideration. The Liberals who apostatised were with scarcely an exception men whose politics had been determined by the accidents of heredity or Dissentership; and who, accordingly, had little of the typical Liberal tendency to ratiocination in politics. The Fitzwilliams, for instance, belong to the barbarian class, as Mr. Arnold would say; and Mr. Samuel Morley's is a case in which the exigencies of evangelical life, acting on a conscience of the Bulstrode order, produce a line of action to fully parallel which we must go back a few centuries in history. The kind of pietism which in Mr. Gladstone is regulated by a highly developed intelligence, is in him an incalculable hysterical force; and his oscillation from his præ-election frenzy of partisanship to his subsequent religious remorse, marks him out as a mediæval survival. In his way, he too belongs to the Tory type. It may be urged that the effort implied in the abstention of the Liberal members in question is a proof of their sincerity, and no doubt that is so, up to a certain point. That is to say, the hostility and the fanaticism which inspired them were genuine enough; just as there was a good deal of genuine hostility and fanaticism on the Tory side. But the point is that while dishonest Tories add dishonesty to oppression, the others, and their quasi-Liberal congeners, are constitutionally prone to injustice, and ought, in the interests of society, to be branded as dangerously vicious organisms in that respect. The apostate Liberals acted under the sway of their ineradicated vice, not on an intellectual decision. Had their action been truly and conscientiously political they would have made a more open and explicit profession of their reasons, and would not have merely stayed away from the debates as in so many cases they did. Their policy was the war policy of Bedouins, capable of abandoning a cause at a critical moment for no better reason than superstition and tribal hatred.

It was not the purpose of this paper to look into the tactics of the Home Rulers who have coöperated with their old enemies in the Bradlaugh case; but it is worth pointing out that their action illustrates the whole of the foregoing thesis; and the matter has practical importance for thoughtful students of politics. The deplorable conditions of past Irish life have produced, in the Home Rule party, a body of men whose idiosyncrasy is clearly near that of the Tory in order of development: who, that is to say, are swayed rather by feeling than by the spirit of speculation; though their situation has developed in them a noteworthy species of adroitness in adapting means to ends. The essentially blind and barbarian character of their main impulse—race spirit and national hatred—makes their moral range at least as primitively narrow as that of the typical Conservative; and their public life is consequently a constant outflow of monomaniac passion and prejudice or profligate slander. There was a scientific truth in the observation of the Parliamentary humorist that "a man must have some principles, unless he is a Home Ruler". All they need to act on is an instinct. Thus we may, unhappily, look to them for the very grossest displays of shameless injustice, and, setting aside as we here may their other misdeeds, we find such a display in their treatment of Mr. Bradlaugh. To the guilt of the Tories they have added that of an unspeakable ingratitude—such ingratitude as belongs to an almost premoral state of things. All Mr. Bradlaugh's services to their nation, his strenuous vindication of its rights when these were for the most part callously ignored in England, his constant sympathy with the Irish people in their hardships, have been not merely overlooked but denied, and calumny has been bestowed where gratitude and help were due. Of all the clouds on the prospect before the Irish people this is perhaps the darkest, that their representatives, with sins enough to answer for where they had some pretext for resentment, have shown themselves capable of doing with light hearts a reckless wrong to a tried benefactor whom they thought it politic to repudiate. Mr. Bradlaugh, when in the House, moved the rejection of the Coercion Bill when the Home Rule leader had timorously deserted his post, and he has had his reward in a hostility and vilification which have out-Toried the Tories. And why? First, because the craven leader, thus compromised, became an unscrupulous enemy, and, having a body of dependent followers chiefly of the emotional and prejudiced type, has been able to sway them to his purposes; secondly, because Ireland is mainly Roman Catholic, and ready to obey its priests so long as they do not resist its main political bias. There are perhaps some other causes, which may one day be made clear.

But if such a state of things promises ill for the moral or social progress of Ireland, no less do the kindred phœnomena of Tory barbarism suggest future trouble in England. Let the unprejudiced reader judge. In the course of the present electoral campaign, of all the hundreds of Conservative candidates who have spoken, certainly not not more than a dozen [I speak under correction: I have only noted four] have consented to so much as support an Affirmation Bill; while of all the hundreds of Liberal candidates, not more than a dozen, if so many, have declared against admitting Atheists to Parliament. And while the Liberals have in certainly the majority of cases protested that they have no sympathy with Mr. Bradlaugh's views, and have thus evidently acted on an intellectual decision, the majority of the Tories have seized the opportunity to more or less brutally vilify the man they are seeking to crush. The language of their aristocrats has in many cases literally been the language of blackguards—one of the decisive evidences of reversion to a prior ancestral type. But it is not only the thinly-veneered barbarians who thus testify to the prevailing tendency of Toryism: the tactics of the leaders clearly point to a calculation that to wrong the Atheist is the profitable course to take. Lord Iddesleigh, sometimes complimented by Liberal journalists in an expansive mood as being a gentleman in comparison with his colleagues, was long ago legible to closer observers as a weak tool, incapable of winning adherence to his own views, and always ignobly ready to compromise them rather than offend his half-supporters. But Lord Iddesleigh's course in the Bradlaugh case has been something worse than ignoble. He is recognisably, by rights, not a typical Tory, but a weak Liberal—that is, a man with a certain endowment of the intellectual qualities which dispose men to Liberalism, and no great share of the barbarism which makes them Tories; but his weakness has kept him where his lot was first cast, in the Tory camp; and the effect of his surroundings has been to gradually worsen him, till his thinking faculty appears chiefly to serve him to lend himself with blundering caution to the brutality in which he has no natural part. His action in this matter has been that of a man who saw clearly enough what was the reasonable thing to do, and who, without the barbarian's excuse of innate ruffianism, yet conformed to the bias of the worst members of his party and ultimately became their mere catspaw, stultifying himself in the process with a facility only less memorable than his moral collapse. So that the man who might have been a decent Liberal becomes in the Tory environment, in a sense, even worse than his surroundings, he doing against his lights what the others do because of lack of light; even as, it is said, when white men settle down among savages they tend to become more slothful and depraved even than their neighbors. It is perhaps well that such a personage as this should be shelved in the House of Lords, out of the way of the strife that may be to come.

Perhaps even a more convincing illustration, to some minds, of the evil influence of the Tory cult on those within its sphere, is to be found in the case of Mr. Arthur J. Balfour, nephew of Lord Salisbury, and late member of the Fourth Party. That gentleman, who is a cultured metaphysician, has written an able and interesting book entitled "A Defence of Philosophic Doubt", in which, with much literary and dialectic skill, he supplements the philosophic achievement of Hume by a demonstration that the beliefs of those of us who call ourselves Rationalists, in regard to the persistence of Law in Nature, have no better ultimate foundation than the constitutional tendency to take a scientific view, while a tendency to believe in mythology is similarly the sole foundation of Mr. Balfour's belief in the religious mysteries on which he spiritually subsists. I believe Rationalists are not unwilling to endorse Mr. Balfour's sceptical philosophy, and are content to explain that organisms of his type, with a constitutional thirst for avowedly unintelligible mysteries, are in process of disappearing, while the scientific type of mind is destined to survive. But I wish here to point out how strikingly Mr. Balfour's conduct in the Bradlaugh case establishes the conclusion that psychologically he represents a transient reversion to a primitive type. He has recently spoken in public on the subject to the following effect:—

"Mr. Hopkinson was of opinion that disabilities on account of opinions on religion ought to be removed at once, and an Affirmation Bill passed. He [Mr. Balfour] did not share that opinion—(applause)—and he would explain why. The practical object of an Affirmation Bill would be to enable Mr. Bradlaugh, who was already prepared to take the oath, to enter the House without taking it. Nobody could deny that to bring in a Bill and deliberately exclude belief in God from the oath taken by a member of Parliament would meet with great opposition, and, mistakenly or not, it would undoubtedly shock the most respectable feelings of the country. He would ask Mr. Hopkinson whether he was prepared to delay public business by introducing a Bill which it would cause a large amount of friction to pass. 'If I have any say in the matter', Mr. Balfour added, 'it will not be one of the first duties of Parliament when it meets to bring in an Affirmation Bill.'"

It would be difficult to imagine anything more nakedly discreditable than the tone here taken. There is not a word of justice or principle: the sole pretext is that many people, to whom Mr. Balfour is pleased to attribute the "most respectable feelings of the country," would be shocked, "mistakenly or not"; on which ground Mr. Balfour would deny Atheists their civil rights for ever and a day—for if there is any meaning in his despicable plea about shocking respectable feelings it will hold good at any time as well as when Parliament meets. I do not pretend to estimate how far Mr. Balfour—who certainly knows something of how the intelligence of the nation is distributed—is sincere in his account of what are the most respectable feelings in the country; but I submit that whatever feelings underlie the nefarious policy he adopts will ere long cease to be respectable in the eyes of decent men. If religion is to be the sole and constant excuse for conduct of deliberate turpitude, the end will be that religion will acquire the infamy of the proceedings it is used to sanction.

Let the bigot and the aristocrat look to it. They have been teaching that tyrannous prejudice may be "respectable" when it inflicts outrageous wrong on a few; and they have also been wont to say there is a danger that the prejudices of the working classes, if given legislative effect to, may inflict wrong on the owners of property. It is possible; though the assurance comes from such authorities. The singular thing is that they thus persistently exhibit to those working classes their own perfect readiness to inflict a monstrous wrong when it suits them to do so, or when they can gratify their own or their allies' enmities by doing it; and that all the while they produce no better reason than that it is their pleasure so to do. Now, the working classes of this country are every day becoming less actively superstitious, and they are at least not growing less disposed to resent iniquitous tyranny, wherever exercised; nor are they remarkable for a capacity to forget those who have espoused their cause. Mr. Bright has averred his belief that they care as little for the dogmas of Christianity as the upper classes care for its practice: however that may be, it is certain that they are now less likely than ever to tolerate an act of high-handed oppression, perpetrated chiefly at the instance of aristocrats, plutocrats, and churchmen, and zealously assisted-in by Papist prelates and unscrupulous Home Rulers. Prejudice might come in there; though, taking them all over, the working classes are less given to act oppressively on the promptings of prejudice than any other class in the community. If there were not abundant proof of this in the past, the facts we have been considering would supply enough. Mr. Arnold, in his famous classification of his fellow-creatures as "Barbarians, Philistines, Populace," lays it down that the characteristic of the populace is to crush by brute force those who oppose it; founding his opinion, apparently, on the Hyde Park riots, so-called, in which connexion, with unwonted facility in fallacy, he has omitted to notice that brute force had been used against the populace to begin with. Mr. Arnold would probably admit to-day, in respect of the Bradlaugh case at least, that blind force has been employed without scruple by the Barbarians and the Philistines; while the populace have remained patient for five years under the outrage done to the man whom Mr. Arnold singled out as their typical leader—that leader all the while fighting his case with scrupulous legality, and never hinting at any appeal to that force of the populace which he is admittedly able to sway. Mr. Arnold will have to revise his formula.

Popular patience might, of course, give way one day; and it is reassuring to be able to cónclude that it will not be tried much longer. But nothing can now alter what has been done, and the lesson of the whole matter for the populace is, as has been said, one that bodes ill for the Conservatives. The people have seen what is the real value of upper-class declamations about justice and class prejudices: they are able to judge of the attitude of mind which is devout about the "sacred rights of property" and is more than willing to violate the rights of citizenship. They have had reason in other ways to scrutinise the devotion to established Christianity professed by men who, as M. Rochefort puts it, make cigarette papers of the Bible; and if there be any risk of their forgetting all these things there are some who will take pains to provide that they shall not. The dice of political destiny are accordingly being loaded against the Salisburys and Balfours, the priests and "respectabilities". But is that all that is to be apprehended?

If there is any force in what has been urged in these pages as to the fundamental barbarism of Tory instinct, it follows either that Toryism must crumble away or that it will manifest itself in various fashions in the near future. Some years ago people began to say that Toryism proper was nearly extinct; but the facts we have discussed have shown how hasty was the assumption. The historic spirit of Toryism did but appear to be dying out because for a time the issues tried between parties were such as only divided the upper and middle classes argumentatively among themselves: the moment an efficient test case arises the old temper is found to assert itself freely. And the Bradlaugh case is in all probability the prelude to a period in which the entire remainder not only of downright disability but of Protean privilege will be assailed with a persistency and vigor never seen in British politics before. Here then are the main elements of the political history that is about to be made in England: on the one hand a Conservative party as essentially anti-popular and tyrannous as ever, as full as ever of upper-class insolence and aristocratic ruffianism; on the other a populace daily becoming more practically educated and more efficiently organised; a populace which has seen the seamy side of Conservative morals unrolled before it with a completeness that leaves nothing to the imagination. And the movement of things at the moment is evidently towards an intensification of Toryism and a counterbalancing development of Liberalism. Some dozen of the apostate Liberals of the late Parliament have either been dismissed from political life or sternly menaced by avenging Radicalism; while on the Tory side, it is plain, the word has gone round to play the card of religion and "respectability". In the ordinary course of things the recrudescence of bigotry over the oath question would have waned in five years, whereas the Conservative attitude on the subject is to-day more determined than it was in 1880; which amounts to saying that the forces of oppression have been deliberately organised and recruited. What are the probable motives of the handful of Conservatives who have approved of an Affirmation Bill it would be invidious to enquire: whether they are all sincerely desirous of seeing one passed, or in the least prepared to push it, is open to question. But in any case their appearance only serves to emphasise the more strongly the damning force of the inference to be drawn from the general Tory policy on the so-called oath question. The slight variation they constitute on the main tendency of Toryism, like the few remnants of determined bigotry on the side of nominal Liberalism, does but establish our conviction that in such an investigation as the present we are dealing with substantial tendencies in human nature, from which we may reason with confidence to a working political philosophy.

PRICE TWOPENCE.

Printed by ANNIE BESANT and CHARLES BRADLAUGH, 63, Fleet St., London.—1885.

SOCIALISM AND MALTHUSIANISM.

BY

JOHN ROBERTSON.

LONDON:
FREETHOUGHT PUBLISHING COMPANY,
63, FLEET STREET, E.C.
1885.

PRICE TWOPENCE.

LONDON:
PRINTED BY ANNIE BESANT AND CHARLES BRADLAUGH,
63, FLEET STREET, E.C.

SOCIALISM AND MALTHUSIANISM.

A REMARKABLE feature in current Socialist propaganda is the almost complete unanimity with which the doctrines of Malthus are there derided, denounced, and repudiated. Alike in the English Socialist journals, in works such as Mr. Gronlund's and Dr. Bebel's, and in semi-Socialistic productions like Mr. George's "Progress and Poverty", that law of population which is one of the foundations of the Darwinian system is bitterly assailed; terms of vituperation being only varied by those of contempt—the latter, however, being too much flavored with wrath to carry any impression of real intellectual security. Such a state of things—whatever be the truth as to the point in dispute—is in itself sufficient to dispose of the claim so often made by present-day Socialists, that their movement is a scientific one. The spirit of science does not assail a patiently and thoughtfully constructed theory with mere cheap abuse and vulgar ridicule. Where it doubts it gives its reasons for doubting; and when it meets a candid, scrupulous, and temperate reasoner, it gives him credit for his labor and his temper, even if it dissents from his conclusions. Such a thinker would Malthus be admitted to be by any student of sociology at once honest and judicial in attitude; but never a word of becoming recognition do his great qualities receive from the militant Socialists. Aware as some of them are that Malthus is endorsed by Darwin, they affect to regard his theory as exploded. Prepared as they are to work with clergymen who share their views, they think it tasteful to allude to him as "Parson Malthus", as if the title in his case served to discredit his theories. We who call ourselves Secularists will not be accused of showing too much respect to priests; but I trust we shall never be guilty of using such *banal* discourtesy to any men who, while holding religious opinions which we reject, have a claim on our respect in the devotion of their lives to humane science and in the tolerant and philosophic cast of their minds.

The treatment of Malthus by Socialists and semi-Socialists of course varies somewhat in tone; and it is only right in this connexion to take note of a recent contribution[1] from the latter school in which, if the acquaintance shown with the subject be inadequate and the spirit unscientific, there is yet an attempt to dispose of Malthusianism by argument instead of by impertinence. The unscientific character of Mr. Wicksteed's method is apparent in the opening sentence of his chapter on Population. "The theory of over-population," he observes, "means, as I take it, that in a given part of the world there are more people than can obtain food and clothing from its surface without an excessive amount of toil"; and he goes on to assume, with professions of a desire to be fair, that Malthusians hold "that as soon as a country does not produce its own food it is over-populated, and the smaller portion it produces the more it is over-populated." Now, this opinion may conceivably be held by persons holding the Malthusian principle; but it forms no part of Malthusianism proper. The law of Malthus—as Mr. Wicksteed knows, for he quotes it—is that "there is a natural tendency and constant effort in population to increase beyond the means of subsistence"; and though Malthus, applying his law to conduct, recommended certain prudential experiments, and Neo-Malthusians to-day suggest expedients they consider better, the law of population remains the law of population, not any set of political suggestions for providing against poverty and misery. Failing to understand this, Mr. Wicksteed proceeds to urge a number of arguments which, while they may tell against the practical politics of some Malthusians, only serve to confuse the issue between him and Malthusianism.

Mr. Wicksteed supposes himself to be arguing against the "population theory" when he proceeds to show that there is poverty in France, where the population increases very slowly; that there is destitution in thinly-populated

---

[1] "The Land for the People: how to obtain it: how to manage it." By Charles Wicksteed. London: Wm. Reeves, 185, Fleet Street, E.C.

countries; and that we may have brisk trade in England a few years hence, as we had some years ago, although population continues to increase. If he would only read the "Essay on the Principle of Population", he will find that Malthus was as fully alive to these obvious facts as he is; and that the question goes a great way beyond such preliminary considerations. What Malthus did was to show that in every country and at all periods, among savages and among the civilised, there is a tendency to produce more children than can be reared to manhood; and that it is by such children dying early, from insufficient nurture, or by general disease, or by war, or by famine, or by vice, that population is always kept, as it must always remain, more or less within the margin of subsistence. What Mr. Wicksteed does at best is to show that in any given country, if men in general were wiser than they are, more people might be comfortably supported than are supported *at present*; which very few people will deny. As for his argument from the fluctuations in national prosperity, that only amounts to saying that subsistence varies in abundance—a truth which Malthus took a good deal of pains to illustrate; as he did the correlative truth that when a positive check happens to bring down population considerably below the level of subsistence, the fall is likely to be followed by a rapid increase in propagation. On that point he simply showed that excess ultimately arises, and that such excess is always removed by one cause or another—war, disease, poverty, famine, or emigration. But Malthus never taught, as so many people seem to suppose, that if only population be restrained by preventive checks, poverty is bound to disappear. He was not given to the headlong reasoning of the Socialist and land-nationalising schools of our time; and if he were alive to-day, and were asked why France suffered from a good deal of poverty, he would probably lay his finger on the true explanation, which is that its enormous burden of militarism largely countervails the advantage of a restricted population. With the fact that in England to-day, as Mr. Wicksteed points out, land is being withdrawn from cultivation, he would only be concerned as constituting a datum to be recorded. For him the fact would stand thus: "Under a certain land system, given certain conditions of industry and free trade in foreign corn, land may go out of cultivation. Either such lapse from cultivation reduces the available subsistence of the population or not [Mr. Wicksteed seems to say it does not, asserting that 'we are not suffering from any shortness of food']—either way the tendency to over-populate remains, and the acute stage of suffering is reached sooner or later as the case may be". If Mr. Wicksteed were searching for scientific truth instead of merely for arguments for land nationalisation (a perfectly proper end in itself), he would see that not one of his facts invalidates the Malthusian law; though they may have cogency as against any fanatical Malthusians who say that no reform in the land laws is needed. To say as he does that "by the Malthusian theory we ought to be getting richer" is simply to quibble very idly over the proposition that as population increases fresh land must be brought into cultivation. Our extra food to-day is got by cultivating land in other countries; and it will hardly be pretended that our population has long been steadily decreasing in proportion to the food obtained.

But besides facts, Mr. Wicksteed offers theories. He "considers that Henry George has shown" the Malthusian theory to be "ridiculously untrue"; and he delivers himself as follows:

"No matter where we look, as Mr. George has so forcibly shown, we find that it is under-population that we are suffering from. Countries once prosperous and rich with teeming populations are now miserable and poor with scant. Read a lecture given by Mr. Arnold Lupton, M.I.C.E., F.G.S., etc., 'Our Inheritance in the Earth' . . . . where the enormous capacity of our earth is clearly shown. Even with our present knowledge, he shows that the earth could well support 100,000 millions of people, or seventy times its present population."

Note here the spasmodic inconsequence of the argument. Not a single detail is given about the countries alleged to be once prosperous and populous and now poor and bare; and it appears to be assumed that to say the earth *might be made* to support so many more millions amounts to a proof that "it is under-population that we are suffering from". But as Mr. Wicksteed invokes the name of Mr. Henry George, it will be advisable to examine that writer's pretended refutation of Malthusianism. Mr. George, like Mr. Wicksteed, believes in a God whose ineptitude almost attains the sublime by exhausting one's sense of the ridiculous. He is Omnipotent, this God, and he "intended" that men should always hold the land in common; but human folly has conquered Omnipotence, and God has never been able to get his own way. With this puerile theosophy men like Mr. George and Mr. Wicksteed recommend their land policy to the minds in which theism operates as a fluid keeping all sorts of inconsistencies in solution. Naturally enough, an irrational theory of the universe is accompanied by an uscientific scheme of taxation, in which rent is singled out from every other form of income for appropriation; the man who lives on dividends from consols being unmolested while the landowner is mulcted. But enough for our present study is the reasoning of Mr. George on the law of population. That is a formidably ravelled process.

After admitting that the principle of Malthus "stands in the world of thought as an accepted truth", and that it is incorporated in the Darwinian theory, Mr. George declares that it is " utterly untenable". He begins his argument thus:

"Population always tending to pass the limit of subsistence! How is it, then, that this globe of ours, after all the thousands, and it is now thought millions, of years that man has been upon the earth, is yet so thinly populated?"

If Mr. George has read Malthus' Essay, "which", as he says, "is much oftener spoken of than read," he has found the answer there: " one of the most crushing answers," as it has been put in an economic treatise not strongly Malthusian in its teaching—"one of the most crushing answers that patient and hard-working science has ever given to the reckless assertions of its adversaries". Malthus showed in the most exhaustive detail how population has been checked in all countries and at all times by one or other of the preventive or positive checks of prudence, vice, infanticide, famine, poverty, pestilence, injurious toil, disease, and war. Mr. George, admitting that there has been plenty of misery in the world, announces that in every case it has arisen " either from *unsocial ignorance* and rapacity, or from bad government, unjust laws, or destructive warfare". Now, to use such language by way of discrediting Malthus is only to show incompetence to gather Malthus' meaning. No man ever did more to show how "unsocial ignorance" hindered human well-being: the very object of his treatise was to dispel such ignorance. But Mr. George in the very same chapter (Book II., ch. ii.), after admitting that "unsocial ignorance" may produce misery, goes on to declare that "nowhere can want be properly attributed to the pressure of population against the power to procure subsistence *in the then existing degree of human knowledge*". Here, besides the self-contradiction, we have one of Mr. George's main fallacies in a nutshell. He virtually tells us that when the savages of the Andaman islands died for lack of the shell-fish they usually picked up by the sea, it was their own fault, because they knew how precarious were these supplies, and they ought to have accumulated other stores of food; that when the Digger Indians live on grasshoppers, and the aboriginal Australians on the worms they get in rotten wood, they are not making proper use of their knowledge. What is to be said of a writer who sociologises in this fashion? He asks us to believe that the savage "knows" how to get better food if he only would; and dies out of obstinacy. What is the meaning of such a doctrine? Any ordinary mind, unpossessed by a pre-conceived theory, will admit that it is idle to the last degree; but it is not more idle than Mr. George's teaching that men and women ought to propagate freely to-day because more food might be produced if only the majority of men were wiser. His thesis is that "in the existing state of knowledge"—that is, of some people's knowledge—it is certain that the amount of food produced might be increased. But what does such an assertion practically amount to? What is the immediate effect of a "knowledge" which the majority have not acquired? Are we to bring children into the world for premature death because we "know" that the land "could" yield more food, if only it were nationalised—while we also know that it will nevertheless not be nationalised for some time to come? Mr. George is not a very clear-headed thinker, and he may not see that his book tends to convey such a precept; but such is the fact. And equally certain is it that his implied denial of the helplessness of starved savages involves an extremely repulsive form of Calvinism.

If the above imputation on Mr. George's clearness of perception be demurred to, let the further steps in his criticism of Malthus be taken as a test. After an untrustworthy, and in any case irrelevant, set of assertions as to the populousness of ancient nations, he deliberately advances as an argument against the law of population the fact that only in recent times has it been formulated. How is it, he asks, that the more civilised peoples of the world have never recognised or admitted this law down to our own time, but on the contrary have always encouraged propagation? It is difficult to deal respectfully with such a question. Would Mr. George allege that the fact that almost the whole of mankind before Galileo held the earth to be flat, is a reason for doubting that the earth is round? What is the purpose of his reference to the "wisdom of the centuries" if it is not a catchpenny appeal to popular ignorance? It may or may not be the outcome of intellectual confusion on his part, but as to his next argument there can be no doubt. "If the tendency to reproduce", he asks, "be so strong as Malthusianism supposes, how is it that families so often become extinct—families in which want is unknown?" And he goes on to argue that "on the presumption that population tends to double every twenty-five years", the descendants of Confucius ought, in 2,150 years after Confucius' death, to have amounted to 859, 559, 193, 106, 709, 670, 198, 710, 528 souls; whereas in fact they only numbered some 22,000. It is depressing to think that such an exhibition of childish folly can have impressed anybody as an argument. Does Mr. George, or does he not, understand the meaning of the words "tends to"? It would really seem not. Setting aside the case of the descendants of Confucius—which simply serves further to confuse the issue, for Malthus never pretended to say what would ultimately happen to a family "enjoying peculiar privileges and consideration" in China or anywhere else— the Malthusian assertion in regard to China may be thus set forth, for the benefit of Mr. George's admirers:—The *tendency* there, as everywhere else, has been to produce children beyond the available subsistence; and the superfluous population produced under the operation of this law has simply been perpetually cropped off by disease, poverty, famine, war, and infanticide; while vice has to a large extent kept the tendency in check. Does Mr. George pretend even to say that the descendants of Confucius have not lessened or thwarted their reproductive powers by vicious practices? It matters not to the argument whether their failure to attain greater numbers result from vice or the enervation of luxury, or whether their particular stock happened to be comparatively infecund—the fact remains that not only is the tendency of population to double itself under favourable conditions in twenty-five years; but it has actually been known to do so, *as Mr. George himself admits*. His Confucian figures are mere dust for his readers' eyes.

After this achievement, Mr. George goes on to argue in detail that in every thickly-populated country where people are chronically miserable, it is not because there are too many of them, but because they might have provided better for themselves if they had been wiser—the old barren formula which nobody ever denied. Mr. George apparently cannot realise that the question in hand is whether or not there were too many people for the food they did produce; and just as little, apparently, can he apprehend the Malthusian argument that, supposing the people of any country at any time had used ever so much better means of producing food, and had good laws, they would on that very account have multiplied to the point of disaster the more rapidly, unless they deliberately practised parental prudence, or impaired their generative powers by vice. A historical case founded on by Mr. George will make the issue clear. He points out that in Ireland, during the great famine, food continued to be exported to pay rent; and he alleges that

"Had this food been left to those who raised it; had the cultivators of the soil been permitted to retain and use the capital their labor produced; had security stimulated industry and permitted the adoption of economical methods, there would have been enough to support in bounteous comfort the largest population Ireland ever had, and the potato blight might have come and gone without stinting a single human being of a full meal."

Now, the Malthusian contradiction to that piece of wild optimism is simply this, that the Irish people had populated up to the limit of the subsistence left them after paying their rents; that, if they had owned their own land without having learned to check their child-bearing, they would have populated up to the full limit of subsistence permitted them by the land; and that when the famine came there would just have been so many millions more to die. Observe, it is not asserted that the Irish people *would* have been so recklessly prolific if they had been their own landlords. Mill, who was a convinced Malthusian, held that property was one of the strongest factors in making people prudent in the matter of their families. But such prudence is action in recognition of the law of population, not a disproof of it. It is the triumph of Malthusianism.

Mr. George, however, not only denies that population has ever exceeded the available means of subsistence: he explicitly declares that "in any given state of civilisation a greater number of people can collectively be provided for than a smaller", and that "in a state of equality the natural increase of population would constantly tend to make every individual richer instead of poorer". Yet, just before, he has declared that "the tendency to increase .... weakens just as the higher development of the individual becomes possible and the perpetuity of the race is assured"; and this tendency he represents as a "beautiful adaptation". So that, on Mr. George's contention, it is a "beautiful adaptation" that the human race tends to fall off in its rate of increase just at the time when its rapid increase begins to be entirely advantageous! Such are the arrangements of Mr. George's "All-Wise and All-Beneficent". But he finds support for both of these propositions among Socialists who are not given to predicating a paternal Providence—whose optimism rather takes the shape of the assumption that only the selfishness of certain classes stands between humanity and unmitigated well-being. Of these Socialists not a few practice the Neo-Malthusian principle which they dishonestly disown: and it becomes every day more important to examine the morality and the tendency of their policy—to see what evidence there is either for the view that as social improvement is promoted, the rate of increase of population will decline to just the right extent without any volition on the part of the part of the people —for that is the argument; or for the belief that under improved social arrangements any increase of population can be comfortably sustained. Mr. George asserts both of these things, and the random and reckless utterances of many Socialists imply both propositions likewise. Let us see what basis there is for either one or the other. Mr. George supplies none. We have simply his word for the "beautiful adaptation"; and when he professes to "submit to the test of facts" his allegation that the denser population is, the more easily it can support itself, he merely cites a quantity of evidence to show that in the most densely populated countries there are found the greatest accumulations of wealth—a statement which is entirely beside the case; and which, besides, is countered by his own contention that in these very countries is also found the greatest poverty. His demonstration simply resolves itself as usual into the protest that men "might" have unlimited food if they would only act more wisely; and such a thesis cannot be sustained by reference to the facts of past history, unless the ideal be shown to have been at some period realised. That of course cannot be shown, and we must fall back on the purely deductive argument of the Socialists —their contention as to what might be accomplished if we adopted Socialism.

In a vindication of Malthusianism against the attacks of Socialists, it is hardly necessary to show that nationalisation of the land cannot abolish poverty. That is asserted by the Socialists against the land-nationalisers. We have rather to consider whether a resort to Socialism would abolish poverty without recourse being had to parental prudence. The Socialists applaud Mr. George's quasi-refutation of Malthus, but tell him all the same that his own principle of land nationalisation is of little more value than that of population. They alone have the cure. Now, it is not easy to say what are the practical proposals of Socialists, seeing that they almost entirely confine themselves to generalities; but for the purposes of this discussion it may be set down that there are two methods by which they propose to apportion the means of subsistence among the workers when all the means of production have been nationalised. One is the payment of what is considered a just wage to the workers individually; the other is the simple bestowal upon each individual of an equal or adequate share in all means of subsistence, education, and enjoyment. By the first method each worker would have to devote his or her wage to the rearing of his or her children while they are too young to support themselves. It is clear as noonday, then, that if under Socialism of this description men and women have large families they will set up serious inequalities of comfort. If Jack and Jill have half a dozen children while Tom the bachelor has none, they will clearly be poor relatively to Tom, who can earn as much wages as Jack, if not more; and if Dick has two children they will be better provided for than Jack's six. If Socialism is ever realised there will probably be payment of wages in the first stage; and we should thus have under a Socialist *régime* poverty and comfort as before. For if the average wage be enough to keep a family of six in complete comfort, it clearly cannot do as much for a family of twelve.

If, however, we assume an equal division of all means of subsistence, &c., or the apportionment to each "according to his needs", the position of the fecund parents and their children will be no worse than that of the prudent or the sterile. But will the prudent and the infecund be content to bear the burden of the philoprogenitiveness of their fellows? Whatever may be thought as to the possibility of increasing the food supply, children are clearly a burden. Is it supposed that in the Socialist state the majority will be indifferent to the selfishness of those who blindly gratify their propensities at the expense of adding to the burdens of the whole? I can conceive no plausible answer to this question save that which falls back on the vague theory—the urging of which is a virtual admission that there has been over-population in the past—that as civilisation progresses fecundity spontaneously diminishes to the requisite extent. What then are the evidences for that? Nothing beyond the fact that under-fed people and animals are frequently more prolific than the well-fed and the over-fed; and the physiological reasons we have for believing that when men and women become purely brain-workers their sexual vigor declines. There is no reason whatever to suppose that healthy working people will for ages to come be incapable of having large families. Many of the loose data on which Socialists so hastily found are really testimonies to the spread of that parental prudence which Malthusians inculcate.

For instance, Mr. Laurence Gronlund, who tells us that Mr. George has "laid bare the utter absurdity of the Malthusian philosophy", gives us the following precious proof that population tends to go all right of its own accord:—"In the beginning of this century families with from ten to fifteen children each were not rare in New England; *now one with more than six is found only among the poor.*" And Mr. Gronlund believes that this is a cosmic pre-adjustment, resting on the nature of things! Is he so ill-informed on the subject on which he writes as not to be aware that parental prudence is deliberately and extensively practised in New England; that women there are very cautious about becoming mothers; and that there have been protests that the native stock is falling off through too great reluctance to propagate? The truth is that, on the one hand, the lessons of Neo-Malthusianism are being widely learned in civilised countries; and that, on the other, women as they gain knowledge and status grow averse to making themselves the mere child-breeders they so commonly were in the past. They see that the old saws about olive branches and replenishing the earth and trusting in Providence have only served to keep them in a state of subjection and domestic martyrdom; and they desire to be something more than overworked nurses during the best part of their lives. And all men who desire to see women cultured and intelligent sympathise with them heartily. But while the more thoughtful men and women are thus practising parental prudence and deliberately limiting their families, sciolists and Socialists actually point to the results of their prudence as showing that no prudence is necessary, and tell the imprudent and the thoughtless among the working classes that they need have no scruple about propagating in the freest fashion—that when they get good wages their fecundity will diminish to precisely the right point! Such advice may be the outcome of delusion; but it is none the less pernicious; and the delusion assuredly does small credit to the intelligence of those who cherish it.

The broad facts of organic life on the earth are patent enough. Even Mr. George can see that vegetable life and the lower animal life beat "wastefully" against their barriers; and Tennyson has sung for theists of Nature "red in tooth and claw", wasting millions of lives to preserve a type, and yet letting even types go. Emerson has told them that all appetites are in excess. Every naturalist knows that plants bear seed a thousandfold in excess of the possibilities of their spreading; that the life of insects and fish rests on the constant waste of myriads of organisms; that birds perish by the thousand in cold seasons; that whole strata of fish are found killed by catastrophe; that beasts die off like flies from drought and famine and murrain; but the Georgian theist, whose "All-Wise and All-Beneficent" arranged all this, believes that the moment you rise in the animal scale to man, everything is for the best; that *his* appetites need never be restrained; that his food can never fail him; that he can always see the right thing to do; and that his miseries are simply the result of his deliberate refusal to do what he knows he ought. And Socialists who have seen reason to eliminate Providence from their scheme of life are not ashamed to join him in a fatuous pæan on the beneficent nature of things—in which every prospect pleases, and only the capitalist is vile! How plausible! how probable! how scientific!

It is time there should be a plain exposure of the evil tendency—be it the outcome of folly or of a nefarious policy—inhering in these Socialist utterances on the law of population. Unhappily one cannot be sure that some agitators are not desirous of keeping up the pressure of over-population and misery in order to facilitate revolution; but there is no room for doubt as to the irrationality which such an aim—supposing it to exist—is promoted by the sentimentalists. Let a Malthusian advise workers to keep their families small, and straightway some Socialist shrieks that the adviser is seeking to rob them of the one solace they had left—as if any good-hearted or sane workman could find pleasure in seeing around him a swarm of poorly clad and poorly fed children, presumably destined to a life of hardship like his own. Of course it is the men who talk so. The Socialist father—to judge by his utterances—is as far as the worst Philistine from proposing to restrict the animal and menial sphere of his wife's duties. She is to go on supplying him with "solace" year after year, going through her eternal round of cooking, washing, mending, cleaning; passing periodically through long spells of weakness and pain; while her helpmeet, in his increased leisure, considers the present and future condition of Socialism. Doubtless many Socialists sincerely desire the bettering of the lot of women; and Dr. Bebel has written a book with that object; but as has been pointed out by Mrs. Besant, he denounces Malthusianism while by implication he is committed to profiting by its lessons. It is for the Socialists to reconcile their professed championship of women with their repudiation of every suggestion for the alleviation of women's domestic burdens.

As for the Georgian chimæra of "the more hands the more food", that may perhaps be left to the common-sense of all who know anything of the processes of agriculture. It is mere impudent nonsense to say that the soil in cultivation can be made to go on doubling its yield as fast as unchecked population doubles. All Mr. George's mock illustrations assume the premature dying-off of a large proportion of the children of the poor, and what Malthusians urge is that these children need never have been born. The scientific Malthusian's message to the workers is clear, consistent, and perfectly sympathetic. He tells them that they share with every other species of organism the tendency to produce superfluous offspring; and that they can only avoid the evil results of this tendency by applying to their parental action the caution and foresight they have to apply to every other department of conduct, and which animals for the most part lack. He points out that by propagating recklessly they not only impoverish themselves, and injure the children they produce, but flood the labor market and perpetuate the miseries of their class. As a Malthusian he does not tell them not to aim at political and social reform; if he carries his scientific method into his politics, he urges them to combine for the reduction and proper apportionment of national burdens, and for the restriction of idle living on the general industry. He does not, as a Malthusian, seek to turn them against Socialism: but he teaches, as Mill taught, that Socialism must positively involve methodical restriction of propagation; while, as some of the really philosophic Socialists hold, it is likely to ultimately involve the most scrupulous selective care in the process. The empirical Socialist ignores the wisdom of his teachers.

One thing more. The worker may sometimes hear it said that pressure of population is necessary to progress. Let him reflect what this means—that his class is to suffer in order that invention and the arts may flourish. And this doctrine he will find half-implied in the teaching of some Socialists, as in this remark of Mr. Gronlund: "If the smart fellows of the Stone Age had been Malthusians and had been able to prevent increase of population beyond the supply of the then existing *caves*, we should never have had brown-stone-fronts or architects." If that sentence—which is certainly irrelevant to its context—has any meaning in regard to present policy, it is that by keeping up the friction and misery of superfluous population we shall secure thoroughgoing reform faster. Let true-hearted workers say whether they will endorse such a doctrine of progress by bringing children into a life of misery and making their wives bear the worst of the burden.

OVER-POPULATION.

THE doctrine, commonly associated with the name of Malthus, that mankind need to guard against a too high birth-rate, is at once an ancient and a modern idea in human affairs. We may reasonably infer, from the extensive practice of female infanticide among savage tribes, that in primeval times the pressure of population on subsistence was frequently felt, reasoned upon, and resisted in that frightful fashion. Among the Greeks and Romans, again, though the avowed opinion and legislative practice was mostly in favor of multiplying numbers, we know that the habit of exposing infants for death or slavery was for many centuries extremely common, people knowing from their own experience that, whatever might be the view of rulers, the rearing of children was burdensome to them as individuals. It is worth remembering, in this connection, that in Terence's comedy, "The Self-Tormentor," in which occurs the celebrated sentiment: "I am a man; nothing that is human is alien to me," the very man who speaks these pretentious words has himself, earlier in the story, insisted on exposing his infant daughter. Such was classic morality in the days of the Republic. The law at one and the same time authorised parents to destroy their children by exposure, and imposed a tax on bachelors by way of encouraging marriage. But indeed the entire public opinion of antiquity authorised infanticide, even where children were not unhealthy, and made it almost a matter of course where they were sickly or maimed.

Among the Jews, on the other hand, we know that the later practice (of the earlier we really know nothing) was extremely philoprogenitive; this being a result not merely, as Tacitus puts it, of their belief in immortality, but of the frequent subjection and depopulation of their country by war, which both stimulated the domestic affections, and favored the view that it was a duty to be as fruitful as possible. And as the higher humanity bred by the unwarlike life of later Rome—a humanity which rather made Christianity than was made by it—gradually shrank from infanticide; and as, further, the sacred books of the Jews, with their exhortations to fruitfulness, became the moral literature of the northern nations, the notion that population ought to be restrained passed for a long time into discredit, or rather disregard. Indeed, the chronic warfare of the Dark and Middle Ages, keeping population in check in a very forcible manner, made the practice of restraint in other forms, as a rule, comparatively unnecessary.

It is only with the advent of what we call the Modern Period—the period after the Reformation had settled down—that statesmen and thinkers are found looking at the question of population in a partially scientific manner, apart alike from the precepts of religious tradition and the conventions of government. Doubtless the revival of letters, reintroducing the study of Plato and Aristotle, prepared men's minds for new views on the subject. Both of these thinkers had seen that human affairs must tend to go ill if population at all times increased without check or control. Plato, indeed, displays little practical wisdom in his social schemes; but at least he saw and taught that, in an ideally well-ruled community, population must not be left to chance; and Aristotle saw it still more clearly; pointing out, further, that any scheme for equalising wealth must involve, in order to succeed, a strict control of births; just as Mill has more recently pointed out that a Socialist or Communist community must above all others control its rate of increase. These views, of course, were not adopted by the humanists of Europe any more than was Plato's prescription of infanticide; but they would at least tend to set men thinking. And in Bacon's essay, "Of Seditions and Troubles," we find expressly laid down this principle of government: "Generally it is to be foreseen that the population of a kingdom (especially if it be not mown down by wars) do not exceed the stock of the kingdom which should maintain them." Bacon's politics, it is true, is a mixture of wisdom and common prejudices; and on the same page we find him teaching that nations can only prosper by beggaring each other—that when one gains another must lose. But on the question of the internal balance of a nation's well-being he spoke with sagacity; pointing out both in this essay and that "Of the True Greatness of Kingdoms and Estates," that in States where the nobility and gentry multiplied fast, the common subject "grew to be a peasant and base swain, driven out of heart." A little later, Sir Walter Raleigh, in his History, points out more than once how population would long ago have overflowed the earth but for the checks of disease, war, famine, and celibacy. And in the next century, Sir Josiah Child, in his "New Discourse of Trade," expressly points out how the extension of population depends on the increase of industry.

But stray teachings like these counted for little: indeed, as we shall see, the most complete demonstration of a great sociological truth such as is here involved gives no security that mankind will act upon it. As has been truly said by the economist McCulloch: "Those who have got together a considerable number of works in any department of science or literature, or who have bestowed any pains in tracing its history, can hardly fail to be struck, on the one hand, with the indications and explanations of sound principles and doctrines to be found among its earlier cultivators, and on the other, with the continued revival of exploded errors and fallacies. But if this be true in general, it is most especially so in all that relates to politics and national economy." It is only towards the latter part of the eighteenth century that we find scientific ideas in regard to population gaining ground even among careful observers. Montesquieu saw how superfluous human beings could at times become, and pointed out that "there are countries in which a man is worth nothing: there are some where he is worth less than nothing." Hume remarked that if legislation were to remove the obstacles to multiplication, the force of reproduction would suffice to more than double the number of mankind in each generation. And his countryman, Wallace, who opposed him on the question of the populousness of antiquity, quite agreed with him that if the checks to increase—which he distinguished as natural, or uncontrollable, and moral, or of human institution—if these checks could be removed, population would greatly increase. And yet again Franklin, looking at the question as a naturalist, saw that there was no limit to the spread of plants and animals save that created by the pressure of these plants and animals upon each other—their struggle for subsistence; and that the propagation of the human species necessarily rested on the same footing. Any one nation, he pointed out, would soon overrun the earth if the other nations had not already occupied it. In all directions, thoughtful men saw the same truth. In England, France, Germany, Italy; travellers, philosophers, and economists had seen and stated the general principle before Malthus came upon the scene. What he did was not to discover a new law but to work out in detail the demonstration of a law that had been grasped by many.

Let us see, then, what the law of population precisely is. Briefly, as put by Malthus, it is that population tends to increase faster than the means of subsistence—that is, faster than the means of subsistence can be increased in the normal state of society. Now by far the greater part of the opposition to Malthus' doctrine arises from, or at least takes the shape of, a misconception of the meaning of his formula. Nothing is commoner, for instance, than to hear thoughtless people say that the law of population is disproved by the fact that on the whole wealth increases faster than population. Those who talk so have not realised what it is that is asserted. In the first place, *wealth* is not "means of subsistence." Wealth is the sum of all desirable objects; but you may amass a great many of these without producing more food. Wealth, too, is calculated in money price, and money price gives no clue to the total amount of the things priced, relatively to the number of people. But that is not all. Even if it were proved that in actual fact, taking periods of ten years, the actual sum of food produced annually is found to grow greater even in proportion to the population, that would still not disprove the law. When we say that population tends to increase, we mean that, where there is no adequate prudential check, *children get born*, but do not live to maturity to beget children in turn. They, as it were, fall over the edge, crowded off in the struggle. Let us take another illustration. At the battle of Ulundi, you may remember, the British force was drawn up in square to meet the Zulus. So deadly was the fire of the breechloaders and the Gatling guns that the attacking Zulus, with all their splendid courage, never reached the British square at all. Their masses were shrivelled up before they got to spearing distance. Now, in that case there was a very distinct "tendency" on the part of the Zulus to reach the square. Any one who should deny the tendency because they never *did* reach the square would be merely stumbling over words. But that denial would be exactly the same thing as to deny that there is a tendency in population to increase faster than subsistence because in the long run the excessive increase does not take place. The Zulu tendency was checked by direct and deliberate slaughter. At home, the slaughter is indirect and involuntary, and the victims are in large part, poor babes and sucklings. That is the difference.

Population, we say, *tends* to increase faster than subsistence, but obviously it cannot in the long run actually make the increase, because people cannot live on nothing. The superfluous births are just translated into deaths—that is, how the tendency is frustrated. But observe, there is a long range of possibilities between comfort and starvation ; and you may very well have, and you do have, not merely children and adults dying of misery, but many more children and adults living in misery, just living and no more. As it was put by one economist, population is like a weighted spring, the weight varying from time to time. The attacking Zulus did not reach the square at Ulundi: at other times they did. And since then there have been battles in which the resisting force was so weak, relatively to the attack, that the square was swept away. *Absit omen*. At any moment, in this country, there are more human beings than there is adequate existing subsistence for; and even if there were enough, and comfort were suddenly substituted for poverty and hunger, with the result of saving alive myriads who, as it is, die, it would only take a few years to make it an impossibility for you to produce the mere food for your doubling population, to say nothing of decent housing—unless in that time your population should learn the lesson of prudence in propagation.

It is strange that, as so often happens, people in insisting on the fact that population does not increase faster than wealth, should forget how it is that it is hindered from increasing. Malthus formulated the causes plainly enough. The tendency, resting on sexual instinct, is restrained by two sorts of causes, destructive checks and preventive checks—the checks which kill off the superfluous births, and those which lessen the number of births taking place. The destructive checks are famine, misery, disease, pestilence, and war. The preventive checks, as seen by Malthus, are late marriages and prostitution. Another check, namely that of parental prudence with early marriage, he did not approve of—a point I shall discuss anon. What remains clear is that without that last check, population is only kept from going to ruinous excess by bloodshed, by disease, by crime, by murderous conditions of life, by the prolonged celibacy of many women, by the degradation of many more, and by the prudence which keeps men for many years of their lives either celibate or supporters of the prostitute.

Now the question in dispute between the old Malthusian and the new resolves itself into that between the Neo-Malthusian and his present day opponents. The position taken up by these always comes to this: that excess of population at any moment is due to the remissness of society in utilising its forces, not to any tendency in the species to breed too fast. If only, say these reasoners, if only society would put its affairs on a sound basis, either by nationalising the land or by nationalising all the means of industry, there would be produced plenty of subsistence for everybody. I would ask you to look into that contention to see what it is worth.

The law of the tendency of healthy species to increase in excess, you will remember, applies to the whole of organic life; and Darwin confessedly took his root principle of the struggle for existence from Malthus. Either, then, anti-Malthusians deny that non-human species tend to propagate in excess of their possibilities of life, or they assert that man forms an exception to the general rule of organic nature. That any one can deny the general statement—that is, as regards non-human species—I cannot well understand. It is a well-ascertained fact that one cod-fish, for instance, can produce in a season two million eggs; and it will hardly be disputed that if all the eggs spawned by all the fish came to maturity, it would not take many years to choke up the ocean. In point of fact, only a small percentage of the eggs ever reach the fish stage at all, and of these the number is constantly kept down by a hundred destructive forces. That is to say, a "viable" species, a species that maintains itself, in a state of nature, is one that propagates greatly in excess of the possibilities of continued life. Among the higher animals, of course,—among the mammals—the germs of life are not produced in such enormous profusion as among the lower, but there too there is always, as it were, provision in excess for the risks to be run. Any one animal could easily overrun an entire country in a few years if it were not checked by other animals or by failure of its food. The power of propagation is always there, and the more increase the more risks arise. Among the animals under our control, propagation is, however, deliberately and systematically checked by wholesale slaughter and artificial sterilisation.

What reason, then, is there to suppose that man is an exception from this general law—that he, of all creatures, has no tendency to propagate in excess of his power of subsistence? I want to deal with the question as one of human science, and would therefore prefer not to discuss purely theological solutions, though it is difficult to ignore these, pressed as they are by many disputants. And the trouble is, that a perfectly baseless theological assumption serves to satisfy thousands of people out of hand. How many people, for instance, have their minds set at rest, their opinions decided, by such a strange doctrine as that of Mr. Henry George—that the Deity *meant* that there should be a particular distribution of the land, but that he has not been able carry out his purpose! Grant this, and of course it may follow that the Deity arranged human affairs to go right in every other particular, if only he had not been frustrated by the landlords. But on such assumptions, science becomes a game of speculation for schoolgirls; and I prefer to suppose that my audience wish me to apply to the concrete problems of human life the methods which alone have yielded durable results in other kinds of research. And in point of fact the theologers do profess to offer us practical arguments, though they so constantly play the card of divinity. I will therefore discuss simply the non-theological arguments of the writer to whom I have just alluded, who is one of the most vehement of the recent opponents of Malthusian doctrine.

To a large extent, of course, Mr. George's arguments come under the heading of nine-tenths of the opposition to Malthus—the heading of misconceptions. I hardly care to say what I think of his way of dealing with Malthus's statements of "tendency"—his fooling about the dog's tail and the descendants of Confucius. Malthus asserted a *constant* tendency in population to excess: Mr. George satirically asks if a dog's tail must always grow because it grows in its puppyhood. As Mr. Harrison has said of some of his other reasonings, "this kind goeth not out but by prayer and fasting." Mr. George, in point of fact, began his argument without mastering the meaning of the word tendency. How is it, he asks, that this globe, after all the ages that man has been upon the earth, is yet so thinly populated, if population is always tending to pass the limit of subsistence? There are two ways in which Mr. George might have got an answer to this question: one being to read Malthus; the other, to stop for a few minutes to think. The reason why the globe is not more fully populated is that the destructive forces of disease, war, pestilence, famine, crime, and cruelty, and in part prudential restraint, and, more largely, vicious or cruel restraints—as among the Greeks and Romans, where slaves were hindered from breeding—that all these influences have kept in check the tendency to increase. Clearly the alleged tendency of population to increase beyond subsistence *must* always be kept in check somehow; and the whole question in a nutshell is this: *Is the check always to be a premature destruction of human beings born, and misery for millions, or is it to be a providing that fewer human beings shall be born?*

But Mr. George has some more plausible arguments than these. He says, for instance, that human misery has always been the result of unsocial ignorance and rapacity. Well, clearly these have been active forces enough—it is unsocial ignorance that I am now arguing against. But to what purpose do we point to ignorance as the reason why a people who in one year are fairly prosperous are in the next decimated by famine? Other nations, you may say, might have helped them. Yes, but in the then state of knowledge and politics the other nations were not going to help them, and the fact remains that subsistence fell short of need. But the main argument is, of course, that if only men were wiser and more social to-day, they might raise a good deal more food than they do. Assuredly they might: very much more: but what then? At this moment, with a given social system and land system, we produce and import a given amount of food. That might be increased if our system were improved. So be it; but in the meantime we have to note that procreation is proceeding in excess, in regard to the present system. If, then, the system be improved, we shall save alive many thousands who now die, and feed better many thousands more; thus making possible a much greater rate of increase than is actually going on. Now we come to the crucial position. Malthus pointed out that where the conditions are comparatively favorable, population has actually been found to double itself in twenty-five years. If, then, you create highly favorable conditions here, you will presumably, in twenty-five years, have twice as large a population as now; and in another twenty-five years, a population twice as large again. Does anybody then pretend that the yield of food can go on doubling at as rapid a rate as that, to say nothing of house-room? That the total yield of the earth's surface can be multiplied sixteen times in every hundred years?

Perhaps some will assert as much: assertion costs nothing; but even the most sanguine are pulled up at this point by the reflection that, while the additional cultivation is going on, the mounting millions must be swiftly building over land that was once cultivated; and that it would only be a question of time when the face of the earth would be covered. It is all very well to talk of emigration; but, to say nothing of the fact that even now emigration is not enthusiastic, emigration *must* one day be played out for mathematical reasons. So the optimists meet us with a new proposition: the tendency to increase, they say, *will spontaneously fall off precisely as men and women are better fed and more comfortable.* This, the most adroit of the arguments against Neo-Malthusianism, has been adopted by not a few publicists, among them Mr. Henry George. That writer, as it happens, has also adopted another early argument against Malthus, which I ask you to compare with the first: the argument, namely, that increase of population means increase of human resources: that the more people there are, the more labor power is there to produce food and everything else. Now, observe the harmony of those two positions. On the one hand: The more people the easier to provide for all, if only you go the right way to work: in Mr. George's own words, " In any given state of civilisation a greater number of people can collectively be better provided for than a smaller." But on the other hand there is this " beautiful adaptation," as Mr. George theologically puts it, that " the tendency to increase weakens just as the higher development of the individual becomes possible and the perpetuity of the race is assured." Then the adaptation amounts to this, that the tendency to increase falls off just at the time when it would be highly advantageous for it to continue—since the more people you have, on Mr. George's own declaration, the more easily they can be provided for! Such are the harmonies of theological economics. Now, I submit that when a man thus employs two mutually exclusive arguments he cannot be proceeding on a clear understanding of the problem: he is over-reaching himself in a headlong attempt to discredit a doctrine he does not like.

And why does he not like it? Here, perhaps, the Malthusians are not free from blame. Malthus, you will remember, began his argument originally by way of refuting Godwin, who maintained that what he called political justice would suffice to redress political evils. Godwin was not a Socialist, though some Socialists to-day seem to think so; on the contrary, he was an ardent Individualist, strongly opposed to State action. The fact remained, however, that Godwin was arguing for reform, while Malthus seemed—I say seemed—to be making light of reform, and refusing to help the poor. In point of fact, there was no more deeply benevolent man in his time; and he has gone so far as to say this: "If all could be completely relieved, and poverty banished from the country, even at the expense of three-fourths of the fortunes of the rich, I would be the last person to say a single syllable against relieving all, and making the degree of distress alone the measure of our bounty." But this, unfortunately, was not the temper of many who adopted his teaching. The late Mr. Senior, who himself was a Malthusian, and came to complete agreement with Malthus in private discussion, wrote to him that in his social experience he had found the principle of population made "the stalking-horse of negligence and injustice, the favorite objection to every project for rendering the resources of the country more productive." It is not unnatural that when democratic reformers are told Malthusianism is against them, they should be against Malthusianism. In point of fact, the law of population is no more opposed to any moral or social reform than is the law of gravitation. Its lesson is simply this, that while you effect your reform, you must also begin to secure a better control of the instinct which brings about reproduction of the species, because without that reform all other reforms will in the long run be futile.

Let political and social reformers accept the law of population, and their position is strengthened a hundred-fold.

To return for one moment to Mr. George. Perhaps the most plausible of all his arguments is that drawn from the circumstances of the great Irish famine. It seems to be the fact, as he alleges, that during that famine, when people were dying of hunger, food was actually being exported from Ireland by way of paying rent to absentee landlords. Mr. George accordingly argues that but for landlordism the Irish would have had plenty to eat during the potato blight. Now the Malthusian answer to this argument involves no defence whatever of Irish landlordism. With the ethics of that we have here nothing to do. I will just point out, firstly, that exportation of food-products from Ireland would tend to go on, to pay for imports, apart altogether from landlordism; and, further, that it is extravagant to suppose that, when the great mass of the people were living on potatoes, their production of other foods could suffice to feed them for a whole season during a total lack of potatoes. But the main point is this. At the time of the famine, the Irish peasantry had for subsistence only what agricultural products were left them after paying the rent. That was what they understood they had to live on. Now we know they populated up to the limit of *that* subsistence. Suppose, then, that for a generation before the famine there had been no landlords, and that the peasantry had all the products to themselves, barring taxation. In that case, one of two things would have happened. They might possibly have intelligently controlled their own rate of increase, as the French peasantry have done. The heightened standard of comfort, or, above all, the feeling that the amount of the land was limited, and that the occupiers must therefore be limited too—this might have made them learn the lesson of parental prudence, and limit the number of their families. In that case, instead of disproving the law of population, they would have acknowledged it and acted on their knowledge. But if they did not do that, they would have done this—populated up to the extended limit of subsistence as they had populated up to the narrowed limit, cultivating cheap food as they had done under landlordism; so that when at length the famine came, it would have found not eight millions but twelve or sixteen millions to decimate, and the misery would have been greater in proportion. Either way, the teaching of Malthus would be vindicated, as the teaching of Newton is vindicated alike when a house stands and when it falls.

But let us come now to that physiological argument that the rate of increase tends to fall off when organisms rise in the scale of culture. That argument, I submit, has been very hastily used against Malthusianism by writers who have not considered the serious practical question immediately involved. Suppose it were true—in some measure it *is* true—that highly cultured and intellectualised people do not have as many children as average working people, what does *that* prove? We are told by some that on this score the proper way to control population is to raise and refine the populace. Well, do so by all means, but how fast are you going to do it? How fast *are* you doing it? At this moment the children of your poor are dying off like flies, and half your adults are stunted, starved, and undersized: are the multitude to go on producing that predestinate host of victims, babes to wither in their cradles, or to grow up to to a life of physical and moral penury, *until* your ideal machinery for elevating the masses is in working order? Is *that* the way to secure the elevation,—saving an ultimate percentage out of the slaughter-house, and letting instinct for a few more years go unchecked, because you believe that one day instinct will not need to be checked? It should suffice to point out to every thinking person that no theory of the ultimate effects of mere refinement on rate of increase can give any help while nine-tenths of the human race are not refined and not visibly in the way of becoming so.

And after all, what does this doctrine really amount to? We admit that people of refined nervous organisation may be less prolific than those of coarse organisation. But let us *quantify* this statement. To what extent, and why, are they less prolific? First, presumably, because delicate women cannot support the strain of frequent maternity. Well, but, in future, are all the refined women to be physically delicate? At this moment, many highly intellectual men are physically robust in a high degree, capable, in a polygamous state, of patriarchal propagation; and the modern ideal of education is the combination of brain power and skill with bodily health and strength. Your delicate specimens of refined people are not, and cannot be, specimens of what the race is coming to: these are already physically degenerate: were all like these there would certainly be no danger of over-population. But just because these are lacking in vitality, other types crowd in in their places. Now, the professed aim of our professed educationists is to produce men and women of high physical vitality; and who will dispute that such men and women, if they merely obey natural impulses, will be capable of having as large families as the multitude of prolific middle-class and lower-class people of the present day?* But the physiological plea is inadequate in other ways. Many of the delicately organised married women who escape over-much maternity do so voluntarily and not involuntarily—by act-

---

* I formerly stated in error, being misled by a biological friend, that Mr. Spencer endorsed the theory that propagation would tend to fall off as people were better fed. His doctrine is in reality very different. It is that "in the human race, as in all other races, such absolute or relative abundance of nutriment as leaves a large excess after defraying the cost of carrying on parental life, *is accompanied by a high rate of genesis*." This, as Mr. Spencer points out, " is exactly the reverse of Mr. Doubleday's doctrine; which is, that throughout both the animal and vegetal kingdoms, 'over-feeding checks increase; whilst, on the other hand, a limited or deficient nutriment stimulates and adds to it.'" Mr. Spencer shows the fallacy of the argument about good feeding. "The cases of infertility accompanying *fatness*, which he [Doubleday] cites in proof that over-feeding checks increase, are *not* cases of *high* nutrition properly so called, but cases of such defective absorption or assimilation as constitutes *low* nutrition." [In other words, a fat man's body does not get the good of his food.] "It may be added that much of the evidence by which Mr. Doubleday seeks to show that among men, highly fed classes are infertile classes, may be outbalanced by counter-evidence. Many years ago Mr. Lewes pointed this out, extracting from a book on the peerage the names of sixteen peers who had, at that time, 186 children, giving an average of 11·6 in a family." (*Principles of Biology*, ii., 483-4.) Doubleday and others have confounded the effects of vice and excess with those of good feeding. For the rest, Mr. Spencer demolishes their argument by a *reductio ad absurdum*. As for his own theory, that in future Man's fertility will decline (which is not necessarily a view opposed to Neo-Malthusianism), I have partly criticised it above, and may here add that Mr. Spencer assumes an ever-increasing intensity of competition, which is far from being a certainty, and overlooks the probable removal of many existing checks to marriage. But in any case I am not here concerned to discuss a theory which really forecasts a distant future: my contention bears on the existing state of things. Indeed, Mr. Spencer might perhaps argue that Neo-Malthusianism is an *expression* of that higher "Individuation" which he says will check fertility.

ing on the teaching of Neo-Malthusianism, by practising prudence. There are delicate women in the slums as well as in the squares. Why, the majority of the women in the slums, whatever their nervous organisation, are necessarily unhealthy, and are therefore unfit for child-bearing. But they *do* go on bearing children : children which die : and they themselves die prematurely, their lives curtailed by futile and joyless maternity as well as by other misery. And the expedients to which many of them ignorantly resort to avoid maternity, just because knowledge of the right expedients is repressed by insensate pietism and Grundyism, for which the blame lies at the door of the middle and upper classes—the respectable classes—I say some of the expedients they do employ are injurious to a degree heart-breaking to think of. It is enough to turn a man's hair grey in a week to go through the warrens of the poor and learn what life there really is; where hunger and lust forever strangle each other in a living death; where the dying child of a few months old seems to carry in its eyes the memory of ages of despair. The righteousness of Grundyism, as a covering for the filthy rags of the East End, is a ghastly enhancement of the spectacle.

And yet, observe, it is owing to the diffusion of Neo-Malthusian doctrine among the workers that the misery at this moment is not a great deal worse. That has been going on despite of terrorism, despite of bigotry, despite of scurrilous and senseless abuse. And, what is more, the results due to it are taken credit for as proofs of beautiful adaptation in nature by its opponents. One writer, for instance, points out that whereas at the beginning of the century it was common in America to have a family of twelve or thirteen children, nowadays it is rare to find one of more than six, *except among the poor*. And this, forsooth, is because it is somehow divinely arranged that when there is less opening for labor fewer children will be born—that people are not poor because they have too many children, but have too many children because they are poor—a singular stroke of Divine beneficence ! Why, these smaller families, unless where they are the result of positive physical degeneration—which can hardly be called a beautiful adaptation—are the result of deliberate prudence, the putting in practice of the teachings of those Neo-Malthusians whom the optimists attack. I should add, indeed, the qualification that some of the limitation of families in America would seem to be accomplished by very undesirable means—namely, by the practice of abortion. I only speak from imperfect knowledge, and may be in error; but there is some reason to suppose that there is in the States a freedom of practice in this regard which is only less injurious than our own usage because we, in our wisdom, add to the misery of an abortion that of punishment (as if anybody would be tempted to resort to abortion for its own sake), and so terrify others into undesired maternity, with the result sometimes of infanticide and often of adding to the misery of the mother that of a child for whom there is no room. We are so zealous that all germs of life shall be cultivated—in order to be indirectly killed and formally buried. We insist that every possible child shall be born; after that, let the devil take the hindmost. The means of checking population without crime, without vice, and without misery are known and have been tested; and one large section of the respectable public contrives to know nothing about them; another is shocked if they are alluded to; and a third would like to put in jail everybody concerned.

On this head let me say one serious and well-weighed word. I am aware that there are many well-meaning people who denounce the line of argument I am pursuing: there may be some such in this audience. They call Neo-Malthusianism by opprobrious names. I will not pause to ask whether they do not sometimes themselves deserve these names: I know that hypocrisy is to the full as common in this as in other departments of English discussion; but I will not dwell on that. I will not even dwell on the question whether behind much of the vituperation there is not vice of other kinds, morbid vice, as injurious to society and humanity as any other. I will just say two things: first, that if there be any impurity in the Neo-Malthusian conception of marriage, as these opponents say, then there is impurity in all marriage, and the whole scheme of nature rests on impurity; and if it has a personal Creator it is all his doing. On the other hand, I would remind the scurrilous vindicators of virtue—and they are sometimes very scurrilous—that not only is constitutional asceticism no more a virtue than constitutional dislike of alcohol or of olives, but the cultus of asceticism has been repeatedly bound up in the world's history with vices of temper and conduct as hateful as mere unbridled sensuality can ever be. If anyone does not realise this, let him compare, say, the clement and sensual Cæsar, in his main aspects, with the mean and ferocious ascetics of early Christendom, vice for vice, and say which type is humanly the more tolerable, and which would in ordinary course—in a peaceful society—work the less harm to humanity.

It is argued by some recent writers, however—and this is indeed the strangest of the many contentions against restriction of families—that we are in danger of under-population rather than of over-population. Mr. Grant Allen has just told us that Mr. Galton has shown that six children per marriage are necessary to keep up our present population, in view of the death-rate. Six children in whose families? Death-rate in what classes? Why, the death-rate is out of all proportion greatest in the poorer classes; and there it is high just because the birth-rate is high. And, forsooth, instead of lessening our death-rate, we are to keep up the birth-rate which feeds it! Among the comfortable classes, a propagation of three children per family would suffice to maintain *their* present number; nay, would more than suffice to maintain it, were it not that the struggle resulting from prolificacy, among the middle classes, with their more luxurious standards, is such that an increasing number of the men are avoiding marriage. On the one hand the large middle-class family: on the other, what shall I say? The brothel for one thing; the army of celibate women for another. And you are to encourage marriage by demanding families of six! It is deplorable that well-meaning writers should publish serious counsels to the community after so little study of the facts.

But that is not the worst. Mr. Galton, according to Mr. Allen, has further "shown" that a certain amount of over-population is necessary to secure the survival of the fittest. Now the murder is out! We are back to the old fallacy of reading the problem of evolution backwards, as Mr. Spencer has too often read it, as Darwin was guilty of reading it, over this very question of population. The doctrine is, that because civilisation in the past has involved a murderous struggle for survival, it must involve it in the future: the struggle, we are told, has caused the civilisation. Do professed evolutionists still think it possible that progress can be made with such a principle consciously taken for guidance? Is it not plain that when once humanity becomes conscious of the struggle *as* struggle, sees what the struggle is, realises that it has been the result of blind instinct in the past—that when once this is seen and understood, an entirely new factor is introduced, and an entirely new problem raised? Conscious progress, under a scientific morality, *must* have different conditions from those of unconscious progress, under a morality merely instinctive. Cannot evolutionists all round yet read the lesson, formulated almost as soon as Darwinism, that the problem of the future is the struggle *against* the struggle for existence?

But, indeed, there could not well be a more hasty assumption than that common one, that the process of survival of the fittest in the past has been so satisfactory to the instructed intelligence that it is desirable to maintain a like selective struggle in the future. What is really meant by survival of the fittest? Fittest for what? Fittest simply to survive in such a struggle: it is an argument in a circle. Are the fittest-to-survive-in-a-struggle, then, the fittest conceivable inhabitants of the planet, the fittest in wisdom, in morals, in intelligence, in refinement? In the terms of the case they are not: they are merely the fittest for a state of struggle, in which wisdom and goodness and refinement are not the main conditions of success. They are the fittest for the life of blind instinct only—or, if you will, for the kind of skill that overreaches your neighbor. We are producing plenty of brains highly fit for stock-broking, for buying cheap and selling dear, for making bad work look good, for producing inferior literature and art, windy religion and shallow philosophy; but are we as rapidly multiplying those fittest to produce the highest literature and art, the best fiction, the best drama, the best music, the deepest thought? I do not deny that the struggle evolves some good gifts; we produce good engineers and chemists: but man shall not live by machinery alone; and match-box houses are not compensated for by the electric light. Now, the pressure of population continually tends to multiply the bad things; whereas the good might conceivably be had without that pressure. Great inventions and great discoveries are the outcome of great brains, not of supply and demand. Great men do not multiply in the ratio of the increase of a population struggling for existence. Survival of the fittest? We have no time to sit still and think wherein true fitness consists; the torrent of population is forever thundering at our heels; we must run for our lives. The struggle for existence is, and always was, not joyous but grievous; and when it is sought to make out that human well-being is to be secured by giving it free play, we have simply an inversion of scientific method, reducing biological science to the very position from which in modern times it has been sought to lift it. Leibnitz saw in the world a pre-ordained harmony, a machinery for working out only the most desirable results. How much more philosophical is the theory that the blind clash of instinct necessarily brings about the highest civilisation? Our naturalists must be reminded that if morality is not the appanage of the pulpit, neither is it that of the menagerie and the museum.

I have undertaken to speak of the menace as well as of the meaning of the law of population. To a large extent you state the menace when you state the meaning; but there is a menace in our present position over and above the evils to which I have alluded.

At the present moment, while, as I have pointed out, preventive checks to population are only in partial use, the growing sense of sympathy is making society more and more disposed to modify the destructive checks. It is becoming increasingly difficult to stand by and let people die of hunger. Mr. Spencer's logic cannot alter the great fact which it attacks, that sensitiveness to the sight of misery is becoming more and more a motive to action. So we have attempts—feeble as yet, doubtless, but still attempts,—to improve the slums, to help the poor workers when they strike, and when they are out of work. Hospitals multiply; we try to take slum children into the country: to feed the multitude of little ones who go to the State schools unfed, whom to think of is to realise the most intolerably pathetic side of human suffering. Now, every one of these expedients, including the State schools themselves, is a stimulus to population; and if unaccompanied by rational teaching as regards future parentage, they all amount to pouring oil on the fire. Save ten thousand infants from death this year, without lowering the birth-rate, and the chances are that you have proportionally more destitution next year. Contrive to save them still, and after some years you will have so many more thousands of unemployed. Find relief works for these—always without teaching prudence—and in a few years you have doubled your number of unemployed.

Is the lesson, then, that we should stop feeding the starving little ones, and trying to better their lives? Certainly not. I don't want to see the penny dinners reduced to farthing dinners: I had rather see them raised to twopenny and threepenny dinners. I would extend every demand on the sympathy, the conscience, of the more comfortable classes, who live on the products of the labor of the poor—extend every appeal to them to do something for the poor in return. And I would do this because I can see no other way of opening the eyes of the so-called educated classes to the nature of the case; no other way of breaking down the insane convention which resists the true cure of the evil. When Mrs. Grundy finds the demands on her purse multiply from year to year, the scales may begin to fall from her glazed eyes: the stuffing may be withdrawn from her capacious ears. Or perhaps, which might be better, Mrs. Grundy may be positively turned out of office by a resolute band of sane citizens grown impatient of the reign of imbecility and nescience, of timid rationalists made bold by extremity of need. On the latter development one speculates with some interest. During the last year or two there have been some stirrings of a movement of respectable people who knew what was needed, these being perhaps emboldened by the fact that an occasional peer and cardinal is beginning to say that there is such a thing as over-population. The respectable people have held meetings without reporters—always without reporters—and they are waiting to see, I understand, what will come of it all. One result has been a lecture or two of a very careful character, under very respectable auspices; lectures in which the strongest sentiment has been fear lest the spread of physiological knowledge should do harm. That is the stage we are in at present. Mr. Howells has remarked that the Anglo-American novel-reading public, for which he so ably caters, recoils in its reading from the most diffident suggestion of adultery, but faces with fortitude bigamy and murder. So it is with our respectable treatment of the population question. The respectable citizen would rather, would infinitely rather, risk all possible evils of infanticide, moral destruction of women's whole nature, the life-long death of their imprisonment, or the life-long suffering of illegitimate children, on whose natures are indelibly imprinted the grief and the despair of the dolorous mothers—our friend would rather face all that than face the risk of what he calls illicit intercourse without these results. He would only give information to people already married, and this privately, by letter. This still passes for scientific morality towards the end of the nineteenth century.

Well, so be it. Go on securing that illicit intercourse shall as far as possible result in illegitimate children—or infanticide; to this end convey physiological knowledge as secretly as possible, so that nine-tenths of the proletariat shall never hear of it; and let us see the result. I am not going to commit myself to absolute predictions. I confess I cannot conceive that this fantastic morality will long survive; in any case, I cannot but believe that the saner policy of at once encouraging and preparing the unmarried to marry, and popularising the knowledge essential to married people, will be carried further and further. But if that hope be mistaken; if we are destined to see sane science trodden under foot by traditional ignorance and pious imbecility, then there is no risk of having predictions of evil falsified by the result. The evil is as inevitable as the course of the seasons. It is resulting in abundance at this moment. But if the conditions worsen instead of bettering, you will see evils of a different sort. At present you have slums, disease, physical degeneration, overwork side by side with want of work, the spread of inferior intellectual standards, the spread of gambling to an extent hitherto unknown, a fostering of brutal tastes, making the prize-fighter the most popular of all heroes. You have also the spread of vice, which distracted respectability hopes to check by suppressing translations of foreign writers much more essentially moral than half our classics, and by bullying the music-halls. All the while the menacing multitude increases.

After a time—I am assuming that the true lesson is not learned—you will feel driven to reform somehow the land laws; the sooner the better, say I, for there is much hope that by putting people on the land with a chance of wellbeing you will put them in the way of seeing the need of limiting their families. But possibly hypocrisy and Puritanism, instinct and ignorance, may still triumph. Then you may try new reforms. But one day, lacking the *sine qua non* of all reform, you will be at the end of your tether. We are accustomed in this country to think we are safe from violent revolution. Well, it is a certified historical fact that the French Revolution was precipitated by the influx into Paris of a large superfluous and hungry population, after a series of bad harvests. I cannot see how an industrial civilisation, which provides ever larger mobs of unemployed, mobs which are learning to organise themselves, can be held safe to escape a revolution in these days.

And to prevent this consummation, what means are being employed—what expedients are there that can compete with the teachings of Neo-Malthusianism—the teaching that men should not postpone marriage but should marry and be prudent? There are still some people, I suppose, who hold with Malthus that the postponement of marriage till late in life is the proper course. On that I can only say that if any man goes among the proletariat and urges on them that course, and gets his head broken for his pains, some of us will not be prodigal of our sympathy. To tell these people that they are to live most of their lives without even the solace of sexual communion, is a folly worse than any of theirs. What are the other respectable expedients? Emigration, to be sure. Well, I am not at this time of day going to go into the good old question, so dear to Mr. Poulett Scrope and Mr. Carlyle, as to how much available room there is for mankind in South America. I will grant any proposition on that head. I would simply ask what prospect there is of any Government of this or any other country getting rid of its superfluous population in perpetuity by emigrating them to South America or anywhere else. Let Messieurs the emigrationists commence. As soon as they get their system in working order, regularly and peacefully shipping off the unemployed and the half-employed, I for one promise to abandon Malthusian propaganda. In the meantime I would deprecate nailing their ears to the pump; but I do maintain that ears have been cropped for less strange philosophy than that which expatiates on the acreage of the planet as a consolation for an annual massacre of infants innumerable, and a state of life for millions which calls up visions of the lowest circle of Dante's hell.

More substantial, on the face of it, is the reasoning which points to the stationary state of population in France, even with an influx of foreign labor. But here, too, the argument is fallacious. The stationary condition of population in France at this moment is the main reason why the burdens of that country are bearable. With an enormous debt, an enormous military system, a vicious system of taxation, which presses on food and entirely spares incomes, you yet have less distress than is seen in England. Compare the poorer parts of Paris with the grimy wildernesses of East London, and you see one of the gains of limitation of families. And let us not pretend that we have less vice than the French, with the whispers of nameless evil tainting all our public schools, and our periodical horrors of " revelation." Were the French poor as prolific as ours, the French system could not subsist. Some say that it were better then that they *were* prolific, and so brought about revolution. Alas, they have had revolutions enough there, if these could suffice. No : the lesson of the case is that French politicians should reform their fiscal and financial system, lessening the burdens on labor, limiting the idle classes : then families will increase as much as it is desirable they should. As for the foreign influx, at worst France will but have to adopt the course resorted to by the prosperous United States, and keep out foreign pauperism, so forcing neighboring nations to look to population likewise— a course which is not unsuggested among ourselves.

But enough of controversy. I venture to think I have given reasons enough to justify an appeal to thoughtful citizens to face and deal with the facts. I repeat that the problem is serious beyond all comparison. Its seriousness, I know, is admitted by thousands ; but the action taken is not adequate to the exigency. One of the most estimable of our politicians—I say this while opposed to him on some important points—Mr. Leonard Courtney, has solemnly declared that "you might as reasonably hope to build a house in disregard of the laws of gravitation, as to secure social well-being in a community where the principle of population is treated as of no account." But how far does any political party recognise this in its practice ? What has even Mr. Courtney done to enforce and publish the truth ? What leading politician in these days has preached it ?* I know of only one—the man who now lies sore sick,† and whose battle

---

* Since this was said, Mr. John Morley, in a speech to the Eighty Club, has spoken of the "vital importance" of the population question, to which he claimed to be "as alive as anybody in this country." "*I wish*," he added, "*that we did not shirk it so much.*" I echo the wish, with special reference to Mr. Morley.

† At the time of speaking Mr. Bradlaugh lay dangerously ill.

in life has been made doubly hard because he insisted on maintaining this truth in the teeth of brutal bigotry, and despite the timorous silence of many who knew he was right but would not openly say so. Now they begin to give him some credit—*after* the worst of the fight is over. He, and those who have wrought with him*—these have done nearly all the work. I know of only two journals which maintain the population principle in England†—neither of them popular—Mr. Bradlaugh's journal and that of the Malthusian League. And that League is now appealing for funds to carry on its propaganda among the poor, and to pay its debts. The sale of cheap Malthusian literature among the workers is large; but it is plain that the buyers must be mostly among the careful and naturally prudent; and you want to reach the thriftless and thoughtless. To this end special action is needed. The "new journalism," so far as I have seen, gives no help—an occasional allusion at most —no steady advocacy; the apparent assumption being that remedial legislation can cure all human ills.

The are a hundred forces of resistance: unreasoning bigotry, convention, tradition, hypocrisy, ignorance; and not only these, but the natural instinct of mankind to deny that the scheme of nature sternly demands forethought of every living creature that would prosper. It is noteworthy that some of the earliest and bitterest opponents of Malthus —Godwin, Coleridge, Hazlitt—were men slow to realise, or too weak to grapple rightly with that necessity: men lacking in force of character in their individual lives. But let us not speak of such men without sympathy because of their weakness, though they spared no asperity in attacking a teaching far more scientific than their own. Nor would I seem to take up a position mainly hostile to any party which has resisted Malthusianism because of being more anxious than some Malthusians have seemed to re-

---

* The lawsuit recently brought by Mrs. Besant against a priest for libel is a reminder of what advocates of prudence have had to meet—and of what treatment they may look for in the law courts.

† I had forgotten the *Weekly Times and Echo*, which has of late very courageously propagated Neo-Malthusianism. And I must not omit to recal the disinterested service done during fifteen years by Mr. George Standring in his journal, sometime the *Republican*, later the *Radical*, now defunct. A less single-minded policy might have led to more financial success.

dress evil in other ways. I appeal to all such not to beat wastefully against an iron law because they do not like the other teaching of some who expound the law; as I would appeal to all Malthusians not to discredit their science by tying to it doctrines which are no part of it. This is no party strife: not even a conflict of class with class, though it is of the profoundest importance to democracy. The final issue is between reasoning man and brute nature; between conscious humanity and the blind instincts which have hitherto swayed human destinies; between ordered life and all the forces of death. Surely those who insist on the impossibility of social well-being under a reign of self-seeking individualism should be the last to suppose that one of the most fundamental of all instincts can possibly be allowed unguided sway without general disaster. And if, on the other hand, there be any who take such optimistic views of the scheme of nature that they cannot bring themselves to admit the need for human vigilance and precaution in every direction, but are fain to cling to the faith of ignorance and instinct, and to let these have free play in the future as in the past—then I would with all possible earnestness appeal to these once more to look around them, and count the cost.

www.ingramcontent.com/pod-product-compliance
Lightning Source LLC
Chambersburg PA
CBHW030236240426
43663CB00037B/1048